One Boy's Flight to Mas Oyama's Japan

UCHI DESHI | BOOK ONE

One Boy's Flight to Mas Oyama's Japan

UCHI DESHI | BOOK ONE

Nathan Ligo

LIGO INK
CHAPEL HILL, NORTH CAROLINA

One Boy's Flight to Mas Oyama's Japan: Uchi Deshi Book One was edited by Annie Gottlieb. Book design and production by Carol Majors, Publications Unltd. Cover design by Nathan Ligo and Steve Hong. Lower front jacket image shows Sosai Masutatsu Oyama (center) and his first-year uchi deshi class in 1990. Nathan Ligo is at left, beside (in the front row) Judd Reid, and (on Mas Oyama's left) Sandor Brezovai. The remaining Japanese faces (from left to right), by family name only, are Messrs. Yamakage, Kato, Kamokai, Ishida, and Suzuki. Upper cover image shows Nathan Ligo at Tateyama, Japan in 1990. Rear cover image shows Nathan Ligo at 18, a sophomore at the University of North Carolina at Chapel Hill in 1989.

The story here told is a true story, and the author has taken steps to conceal the identities of private individuals. He has reconstructed both that story and the voice of the 19-year-old version of himself that lived it, using that youth's words, thoughts, and feelings to recount actual events as best he can remember them. In addition to the inherent potential for error due to 25 years of separation from actual events, the reader can also expect to encounter a 19-year-old's worldview, encompassing his naiveté, his virtue and vice, his bias and prejudice, his blind ambition, and his human potential for misinterpreting the truths that he beholds.

LIGO INK
www.ligodojo.com/LigoInk
ISBN: 978-0-9905522-0-8

PRINTED IN THE UNITED STATES OF AMERICA

For my Father

And for Master Choi
to whom the entire work,
Uchi Deshi, will be presented
once all installments are complete.

"It is said the warrior's is the twofold Way of pen and sword, and he should have a taste for both Ways. Even if a man has no natural ability he can be a warrior by sticking assiduously to both divisions of the Way."

– Miyamoto Musashi, *A Book of Five Rings*

Introduction

THE MAIN BODY of this work is nonfiction narrative meant to be read like a novel. It is both a stand-alone work, and Book One of a longer story that will take at least a trilogy to complete. More so than a simple history, its telling involves the reader in the life that I lived as an uchi deshi of Mas Oyama in such a way that the reader can experience what I experienced as I experienced it, feel what I felt as I felt it, and learn what I learned about uchi deshi life, in real time, as I myself learned it. Accordingly, there is a lot of my own life story present. To those who want *that other* book, I apologize that this one is not merely a book about the uchi deshi program; it is, rather, the story of the young Nathan Ligo *who happened to be in* Mas Oyama's uchi deshi program during much of 1990 and 1991.

In order to recreate that voice, my own as a nineteen-year-old, I looked to a form of prose-poetry that intertwines real-time voice and experience with the *inner* voice of real-time conscious thought, and also with the *artificial* voice of subconscious *interpretation* as real-time moments of experience are seen through the lens of all that I knew, and believed that I knew, prior to the moment in question. The prose-poetry main body of this book can be read normally, flat off the page like any novel, although some readers might prefer to read it "internally aloud" so that they can "hear" its lyrical element.

There is a subtle but consistent set of poetic licensure taken throughout intended to facilitate that kind of read.

My intent is to have an audiobook version available online that I strongly recommend to any reader who wants either a richer experience, or easier access to the voice in which the story is meant to be heard. (Please find updates on the Ligo Ink page at ligodojo.com if the recorded version is not already available on Amazaon.) I do strongly recommend the audio version. In it, I read aloud the work's 31 chapters in just over five hours.

As for the sections of nonfiction historical essay that follow, I would actually invite the reader who would sooner choose a novel to skip it completely for now, and go straight to Chapter One of the main work. For that other set of readers, however, those who will have surely chosen this book for its historical reference to Mas Oyama's uchi deshi program, I am pleased to offer the ensuing passages of introduction as well, along with several photographs chosen to illuminate the experience. As I currently envision this book's sequels, each part of the ongoing *Uchi Deshi* story will be introduced by several additional sections of introductory essay, each with additional photographs. These subsequent essays only barely begin, of course, to introduce the totality of the uchi deshi experience.

The Young Lions' Dormitory
of 1990 and 1991

IN MAY OF 1990, when I entered Mas Oyama's Young Lions' Dormitory at a very young nineteen years of age, no foreigner had ever completed the full three-year course. Mas Oyama was sixty-seven years old and he was the epitome of health. Every day he read my journal entries, which I wrote each day in Japanese (I was the first non-Japanese ever to do so for the entirety of the time that I was in Japan), he lectured us every morning at the Honbu Dojo Morning Ceremony, he ate dinner with us in the dormitory every Saturday night, and he taught us personally as many as four times a week, depending on many variables, not the least of which was whether he was in country, rather than traveling for his work promoting Kyokushin worldwide.

Mas Oyama must have become aware, during the something less than two years I was in the dormitory, of his cancer diagnosis, but *we* certainly were not aware. He died in 1994, less than three years after I ceased to be a full-time dormitory resident.

When Mas Oyama wrote to my parents, officially accepting me as his personal student (*uchi deshi* means "live-in disciple"), he wrote that 120 foreigners had previously been admitted to the program, and "none of them managed to complete the period of time that they'd promised to stay." Arriving in May, I joined a class of seven Japanese and one Korean who had been admitted one month earlier, on the annual official start date of April 15. (The Japanese were Messrs. Suzuki, Yamakage, Kato, Ishida, Kamokai, Oshikiri and Kuruda. The Korean's assumed Japanese name was Furuyama.) Also present in the dormitory when I arrived was an older, standoffish white-belt Ukrainian, named Stanislav, who would complete just six weeks in Japan (the length of his visa) before being sent home to Ukraine with a very premature shodan, and with the daunting task of introducing Kyokushin Karate to that country.

On my third day in the dormitory, Sandor Brezovai arrived from Hungary and stayed for 90 days, the length of the only visa he could obtain in that, the very year the Eastern Bloc wall came down. He, too, had been admitted as a special case, to spend just those three months. On my 17th day in the dormitory, the nineteen-year-old Australian Judd Reid, who would become my closest friend during the time I was in Japan, arrived to begin three years of training. Soon after that, our Korean classmate ran away in the night, the only acceptable way to "fail" when the lifestyle became too much to endure. Judd Reid would become the first non-Japanese uchi deshi to go full term, and graduate along with the seven Japanese members of our class.

The story of my failure to complete has never been disclosed, and therefore never fully understood by anyone,

A photo taken at the end of one of our Thursday Uchi Deshi Trainings at the very end of Sandor's third month in Japan. Since he arrived on my third day, this is also the very end of my third month. From left to right that's me, Yamakage, Judd Reid, Kato, Sosai Mas Oyama, Kamokai, Sandor, Ishida and Suzuki. All of us were members of the same first-year class. Absent, here, are Kuruda, Furuyama (who had dropped out), and Oshikiri (who was in the hospital with an injury).

and one should not jump to conclusions based on what others might conjecture or conclude, certainly not before hearing what actually happened. If anyone says that I was not strong enough, at the age of nineteen and twenty, to endure the rigors of the uchi deshi program, I would be obligated to refrain from disputing that judgment in order to commend the accomplishment of Judd and our junior, Nicholas Pettas, who did. There IS a deeply personal story to be told, however, and part of that story includes extenuating circumstance of which no one is aware (least of all Judd Reid whose recent book presents, in this case, a distorted recollection of actual events). Within two years of my return to America, in 1993, and thanks to work that I was doing for Kyokushin at home, Mas Oyama awarded me an uchi deshi graduation certificate "as a special case," having crossed out the words "three years" on the diploma and replaced them with "500 days." That award was unsolicited – I never would have expected it – and I was both very honored and very ashamed to receive it.

Of the uchi deshi class one year ahead of us, our second-year sempais, only two remained: Hashimoto Sempai, the only remaining Japanese, and an Algerian Frenchman named Mocaram, one year younger than I, who had been admitted as a favor that an associate of Mas Oyama had arranged for Mocaram's father. Mocaram was a bit maturity-challenged, and at first Judd and I, and later I alone, fell victim to his de-linquency as it combined, unhappily, with the ultimate power *sempai* (seniors) were granted over their *koohai* (juniors) in the dormitory. I am told that he improved after I was no longer in Japan, but nevertheless, Mas Oyama kicked him out of the program, amazingly, just three days before his graduation, so there still must have been significant problems. The other Japanese members of that second-year class, whom we never met, were reported to have been beaten (tied up with karate belts and beaten with baseball bats, no less!) by their sempais, members of our third-year sempais' class, at least one of whom I never met because he had been kicked out for that abusive treatment of his koohais.

The comings and goings of the four remaining members of that third-year class (two years ahead of us), Messrs. Iwaya, Ishiguro, Yoneda, and Kawaminami, are a bit complicated, and I will save that description for later. In my first days in the dormitory, I helped my sempai Mocaram help Yui Sempai, the just-then-retired dormitory chief, move all of his belongings out of the dormitory, as he had just recently been asked to leave by Mas Oyama after a dispute over bodybuilding (Mas Oyama didn't approve of bodybuilding per se[1]), and we lived without a dormitory chief for the better part of a year before Minami Sempai came on board. Dormitory chief was a position held by a graduated uchi deshi. Yui Sempai had graduated about five years before we arrived, and Minami Sempai was his koohai.

After I had been in the dormitory for ten months, a new class of four Japanese arrived; three of them quit very soon afterwards for some reason that we never understood. They certainly experienced no severe hardship. Soon after that, Nicholas Pettas arrived from Denmark to join the one remaining Japanese, and he, Judd, Mocaram Sempai, and I were the foreigners present in the dormitory until my departure less than a year later. Nick would become the second, and only additional, non-Japanese to complete three years in the program. To my knowledge, the three of us, Nick, Judd, and myself, are the only three foreigners to hold graduation

---

[1]   The Kyokushin of the 1990s was just then approaching its pinnacle of extra-karate body conditioning training, employed by tournament fighters seeking power and increased body mass in open (no weight category) tournaments, and Mas Oyama was concerned that this training was occurring at the expense of the vital pursuit of karate basics.

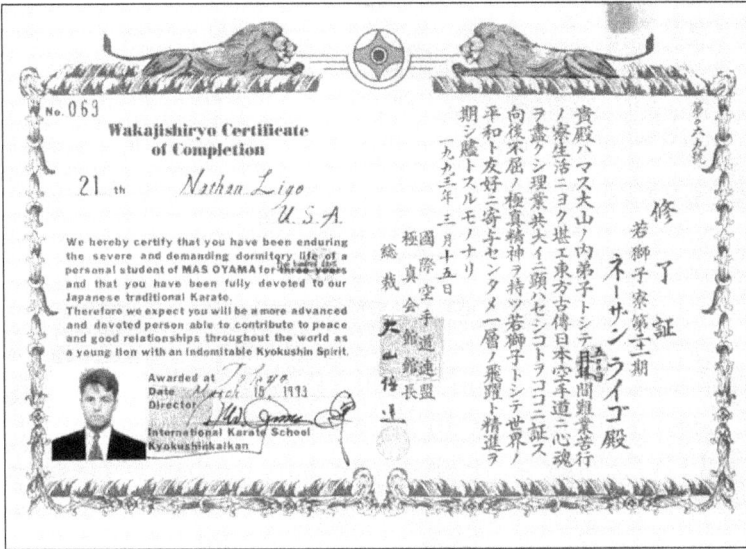

Sosai ordered his assistant to prepare my uchi deshi graduation certificate, altered to read "500 days" instead of "three years." He signed it personally and awarded it "as a special case" during a Honbu Morning Ceromony on one of my return trips to Japan, after Judd's graduation (with the rest of my classmates) but before Nick's (a year later). I stayed in the dormitory for those few nights (when no longer an uchi deshi) and, during Saturday dinner with the other uchi deshi, Sosai told them he would award me this certificate in recognition of the work I was doing in the US, and, in front of everyone, he ordered me to come back in February to test at Honbu for my nidan (I was still a 1st kyu brown belt at the time). Nidan was the minimum requirement to appoint an overseas "Branch Chief," and the challenge, I knew, was to fight twenty consecutive fights, rather than merely ten.

certificates, although mine is certainly not what theirs are, because I did not go full term.

No other American in history spent more time in Mas Oyama's daily, direct tutelage than I myself did, although one of my sempais, Shihan Fujiwara Kenji, was a Japanese uchi deshi graduate who later became an American citizen, and several Americans, including especially the timeless greats Shihans Bobby Lowe and Jacques Sandulescu, spent many more *years* as students of Mas Oyama from afar, following initial periods of concentrated study in Hawaii and New York City, respectively.

Eras of Dormitory Life

EVEN DURING the short time that I was in Japan, there were several distinct eras during each of which dormitory life could be defined as dramatically different than in previous ones. Since the students in the dormitory were always divided up by class – first-year, second-year, and third-year students – and since we were expected to respect and obey our sempais, *those* three eras of uchi deshi life would have applied to all dormitory residents, even before and after my tenure. The first year was always the hardest. First-year students were the dogs of the dojo, whose training was also the hardest because first-year students were, by definition, weaker than their surviving second- and third-year sempais. First-year students were required to do most of the hard work around the dojo, and, in the case of the Japanese, it was often work that was so voluminous that they would only sleep a handful of hours a day. Third-year students, on the other hand, by definition, had fewer supervisors, and therefore more freedoms. They were stronger, because they'd been training longer, so the trainings generally tended to be less dangerous for them. One easy example to cite is that, when we arrived, we were required to wash our clothes by hand in a tub of ice-cold water in the street in front of Honbu, wring them out by hand, and hang them on lines to dry. Meanwhile, the third-year guys used the washing machine and centrifuge in the dormitory without remorse. Certainly when we fought (*dojo kumite*) with our sempais, they were stronger than us, and it was we who had a greater chance of coming away broken.

Beyond this natural distinction, however, there were also distinct eras that occurred during my tenure that would have been unique to 1990 and 1991, and to the experience of those who lived there with me during that time. One of the most significant era changes that occurred, for example, occurred after I left the dormitory and before Judd's graduation; it was one that I only became aware of when I returned to Japan to attend my classmates' graduation ceremony after a year back at home in college. That era change occurred when the foreigners in the dormitory, mainly Judd and Nick, started to become the strongest fighters at Honbu. It was a dramatic change because when I was a first-year uchi deshi, along with Judd (and Sandor for our first three months), we were certainly NOT the strongest in the dojo, we were outnumbered, and we were discriminated against, in various subtle and overt ways, as foreigners. In a life where so much of relations between dormitory- and dojo-mates depends on who can beat up whom in kumite, it was a shocking change to behold when I returned to Japan to visit, and heard enough stories to know that, all of a sudden, it was the foreigners who were becoming the terrors of the dojo.

The most significant era change that I personally bore witness to, however, occurred soon after Judd and I had embarked on our second year, and, perhaps, just a little before Nick arrived. That era change had to do with a degree of violence and hazing employed by our sempais, a practice that Mas Oyama abruptly put an end to, finally, when a classmate of ours with a broken rib was beaten up by Hashimoto Sempai (in the dining room during lunch) for telling him that he would not be attending training because the doctor had told him to rest. This angered Hashimoto Sempai, and he ordered Ishida-san, our classmate with the broken rib, to

The dormitory dining room with about half of us lined up for every morning's 8 a. m. Young Lions' Dormitory Morning Ceremony (not be confused with Honbu Dojo's Morning Ceremony, which Sosai attended from 9:30 a.m.). Here we recite the Dormitory Oath, the Dormitory Rules, and sing, at the top of out lungs, the dormitory anthem. From left to right, that's Hashimoto Sempai, Kato, Judd, myself, Yamakage, Kuruda, and Sandor. This was Sandor's last morning in Japan (when the camera came out), and therefore the end of my 3rd month.

assume *sakadachi*, an on-your-fists handstand position, leaning your feet against a wall, that was historically used by our sempais as a tool of punishment and intimidation. Clearly, beyond just a few minutes of standing upside down on one's knuckles, this became a very difficult and painful position to hold, and the standard punishment was for the sempai to beat up the koohai (physically) should he fall down from the handstand position before being given leave to do so. (Before going on with my story, I should note that, although I spent plenty of time in sakadachi *as training*, we, the foreigners, avoided a great deal of this particular activity *as punishment*, since our sempais feared Mas Oyama's wrath should he hear that they had mistreated us. As a result – full disclosure – I witnessed more sakadachi intimidation sessions than were inflicted on me.)

In this particular case, however, Mr. Ishida, as politely as he could, declined to follow Hashimoto Sempai's order to assume sakadachi – we were not allowed ever to stop eating, or pay any attention to what the sempais were doing *while* we were eating – and Hashimoto Sempai did just as he was trained to do by his own sempais: he beat Ishida, including by punching and kneeing him in the rib that was broken right there in the dining room. Someone, apparently, reported this to Mas Oyama – and part of the difficulty of ever breaking free of such an era was that, even though we all wrote journal entries that Mas Oyama read every day, we almost never reported to Mas Oyama any hardship that we faced. To do so in this case would have been to invite the reprisals of our sempais, either in kumite or in nighttime sakadachi sessions. In that era when the koohai had no rights whatsoever to stand to up the sempai, it was almost unheard of to report even the most dreadful of treatment. In this one case, however, someone must have reported the event to Mas Oyama, and he was extremely angry the next morning at Honbu's Morning Ceremony, where he greeted us each morning and lectured us, every day but Sunday, for at least several minutes and sometimes even as long as half an hour.

This particular morning Sosai (honorific for chairman) told us in no uncertain terms – and I had been in Japan long enough by then to be able to understand at least this much of his Japanese – that we were to band together, and put even our sempais in the hospital if necessary (by beating them that severely) should we all agree that their treatment of us was inappropriate. It was a command that rocked the dormitory like no other event during the time I was there.

Judd and I would 100 percent agree, I think, that although Nick, our koohai, became so accomplished, and so
famous, actually, as a fighter before he retired from Kyokushin
altogether, his first year in the dormitory, with our class as
his sempais and Minami Sempai as dormitory chief, didn't
even come close to comparing to our own first year in the
dormitory, when violence and intimidation at the hands of
our Japanese sempais was allowed to proceed unchecked.
I can only guess what life was like for Nick and Judd when
they were third-year uchi deshi and teaching classes every day
at Honbu; I would never claim to know since I wasn't there.
But, at the same time, I can say with certainty that Nick can
have no idea what life was like for Judd and me as first-year
students, and, for that matter, even Judd can have no idea
what life was like for Sandor and me for the two weeks we
were together with our sempai Mocaram, and the Korean
Furuyama, before Judd arrived two weeks later.

Within a day or so of the day that Judd arrived, my 19th
in the dormitory, I was out of training because of a torn left
pectoral muscle, or some other nerve strain or tearing of con-
nective tissue that left me virtually unable to get up off my
back. (Note that no one beat ME up at that time for being unable to train, probably because I was a foreigner.) That morning, in morning training, two of our third-year sempai beat
up one of our lightweight classmates, Oshikiri-san, so badly
that a broken rib punctured his lung, and he spent the next
half year of his uchi deshi experience in a hospital. Whether
it was true or not, we were told that he almost died. Some
weeks afterwards, Sosai (Mas Oyama) kicked out two of our
third-year sempais, Iwaya Sempai and Ishiguro Sempai, who
were the reason why Sandor's and my lives were particularly dangerous prior even to Judd's arrival, and they were
replaced by Hashimoto Sempai, initially, as the dominant
controlling force in our lives. He was that same second-year

I can be certain that this photo was taken during a Morning Ceremony in my first month in Japan, because that's the Ukrainian, Stanislav, in the print shirt in the second row, behind me and Judd. The photograph was taken for an article in Power Karate Magazine. Faces, from left to right, are Kawaminami Sempai, Hashimoto Sempai, Sandor, myself, Kuruda (way in the back), Suzuki, Stanislav, and Judd. The FG on my T-shirt is for Fetzer Gym at the University of North Carolina at Chapel Hill.

sempai who would beat up Ishida in the dining room nearly a year later, and Sosai would ultimately allow Iwaya Sempai and Ishiguro Sempai to return.

During that era, our sempais' power was absolute, and because that was the only way we knew, we didn't know until Sosai finally set us straight that that's not how life was supposed to be in the dormitory. The very next morning after Sosai's telling us to band together and even hospitalize our sempais if necessary, it actually nearly happened. There were nine of us in our class, seven Japanese plus Judd and I, and that morning Hashimoto Sempai became angry at our class for some reason I don't think I ever knew. When we arrived for morning training at 7 a.m. in front of Honbu, he ordered all of us into the first-floor dojo for *sakadachi*, foreigners included. It's not at all that Judd or I were in any way majority decision makers at the time, so when I say "we refused his order," it's rather that the Japanese members of our class refused, and Judd and I were on the periphery, as we often were, foreign observers to the sometimes-mystery that was the politics among the Japanese uchi deshi.

The experience is one that I can recall like it was yesterday.

We stood there for the full hour of morning training in a perpetual standoff, many of the nine of us on one side, and the enraged Hashimoto Sempai on the other. Mostly it was our classmate Suzuki-san, a best friend of mine among the Japanese, and one who was known for not putting up with much before resorting to using his fists to solve whatever the problem was, who stood nose to nose with Hashimoto Sempai, "politely refusing," for the entire hour, to do as Hashimoto Sempai was ordering us to do.

It is a good time, perhaps, to mention something about my character as it fit into the dormitory average. I was never the strongest one, and, among the foreigners, I was the one for whom fighting was the most unnatural of activities. I was the only even remotely educated uchi deshi in the dormitory, I had never fought with my peers growing up, and whenever I did fight, even in Japan, I always had to overcome, within me, the notion that the activity was not really all that sensible. I don't remember feeling afraid that morning, per se, but I shudder to remember how violently my thigh muscles shook on my bones, quite literally, in response to the tension of the sea change that was under way. Even though there were nine of us, essentially, against one, there was so literally no precedent for us to stand up to our sempai, and since we had witnessed, so exclusively, only one-sided violence directed downwards, sempai to koohai, there was almost no way for me to compute that what we were witnessing wouldn't result in something very, very bad.

While it is true that I'd been beaten up my share of times *in kumite*, with legal, punishing body and leg blows, and although I'd *witnessed* a lot of one-sided, abusive, *illegal* blows, such as my classmates getting punched in the face as they stood at attention (and were required to remain standing at attention), and while it is true that our muscles sometimes behaved in all kinds of new and unusual ways due to the extremity of our training, that was the only time in my life that my legs ever actually shook like that, so much like what one might call "shaking in one's boots." It was really quite embarrassing. I'm not sure anyone even noticed me, there on the periphery, but, like the rest, I stood for that entire hour as part of that standoff, and for a portion of that time I could not make my thighs stop shaking.

I suppose I knew that I would not be beaten – we as foreigners never were, except in kumite – so the greatest actual risk to me was that I would wind up upside down on my knuckles in the first floor dojo, threatened with violence if I fell down, while most likely watching my roommates actually get beaten when and if they fell down. I think it was probably rather the cumulative stress of the entire one-year experience, combined with the fact that (it was a bitterly cold winter, and) our thigh muscles often felt like inhuman sides of beef strapped onto the fronts of our legs, due to the hundreds of jumping squats that we'd done the day before, that resulted in that bizarre phenomenon that was my thighs shaking so violently.

In the end, the hour passed, Hashimoto Sempai was not so stupid as to take a swing at Suzuki when it was clear everyone would have swung back, and Suzuki and the rest of us held our ground. Hashimoto Sempai shouted, and growled and cussed and spat, and threatened us with everything under the sun; Suzuki, as our spokesman, stood nose to nose with him and refused the order. At times during the hour, Hashimoto Sempai called us out by name, including even myself and Judd: "Ligo, Juddo! *Hiyaku!* Sakadachi! *Baka-yaro!"* ("Ligo, Judd! Hurry up, you bastards! Go do sakadachi!")[2] Perhaps it was then that my thighs started to shake; it was the first time I ever refused a direct order from a Japanese sempai. Hashimoto Sempai looked at me like he wanted to approach and punch me, too, but Suzuki was in his way. And so was everyone else. We held our ground, and that was it. The hour passed, and Hashimoto Sempai finally dismissed us to the dormitory to get ready for breakfast.

And life in the dormitory completely changed.

An era had come to a close.

Of course it was Sosai's command that had changed everything. He let us know that not only was it our right, but it was actually our responsibility to stand up to our sempais if we agreed that how we were being treated was unreasonable. The stand-off in morning training was merely the manifestation of Sosai's command. Although we continued to see beatings in the dojo, *in kumite,* I never again, after that day, saw the one-sided beatings of the type that Judd and I witnessed during our first year. In Minami Sempai's dormitory, there was one morning that the entire group of us did 1500 consecutive jumping squats for the entire hour of morning training because we had overslept our alarm clock. That's a story for another time; the amazing piece, however, is that all of us did all 1500 of those jumping squats without fail – and the point to note here is that we did them because

---

[2]   Japanese curse words are implied by tone and "levels of speech." Baka means "fool," not "bastard," but taking the tone into consideration, it's really far more harsh than simply "fool."

we were told to do so *by our sempai who also did them with us*, because we had been in the wrong. We did not do them under threat of violence.

It does occur to me that to begin my description of uchi deshi life in this way is a little bit like capitalizing on gratuitous violence to win over an audience, because although the stress of this first-year atmosphere was all-prevailing, it's not like we had incidents like this every day. The experience

That's me on my futon in the corner of the room in which twelve of us slept, the tatami-floored Obiya (the "big room") on the second floor of the dormitory. We folded the futons each morning and stacked them in a corner, since the closets were full. Life wasn't always constant activity, particularly for the foreigners. Especially in our second year, we passed many daytime hours here as well, reading, writing in our journals, and deeply sleeping so that our bodies might recover from our daily training sessions. In our second year we were allowed to go out into the city one afternoon every fourteen days on a "rest day." In our first year, we never left the dormitory or dojo without special permission.

of being the personal students of Mas Oyama was the most noble of all things we could imagine, and we were sustained through hard times by this intense feeling of pride.

During my first two weeks in the dormitory before Judd arrived, there was one night when, at 3 a.m., our Japanese classmates were torn from their sleep and ordered to the first-floor dojo for punishment. Mocaram, Sandor, Furuyama and I remained behind and listened for what seemed like an eternity as the shouts and cries of our classmates being terrorized in some unseen way fought their way in through the back wall of the dormitory. Mocaram, who had been in the dormitory for one year already, was a bit crazy from the experience, I think, and he told the three of us newcomers that the Japanese "hate the foreigners" and would be coming for us next, and that they "might kill us." He gave us half baseball bats[3], and a *boken*[4] – Furuyama was content with his sheath knife – and told us to keep them with us under the blankets, and to pretend we were sleeping, and to be ready to fight.

Of course the Japanese did not come for us, but how was I to know?

I was in Rome doing as the Romans told me it was supposed to be done. Our Japanese classmates merely returned, bloodied and drenched in sweat, and plunged directly back into a deep sleep all around us. I lay awake for some hours after that still clutching my bat. That was my first experience of real fear – that is, for my physical safety from actual physical attack – and there was more than one night like that in the very beginning, during which we did as Mocaram told us to do, and slept with weapons under our blankets. It was as though the night was a different place altogether than was the

---

[3] Kyokushin karateka break baseball bats with low shin kicks in demonstrations, and for training. The half-bats in the dormitory were salvaged to be used as billy clubs.

[4] Japanese wooden sword.

dormitory in the daytime. Mas Oyama was just on the other side of the dormitory wall, all day, every day except Sunday. We could feel his presence there. In the nights, however, we were at the mercy of our sempais.

Three or four weeks into my dormitory experience, I was cleaning the basement locker room with the Korean Furuyama and our classmate, Yamakage-san, as we did every morning after morning training, the dormitory morning ceremony, and breakfast, and before Mas Oyama arrived for Honbu's Morning Ceremony. Furuyama, in an apparent moment of insanity, decided he needed to fight with one of the Japanese – God only knows why! – perhaps to assert that he was not afraid. Unprovoked, he rolled up his T-shirt sleeves and punched Yamakage in the mouth, just as our former dormitory chief Yui Sempai walked in (by chance). Without thinking, I grabbed Furuyama by his T-shirt, head, and neck and hurled him away from Yamakage to where he crashed into the lockers, myself between the two of them. (I was a lightweight then, but Furuyama was even more so.) Yui Sempai asked angrily what was going on, and Yamakage could only apologize, tasting his bleeding lip.

It was amazing to me that, although I had most certainly saved Furuyama from an extreme beating (and believe me, I was thinking about myself, not him, because we foreigners were of a different class than the Japanese, and I feared repercussions against all the foreigners), Furuyama was so angry with me (for touching his head, he said) that back in the dormitory he told me he was going to slit my throat, or maybe just cut my ear off, as I slept. Of course I had no way of knowing just how crazy he was – he looked like he was dead serious – and I fell asleep to *that as well* for the next several nights of my life. We all shared a room, lined up on futons like sardines when we slept, and Judd, who slept between me and Furuyama, told me he would help watch out for me, although it was Sandor, a special forces para-trooper in Hungary, who took this very seriously, and looked as though he'd watch out for me in a much more knowing and experienced way. Judd gave nearly all of our roommates nicknames that stuck, particularly to the Japanese, because it meant that we could talk about them *in code*, without them knowing who we were discussing. Furuyama got the nickname "Freddy Krueger" after those nights, because of the

It's remarkable how cheerful we look in some of these photos given the hardship that we faced. I think one can see the fatigue in my face, however, here looking very cleanly head-shaved. It's also an unusual photograph because Mocaram (center) looks so light (he was heavier than me). That's Kato in the background and Kuruda, far right. This is the Obiya, the dormitory's 2nd-floor "big room" where a dozen of us slept on futons. All of our personal belongings were stored in cardboard boxes on a shelf that ran around the perimeter of the room. One can see "Kuruda" written in Japanese in black magic marker on the one just above me.

knife, and because he had gone completely insane. Some days later he disappeared in the night, and, although I can't remember the circumstance, we came to know that he had gone home to Korea with Sosai's help.

Perhaps one way to put all of this into perspective is that we lived an entire life in Japan; we weren't tourists, merely visiting. Life has ups and downs, hard times and easier times, and the same held true for dormitory life. It was largely thanks to the most significant era change that I witnessed while in Japan that I have always assumed that the reason why no foreigners had ever graduated before was because dormitory life must have changed enough so that it became possible, somehow, for foreigners to make it through. If our life had remained as it was for Sandor, and Judd and me, in our first three summer months, I wonder if any of us could have made it as long as we did. There were times in the dormitory that we slept for hours and hours of our daytimes, both to recover physically and to escape the stress of it all. It was Judd who coined the phrase "sleep training"; we used it as a means to deal with the hardship, yes, but also the monotony, of dormitory life.

Months after my eventual departure, I returned at the time of Judd's graduation, and I was amazed at the extent to which the dormitory atmosphere had changed. My then third-year classmates seemed so comfortable (with added freedoms that I'd never known) that it seemed like summer camp. And yet, it was Sosai who made the point that there were always hardships associated with uchi deshi life, and that we foreigners would face a set of them that even the Japanese never faced. I never saw a Japanese uchi deshi engaged in "sleep training" since they were working to the edge of sleep deprivation, but, as Sosai said, we foreigners had to deal with the language barrier, and a type of homesickness that the Japanese would never face. We all missed our families and friends at home, but we foreigners were also denied our culture, and cast headlong into a new one that was unfamiliar and often fairly unforgiving. Uchi deshi life was always hard, but to suggest that it was consistently hard in the same fashion would not be accurate. Until the day I die, I will always regret not going to talk to Sosai about the situation that finally broke my will, and I will regret it, also, because I know now, beyond a shadow of a doubt, that I had already made it past the hardest part. The hardest eras of my own uchi deshi experience were already behind me.

Full-Contact Kumite

IT WOULD BE impossible for me to liken the history of my fighting experience at Honbu to that of Judd or Nick. I was beaten far more times than I won fights, and I was not present for that dojo era of Judd's third year (and Nick's second) when they started to become the dominant force in Mas Oyama's dojo. Nevertheless, I did have some heroic moments on a lesser scale, which counterbalanced the rest enough for me to know that I was learning to fight well enough to defend myself against stronger opponents, even though I have to admit I mostly preferred not to. I was at such a disadvantage in terms of experience and temperament, and, as I'll describe, the activity was really a very risky one given how violent some of our sempais were.

The routine for uchi deshis was to enter the dormitory as white belts no matter what prior experience or rank the uchi deshi had. Sandor, who was already a Kyokushin lightweight champion in Hungary, retained his shodan since he was only to be in the dormitory for three months, and, Judd, who was also at least a *junior* champion in Australia, followed suit. I had a nidan from my first teacher after six years of training as a teen in the States, but I would discover very quickly that the hard fighting we did in North Carolina under "Master" Choi (the youngest son of Mas Oyama's oldest brother) was never really true full-contact fighting, so I was very happy to don a white belt again. Probably the way that unfolded was that I arrived first, following a period when there hadn't been foreigners admitted since Mocaram a year earlier, and I didn't have any prior rank that was officially recognized by Mas Oyama's organization, so it was easy to make the case for white belt. Sandor, who arrived three days later, already had a shodan, and would only be present for three months, not long enough to grade, so he was told to keep his shodan. Then Judd arrived, and even though the routine would have been for him to start with a white belt again had he been Japanese, it didn't make sense to ask him to do what Sandor had not been asked to do. At any rate, my prior fighting experience upon entry didn't compare to that of Judd, and definitely not to Sandor, who is five years older than us, and who I would later discover to be one of the most dangerous street fighters I've ever known.

I was a brown belt when I left the dormitory towards the end of my second year, and I did not test for my first dan until the better part of two years later, when Mas Oyama requested that I return to Honbu and test directly for nidan, instead, in 1993. One should keep in mind, therefore, that the fighting that I describe in this brief introduction is fighting as I experienced it as an uchi deshi, starting at white belt and never, yet, earning shodan. I was smaller than most, and fighting was an unnatural activity for me. I was almost always the underdog.

At Honbu, there were three two-hour classes per day, and we usually did one of them each day in addition to morning training and self-training. In general, the fighting got harder as the day progressed, by nature only of which of our non–uchi deshi sempais showed up for class (and who was teaching the class). Fighting tended to be the least dangerous in the 10 a.m. class, a little bit more intense in the 4 p.m. class, and sometimes quite dangerous indeed in the 7 p.m. class, when most of the "old guard" black belts came. There was a difficult politics of kumite at Honbu during my first year that was very frustrating for me at first in how hard it was to navigate. If we hit our sempais (of that era) too hard, they would click, like a switch had been thrown, into a full-contact "time to destroy the koohai" mode. At the same time, if we didn't hit them *hard enough*, the same thing would happen. In most cases, at 65 kg (143 lbs) during my first summer there, I was smaller than all of my sempais, and during that first year it seemed that it was the unwritten policy that every sempai would fight just hard enough for us to feel battered before then throwing in a handful of really hard blows near the end of the round, as if they wanted to make sure we knew that they weren't using their all after all. We would fight in consecutive one-minute rounds, usually 10 to 15 at the end of each class, rotating on after each minute to face a new opponent. If the majority of these were my sempais, that experience was kind of like entering, each day, a meat tenderizer with one's "meat" still painfully tenderized from the day before.

As a brown belt, I fought in, and lost in the first round of, the Osaka Weight Category Tournament about midway through my second year. My weight had increased to 68 or 69 kilograms, and I made a poor choice to try to cut weight to 65 again, so that I could fight in the lightweight division. I fasted the day before the tournament, and relied on my high school wrestling experience, and an Osaka sauna, to cut the necessary weight. I almost did not make it – weighing in alongside Midori Kenji and Kurosawa Hiroki – and I lost that fight (to someone not famous) by decision at the end of a two-minute round.

This is perhaps two months into my time in Japan, at Tateyama, the beachside location where Honbu's annual summer camp was held. It was also where Mas Oyama's most famous barehanded bullfight had occurred. That's Sandor at left (who was in Japan for my first three months), then Judd, and myself at center. With us is Yui Sempai, the former dormitory chief.

Some weeks in advance of that tournament, the world champion, Matsui Akiyoshi (who would become Kancho Matsui Shokei), ran a special training one afternoon at Honbu for the dozen or so of us who would be fighting. It's ironic that I was the first foreigner of my class to fight in a tournament in Japan – Judd did not, this time, and Sandor was gone by then – given how it would be Judd, and our koohai Nick, who would become such forces in the Japan tournaments in the years to come. Accordingly, they were not present that day; no foreigners were. It was me and "the Champ" (Judd's nickname for Matsui), and the dozen or so of Honbu's sempais who were fighting in Osaka. It was decided that each of us would do a 15-man kumite (15 consecutive one-minute fights), each of us also contributing individual fights to everyone else's consecutive 15, and I have to admit that although we were fighting hard, it was not a slaughter, especially because I had gotten better at the politics of dojo kumite. I was being very cautious since I felt myself to be in a precarious position, being as I was the youngest, among the smallest, the most inexperienced, and the only white guy in the room.

Unfortunately for him, that same kumite session did not go so well for a third-year sempai of mine (who would, at that time, have just recently graduated). Yoneda Sempai was the smallest in the dormitory, certainly the least strong among the four third-year guys we knew, and the only one of them who didn't make me feel threatened when I fought with him. I don't know what he did to piss people off that day – I suspect it was that he showed that he was beaten by some exchange of blows when the others thought he shouldn't yet have shown that he was beaten – but the others bashed him till tears were running down his face. That angered them more, and they bashed him like no bashing I'd ever seen. He was sobbing and collapsing finally, that angered them more, and they didn't stop bashing him until his rounds were complete. Of course by then he could no longer stand, but they kept making him stagger back into his "ring" to take more blows.

I, myself, wept once *in wrestling practice* in high school (and I would eventually get my chance, in private, *following* a 7 p.m. training at Honbu later that year), and I probably would have been more sympathetic – I feel that way towards Yoneda Sempai now – except that he was part of that third-year class that had been so rough with us, and, also, I was too busy taking care of myself. That was the way at Honbu: to remain disinterested when someone else was getting bashed by one's sempais, in order to protect oneself.

I was not beaten like that, that day – *the Champ* was very kind with me when we fought – but the same could not be said for my sempai, a 90-kg non–uchi deshi sempai of mine named Oda. He was part of the old guard at Honbu, friends with Yui Sempai and the rest, and I made the mistake of kicking him in the head during our round. The problem was that I knew it to be a mistake, but I couldn't stop it in time. I realized that he was going to fail to block it just soon enough to not focus the blow completely, but not soon enough to stop it. It smacked him in the ear, that psycho switch got thrown that was the norm for our sempais during that era, and he lifted my ankle off his shoulder (where it had landed after the kick) with an upper block that trapped it, his wrist under my heel, and he charged forward, causing my other foot to lose contact with the floor, body-slamming me, back first, his 90 kg to my 68, into the wall. Unfortunately there was a heavy piece of equipment in the corner of the first floor dojo – a water heater or whatnot – that was covered with a protective heavy plywood box cover, and as he threw me into the wall, that psycho switch convinced him that that protruding corner of wood would be the best thing to body-slam me into. I crashed into it with the small of my back, breaking the skin just about an inch to the right of my spine, and I had to writhe on the floor for a while, safely out of my mind for a few moments, before getting up to continue fighting. I can only remember thinking that I was lucky that I fared so well, given how badly it had gone for my sempai Yoneda.

There was a long period of time during my first year that I specifically chose the 10 a.m. class, or alternately the 4 p.m. class on those days when I couldn't muster the strength to go for training so soon after morning training (7 a.m. running, sprints, push-ups, jumping squats, sit-ups, sakadachi, etc.), in order to avoid the more dangerous kumite of the evening class. I developed a front-leg side kick that I became famous for in those classes of mostly colored belts, because it was enough different from the normal Kyokushin side kick that it got – uncannily – to where I was near 100 percent certain

I could knock down anyone with it *provided they were my height or less*. I don't know why I couldn't make it work on taller guys – even one inch taller – but there were a handful of really surreal classes when I would knock down eight or ten opponents during single kumite sessions. Unfortunately, these were blows that *knocked down* my opponent due to the timing of the kick, but they were not kicks that injured my opponents. So, unfortunately, they always got back up again, sometimes angry ... and sometimes I would knock them down again. I think of Judd and Nick as I write this, and therefore must emphasize that it was a 100 percent defensive kick that I developed in order to protect myself from getting bashed by the average Joe, during an era when the norm for me was to be so often bashed, helplessly, by my black belt sempais.

There were two full-contact fights in which that kick came to my aid, in both cases in the exact same fashion. When I say "full-contact fights," I should stress that there were full-contact elements to all of our fights, in every class, every day, but the times when there was really no ambiguity at all was in situations like gradings or tournaments where there was a referee, a time-limit, and a *"Hajime!"* ("Begin!"), and it was 100 percent clear to both parties that the intent was to knock out or injure the other before the other managed to do the same to you.

One such instance was at the end of a 4 p.m. training that was being led by a graduated uchi deshi sempai of mine named Ishida Ishii (not the same Ishida that Hashimoto Sempai bashed in the dining room). He was finally one of the nicest guys imaginable when I knew him later, but like all the rest, he was a bit crazy during that first year, and most certainly one whom we gave a wide berth whenever possible. He was famous for escaping from the uchi deshi dormitory at the end of his second year, and Sosai would only readmit him if he started over at day one, so he did, and as a result he spent five full years in the dormitory. We always assumed that that's why he was a bit off, but I would learn later that *crazy* was just something that all of our sempais were on occasion during that first-year era.

I was still wearing a white belt that day, and once training was over, Ishida Sempai sat everyone down and called me up, alone, to the front of the dojo. "Oh shit, here goes," was all I could think, "what now?" I guess I should have been relieved that he called another student up, rather than standing across from me himself, because, had that been the case, I surely would not have fared so well. As it was, though, I had no time to be relieved, since the brown belt student whom he called up was known to us (Judd and me) as a tough guy, a bodybuilding type who was taller than me and outweighed me by ten kilograms. Time kind of stops for me once I know the fight is inevitable, and so I have this hazy, surreal recollection, only, of Ishida Sempai handing us each the pair of one-inch wooden pencil-diameter sticks that we held, one in each hand, during full-contact fights to ensure that we kept our fists closed, and prevent people's hands and fingers from getting broken. When those sticks came out, you knew it was going to be a fight.

"One minute only," Ishida Sempai told us, he had us bow to each other, and "*Kamaite*! Hajime!" he said, and there was no ambiguity, it was kill or be killed, with one interesting different dynamic. This had happened before – it was rare, absolutely not a normal part of our trainings, that two of us would be asked to fight alone at the end of class – but it had happened enough times around us before for us to know that the purpose of the fight was to pair up someone the teacher wanted to see bashed with someone he chose that he was fairly certain could do the bashing. Unfortunately, I knew myself to be the one who was meant to be bashed that day, hence the death-sentence-like surreal quality of the recollection. I was smaller and a white belt; my opponent was much bigger and a brown belt; and I knew myself to be in a self-defense situation. He was going to try to break me.

My opponent was taller than I, and my front-leg side kick did not knock him down when he tried to break my leg with his biggest, strongest low shin kick, but it did stop him, and he was visibly miffed. He redoubled his efforts, and tried to break my leg with an even bigger kick to my thigh, and I stopped him, once again, with that same side kick. This one also did not knock him down, but it hurt him, I could see it in his face. Remember, however, that wasn't always a good thing in the dojo politics. I'd hurt one of my sempais (albeit not one of my *old guard* black belt sempais), and it was now his turn to flip his psycho switch and enact his revenge. He came at me a third time, with an "I'm going to kill you now" intensity, and this time I kicked him in the left side of his skull as hard as I could, just about directly in the eye. And it rocked him. From that point, I can't recall what happened. He had been rocked, and so I was able to match him and defend myself. He punched and kicked me, and I punched and kicked him in a desperate attempt to stay safe – that's what those mismatched fights were all about – and before I knew it the student Ishida Sempai had designated to be the timekeeper struck the great drum in the corner of the room to indicate the end of the one-minute round, and it was over. Ishida Sempai nodded at me in approval, and lined us all up to dismiss the class.

It wasn't until that nod of approval that I realized that, whereas Ishida Sempai had indeed wanted to see me bashed, it wasn't for any really important reason that meant he was going to be sure that it happened. He could have had us fight another round, after all. He could have fought me himself. It was probably rather a result of the growing reputation of the other foreigners in the dormitory, particularly, at that time, Sandor.

It wasn't until several years later in Hungary that Sandor told me, once his English was better, a story of an occasion in that same era when Yui Sempai, who was teaching a class, had done the exact same thing *to him*, and called up none other than Ishida Ishii Sempai to be the one who bashed him. In his case they had real cause, because, unlike me, Sandor was strong enough to threaten the *old guard*'s idea of itself as unbeatable. Sandor didn't know that it was supposed to be a blood match, and was caught off guard as Ishida Sempai tore into him like a wild beast. He drove Sandor onto the *Shinden*, the shelf-like Shinto altar at the front of the room, and Sandor, still taking body blow after body blow, looked up at Yui Sempai, expecting him to stop the fight. Much to his surprise, however, he saw that Yui Sempai was cheering Ishida Sempai on with every bit of his unbridled excitement. Sandor realized only then that he was intended to be beaten, gangster-style, and he flipped his own psycho switch and dropped Ishida Sempai to the floor with a side kick to the jaw (Sandor's hands were still planted on the Shinden), and he pounced on Ishida Sempai, MMA-style, and started punching him in the face. In that case, Ishida Sempai did not recover, both sempais were clearly miffed when the fight was over, and Sandor and Yui Sempai would become great friends in the days, and for the years, to come. I once met Yui Sempai in Hungary years later when I was living there, and when Yui Sempai came to visit Sandor.

There are too many of these stories for this brief introduction, including one in which I was so badly beaten, including by Judd and Nick, in a 7 p.m. evening training in my last month in the dormitory that I collapsed and wept under the shower in Honbu's basement, accusing them, and mostly crushed that they, too, had bashed me along with the other dozen or so black belts who had bashed me that night. And there's another in which, in front of Sosai during a five-minute full-contact endurance round, I managed to pull off virtually the exact same defeat of the brown belt described above, this time against a nidan Sempai of mine named Minami (not the same one who was our dormitory chief), breaking his lip with a side kick and kicking him in both eyes with high roundhouse kicks until both his eyes swelled into black slits he could barely keep open enough to see through. This Minami Sempai was known to us in our first year to be one who always bullied weaker students, including me, and also even Judd in the very beginning. Judd and Nick would chuckle, though, because although that was a big moment for me, to defeat someone who had bullied us, Judd and Nick would both become so strong in years to come that they would have knocked down Minami Sempai as an afterthought. All fighting at Honbu was relative to who was fighting whom, and how strong each of them was during that particular era of their tenures.

There is one fight of mine from that era floating around the Internet (on YouTube) – the seventh fight of Masuda Akira's 100-man kumite – so the reader can actually see what my fighting experience was like. Masuda was the All-Japan Champion and I was just me, and I was very afraid. I drew the number 7 out of a hat while Judd drew something like 49. Nick was a white belt and was not invited to fight. Masuda, I knew, would just be warmed up, and therefore at his most capable, after just six prior fights. The rounds were 90 seconds each, and I was scared enough, and Sosai was watching, and that combination was one that always threw my own psycho switch, and I resolved to do my best to kill him. Of course, I couldn't possibly have – I was so much less than he was – but the 100 percent commitment of resolving to kill him, I knew to be the best way to survive the fight without being seriously hurt. He was taller than I was by an inch or so, and you can

Stills from the video of my fight against Masuda. Punches (and defense against punches!) were definitely my weakest point when I was 20, and in this top picture you can see me risking a penalty to hold Masuda's punch at bay, and setting him up for a front-leg sidekick. Below is the instant I kicked him in the eye, and therefore just a few seconds before he finally knocked me down.

see me stop him with my side kick several times before, in the final ten seconds of the fight, I kick him once in the eye with my high roundhouse kick. That focuses his resolve, and he drops me with a TKO, mid-section roundhouse kick to my solar plexus that completely shut off my ability to breathe. I fly through the air kind of like a rag doll, but as Judd would say, and probably did, in fact, in his thick Melbourne accent, "that was a fair effort, Ligo!" There was no chance I could have beaten him.

The backstory of the era change of that moment in the dojo is worth mentioning. Masuda, I'm quite certain, had heard about the just-then rising force that was the foreigners at Honbu. That rising force would have been Judd and Sandor, and Masuda was on foreign turf since he was not a Honbu student. The six Japanese fighters that fought him before me had all been fairly lame in their resolve to beat him, either because they were afraid, or because they were being kind to their sempai who they knew would fight 100 more opponents. Either way, they didn't go after him very hard, and Sosai was angry. I was so afraid, however – also of looking weak in front of Sosai – that I had decided to bash him, he saw that in my face, and that played right into what he must have heard about the rising force that was the dangerous foreigners at Honbu. In retrospect I am flattered that the look in his face as we fought was one of acceptance of the fact that I was dangerous to him, even though – I chuckle – I was not at all one of the foreigners around whom that reputation was building. At any rate, it worked to my advantage and I got some good psycho-switch blows in before he knocked me down. Interestingly, you can see later, when Judd fights him, that Judd did not commit, and Masuda knocks him down too easily with a leg sweep. Judd was unquestionably strong enough then to beat him – certainly 49 fights in! – had he committed like I had. As I mentioned, that was a transitional moment. The era of the dominant foreign fighter at Honbu was only just then on the horizon.

Daily Interaction With Mas Oyama

AMONG THE MANY thousands of Kyokushin students around the world, we were the only ones who were Mas Oyama's own personal students, and we knew it. It was a fact that made all the hardships that we faced worth facing. I used to tell myself that "the one thing that I can't overcome is the one thing that I must, and then I'll make it through." In the end I wouldn't overcome that one thing in terms of the uchi deshi program – I will eventually tell that story, and it's not what most might imagine – but I loved Mas Oyama with all my heart and soul, and I am lucky enough to have reconnected with him and sacrificed for him once again before he died (through work for Kyokushin in the US), and to have benefited from his powerfully voiced approval of me, once again, before the world lost him in 1994.

As an uchi deshi I was lauded by Mas Oyama for one thing or another that I did, or said (or wrote in my journal), enough times that I feared the reprisals of my classmates, many of whom were more natural fighters than I was. I had been his nephew's student for six years prior to arriving in Japan – my love for my first teacher, Master Choi, was an overcompensatory love born, also, of the gradual erosion of my relationship with my father – and Mas Oyama had his nephew's same eyes. In one sense, therefore, I'd had six years of practice before I ever met Mas Oyama. I had always connected with my teachers in a more direct way than with my peers, even in grade school, and the same pattern held true with Mas Oyama. Mas Oyama called me to his office one time to ask me if I was sure I wanted to continue on in Japan, because he could see the extent to which, being weaker than some, certain elements of the lifestyle were not in my nature. And yet, other times, he would praise me publicly in front of my dormitory-mates to the point where I would have wished he'd stop had he not, of course, been Mas Oyama.

Mas Oyama used to call me to his office on the second floor of Honbu Dojo, from the second floor of the dormitory, to recite the Dojo Oath in Japanese, to show some business associate or another how he had foreign uchi deshi who were learning the Japanese way. Since the dormitory and Honbu Dojo were back to back, with no way to cut through without running all the way around the block, that was quite the experience, even just for the sprint of it.

"Ligo!" the Japanese uchi deshi on kitchen duty would call up from downstairs, "Sosai is calling you!" and I'd take off at a sprint down a flight, all the way around the block, and up four flights, to show up at Sosai's office within about two minutes, panting, and a little less than terrified (since being called to Sosai's office was such a rare thing), only to be told by Sosai, "Ah, Ligo, please! Recite the Dojo Oath for us!"

"Osu!" I'd shout, and hyperventilate my way through the oath in Japanese.

Once through, Sosai would say, "Ah, very good, Ligo! Nice job! What's your weight now?"

"Osu! It's 69 kilograms!" I'd tell him.

"Okay, 69 kilograms! Good, but you must eat more!"

"Osu!" I'd shout.

"Okay, okay," he'd chuckle, using one of the few English expressions he was comfortable using. "You go back to the dormitory!"

"Osu! *Wakarimashita! Shitsurei Shimasu!*" ("Osu! I understood! I'm going to be rude and excuse myself now!")

During that aforementioned five-minute endurance-round fight that I fought against the then-bully Minami Sempai (the fights were held because 24 students wanted to fight in Osaka, and Mas Oyama said only 12 could go), I immediately repositioned myself so that I'd have Mas Oyama at my back (it was always unnerving to be looked at by Mas Oyama), and when I kicked Minami Sempai in the teeth with my side kick (some minutes before I eventually busted both of his eyes with roundhouse kicks to the head), Mas Oyama slapped his table, and exclaimed, "Be careful, You! This guy's kicks are fast!"

"Osu!" Minami Sempai responded, and I knew from that moment that I had a chance. Minami Sempai was off balance, and even Mas Oyama was cheering the underdog.

I'd completed nearly two years of college before entering the dormitory, including one at the nationally-ranked private college from which I would finally graduate, and I had studied just enough Japanese so that when I was injured and out of training for a week, just about the same time Judd entered the dormitory, I was so ashamed that I spent an entire day writing my first journal entry in Japanese. Although all the Japanese wrote journal entries, one half page each day of tiny, meticulously printed Japanese characters (a half page of printed Japanese is like two pages of English), which Mas Oyama read, every single day, and stamped with his *hanko* (his signature stamp read "O-YAMA" in Japanese), there was no expectation that I, as foreigner, would ever do so. No foreigner had ever done so before. I started writing my journal out of shame, and I never stopped – even today I have in my possession nearly 500 journal entries that I wrote in Japan as an uchi deshi that Mas Oyama read and stamped – and Mas Oyama sang my praises in the daily Morning Ceremony for doing so, enough times that I was ashamed to be thus praised in front of my peers.

Soon after that major era change described above, soon after our one-hour standoff against Hashimoto Sempai in front of Honbu that morning, Shihan Oishii Daigo (who was forty-five, and famous, as he had been a favorite to win the First

World Tournament in 1975) moved into the dormitory with us to train for a month – and to try to resist smoking cigarettes! – prior to the 50-man kumite he would attempt for his fifth dan grading. During that era, I commented one day in my journal that life had changed in the dormitory after he arrived. The year before, I wrote, we always heard phrases and tones in the dormitory like *"Urusai!"* and "Baka-yaro!"—literally "You're noisy!" and "You're being foolish!" but actually fighting words of contempt, rendered Japan's greatest curse words *by the tone* in which they're sometimes spoken. ("Urusai!" means "Fuck off!" and "Baka-yaro!" means "You motherfucker!" when spoken in aggressive, guttural tones.) I wrote that after Shihan Oishii arrived, however, I started to hear kind words spoken in the dormitory, sempai to koohai, such as *"Onegai!"* and *"Doumo!"* ("Do me this favor?" and "Thanks so much!") Mas Oyama loved that, he loved that I'd thought to write that in my journal, the American who couldn't even write Japanese well, and he shaped a lecture out of it the next morning in our daily Morning Ceremony.

Mas Oyama would stamp our journal entries twice, with his *hanko*, when he was particularly pleased with something we'd written.

My days 105, 106, and 107 in the dormitory, September 19, 20, and 21, 1990 (photo right). I was the first and only foreign uchi deshi ever to keep a journal in Japanese, which Sosai read every day (as he did with all of the Japanese uchi deshi) for the entirety of the time that I was in Japan. (Nick was making an effort, too, by the time I left the dormitory.) Each day Mas Oyama would stamp his approval with his hanko (signature stamp), the small circle insignia shown here, and comment to us, either at dinner on Saturdays or in Honbu's daily morning ceremony, if anything that we'd written caught his eye. We never spoke to Mas Oyama directly without being spoken to by him first.

We uchi deshi were the only students in the world that Mas Oyama taught privately, day in and day out, and the most intense of that private teaching came in the form of our every-Thursday Uchi Deshi Training, from 1 p.m. until 3. (He taught an open class for all students on Saturday mornings, and brown and black belt classes on Wednesdays and Fridays,

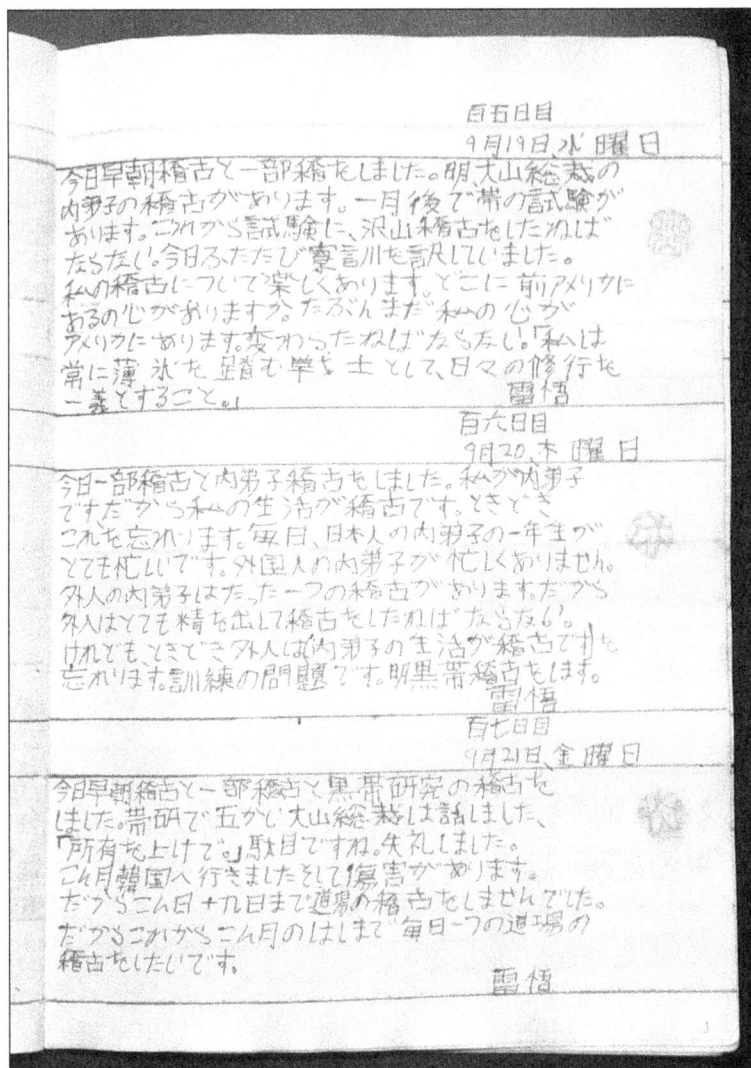

百五日目
9月19日 水曜日
今日早朝稽古と一部稽古をしました。明大山総裁の内弟子の稽古があります。一月後で帯の試験があります。これから試験に、沢山稽古をしたければならない。今日ふたたび豪言川を訳していました。私の稽古について楽しくあります。どこに前アメリカにある心がありますか。たぶんまだ私の心がアメリカにあります。変わったねばならない。私は常に薄氷を履む武士として日々の修行を一義とすること。霊悟

百六日目
9月20日 木曜日
今日一部稽古と内弟子稽古をしました。私が内弟子ですだから私の生活が稽古です。ときどきこれを忘れります。毎日、日本人の内弟子の一年生がとても忙しいです。外国人の内弟子が忙しくありません。外人の内弟子はたった一つの稽古がありますだから外人はとても精を出して稽古をしたければならない。けれどもときどき外人は内弟子の生活が稽古ですを忘れります。訓練の問題です。明黒帯稽古をします。霊悟

百七日目
9月21日 金曜日
今日早朝稽古と一部稽古と黒黒研究の稽古をしました。帯研で五かじ大山総裁は話しました、「所有を上げで」駄目ですね。失礼しました。こん月韓国へ行きましたそして傷害があります。だからこん日十九日まで道場の稽古をしませんでした。だからこれからこん月のはじまで毎日一つの道場の稽古をしたいです。霊悟

so there were times when he taught us four times a week. Starting at green belt level, the uchi deshis' first colored belt color, he told me to attend the black belt classes as well.) Mas Oyama often traveled, and sometimes was away for medical treatment, and I could go through my journal and count, but I would estimate that we had Uchi Deshi Training an average of three, not four, times per month for the entirety of our life in the dormitory. Many months were four, but others were probably just two. These were among the hardest trainings of our life, but it is certainly remarkable that they were that hard because our fight to impress *him* forced us to fight any tendency we might have had to hold back, rather than testing us by having us fight opponents. None of Sosai's Uchi Deshi Training, or brown and black belt training, was kumite. The content was almost exclusively kata and bunkai (one-step and three-step application drills).

In the beginning, in each class we would do one single kata sixty or seventy times. I learned all of my kata that way, in fact, as a first-year uchi deshi. Having never seen Pinan 1, for example, I would enter the dojo, we'd do the warm-up, and then we'd begin. Each of us in sequence would announce the kata, "Pinan sono ichi, *yoi!*" and then "Hajime!" and then when that repetition of the kata was over, "*Naore!*" and "*Yasume!*" and then the next person would do the same until everyone (usually about ten of us) had led the kata once each, and then we'd start over with the first person again, and continue until Sosai decided it was enough. It was usually an hour, or a little more, and since our basic kata generally take less than a minute, I estimate 60 or 70 reps. We wasted no time between kata, there was no pause for discussion, and we wasted no energy in the execution of the techniques. Mas Oyama was watching, after all. Of course I never forgot a kata after doing one that many times. Each week there was a new kata, and I can list the ones that were introduced to us by Sosai personally: If not Taikyoku 1–3, there was definitely Sokugi (kicking) Taikyoku 1–3, Sokugi Taikyoku 1–3 Ura, Pinan 1–5, Pinan 1–5 Ura, Yantsu, Tensho, and Saiha. That's a summary of 23 weeks of Mas Oyama's weekly Uchi Deshi Trainings right there, each one of those kata for the first half of each two-hour class. We never once practiced more than one kata in the same class.

There was another particularly memorable era of Uchi Deshi Training in which Mas Oyama had us focus on Ido Keiko in *sanchin dachi* for thousands and thousands of reps of our basic techniques. Advancing in sanchin dachi, we would take five steps while executing prescribed techniques at each count, before turning around and taking five steps back to where we started, to turn again, and start again, each of the ten of us counting one round-trip each, before the ten of us started all over again, for longer than an hour. Ten people counting ten reps meant only 100 reps of the technique in question, but, having started with *gyaku-tsuki*, the second time through we'd add a second technique, *chudan uchi-uke*, and so when everyone counted that time, we would have done 200 techniques in 100 counts. Each time we'd add a technique until finally we were execut-ing eleven techniques per step! They were, in this order, 1. *jodan-soto-mawashi-geri*, 2. *jodan-uchi-mawashi-geri*, 3. *jodan-mawashi-geri* – these three were kicks high up over our heads – before starting in sanchin dachi with 4. gyaku-tsuki, 5. chudan-uchi-uke, 6. *uraken-ganmen-uchi*, 7. *hiji-ate*, 8. *tetsui-soto-uchi*, 9. a rising elbow strike, 10. a back-fist strike to the nose (as in the kata Gekisai-Dai), before, finally, 11. a descending elbow strike that we threw from over head level all the way down to the floor, dropping us, each time, into a full squat (as in the kata Kanku), before popping back up to sanchin dachi again, ready for the next count. All eleven of those techniques would be performed with the

I apologize for the poor quality of some of these photographs; some of them only exist as badly battered original prints left over from that time. This photo was taken at the end of one of our Uchi Deshi Trainings after Sosai had left the room. That's Judd in the middle, and from left to right, myself, Komokai, Kuruda (kneeling), Judd, Kato, Mocaram, and Yamakage. Ishida must have been on lobby guard duty, and Oshikiri was either with him, or already in the hospital with his broken rib and punctured lung.

---

same arm or leg, in rapid sequence. Note that ten people, counting ten reps each of eleven techniques, means 1100 techniques! Since we started with one technique and added one each time, 100 reps each to complete the sequence, we would do 100 techniques, plus 200, plus 300, plus 400, plus 500 … etc., all the way to 1100, and that's already *6600* techniques in one single session! Now imagine performing them fast enough to complete them all in half a class. Of course the count was normal, *"Ichi, ni, san, shi, go,* turn!

Ichi, ni, san, shi, go, turn!" but the speed with which we did the multiple-techniques-per-count was uncanny, maybe even 3 or so per second for the rapid arm motions. Add to that power and focus per each technique that conserved nothing, and kiais (shouts) that were at the very top of our lungs, and I used to feel as though we were trying, with all of our power, to wring every last drop of water, and every last calorie of energy, from our bodies until there was nothing left. It was not unusual to drop four or five kilos of water weight in a single Uchi Deshi Training, particularly in summer.

There was one such training in which Judd and Mocaram, to my right in the lineup (since they had belts of higher rank), decided to conserve energy as they performed those exact techniques, frustrated at that point that the thousands of repetitions would undo the work they'd done on the bench press the day before. That encouraged me to work even harder – I could see that Mas Oyama was displeased – and Mas Oyama snapped at them and told them "Do as Ligo is doing!" That was not a particularly good moment for my sense of security in the dormitory, since both of them where actually stronger than I.

Since Judd and Nick are the two readers of this introduction that I most imagine reading this as I write – they are the ones who will fact check my work – I will qualify that as follows:

I was often guilty of conserving energy *in general trainings* in Japan because there was so much training, and it was so hard, that I often held back in order to be able to endure it all. We all did at times. As I mentioned, I also tended to opt for 10 a.m. trainings, rather than 7 p.m. trainings, because the kumite was less dangerous. Judd, certainly once Nick started to become more powerful, started to opt for the classes in which there was harder fighting. I never did, at least not so eagerly. Judd tended not to conserve energy when competing with his

This is a still taken from a video of one of our Uchi Deshi Trainings. That's Komokai in the foreground and Suzuki just in front of me. The fact that we were all white belts indicates that this was very early in our first year. There were often cameras around in our earliest trainings, because Mas Oyama and Kyokushin were so famous, and during that era he was touting the fact that he had foreign uchi deshi.

peers; meanwhile I was overly cautious and tended to conserve in order to remain safe. I tended to choose my battles in the name of self-preservation. This was the major character difference that ultimately separated Judd and me. I would fight like a badger to please Mas Oyama, because being in front of Mas Oyama tended to empower me – and encourage me! – like nothing else. Yet I would conserve at other times, to protect myself and my physical safety as underdog. Not very often, of course, but Judd had it in him to slack off that once, for example, in front of Sosai, but then he would fight like a badger when fighting against, or competing with, his peers. In short, at the age of 19 and 20, I sought the validation of my teacher, Mas Oyama; I was well practiced at it, and I did it well. Mas Oyama loved me for my efforts to please him *as he expected us to please him in the moment.* Judd was becoming a fighter, a much more natural one than me, and it was winning vs. losing that was the stronger force that drove him. Note which one of us became the champion tournament fighter, and which one has dedicated his life to teaching.

Mas Oyama challenged us to read 100 books in 1000 days, and make our uchi deshi experience like a university education as well. I *did* read 50 books in 500 days. Nick read a lot in both English and Danish; I seem to remember that Judd read at least James Clavell's *King Rat* – the story of an American POW in a Japanese prison camp! – after I finished reading it. I wrote in my journal, practicing my Japanese every day, and I imagined the books that I would write after gradu- ation. I taught Nick a fair amount of his first expressions in Japanese. While Judd and Nick ultimately pursued only tour- nament victory, I pursued making myself the one-day karate *teacher* that could change the lives of other young people in America as my teacher, Master Choi, had changed my own.

I digress, but the difference speaks directly to the concept of the uchi deshi's role in defending Mas Oyama's legacy, and the point is that there are multiple ways to defend the Kyokushin legacy. Mas Oyama was multifaceted enough that he was a father-like role model to us all, and we were not all of the same mold. Accordingly, what Mas Oyama taught us before sending us out into the world as ambassadors – and protectors! – of Kyokushin extended far beyond the mere kicks and punches of karate. Nick is not active in karate today, but everyone knew he had been Mas Oyama's uchi deshi when he honored us all by becoming K-1 kickboxing champion of Japan. I did not become champion – or really ever seek becoming champion – but I did learn self-defense against stronger opponents, and my teaching today, and my books, are making a difference in America, certainly in my own expanding community. Judd falls somewhere in between. He completed a 100-man kumite two years ago, he's no longer associated with a Kyokushin organization led by one of Mas Oyama's original Japanese instructors, but he is still teaching, and he is a powerful credit to our teacher, Mas Oyama, in that he's fostering the Budo Karate way. There is no question, in my life today, that I have the feeling that Mas Oyama is watching over my shoulder in virtually all things that I do. I feel his pleasure when I succeed, and his displeasure when I make poor choices. More than anything, I feel his backing when I'm fighting difficult odds, particularly when I know he would have approved of what I'm fighting for.

Having been Mas Oyama's personal student, I would disagree with any assessment that Mas Oyama's only priority for his students was to develop in them unbeatable fighting ability. He did encourage that as well, but he also preached that his students must become strong *so that they could become better role models for society,* and becoming that-kind-of strong *also* meant winning full-contact fights against other karateka, but I would object if anyone ever said that Mas Oyama believed every one of his student's first priority must be to become a champion before ever being content. He also encouraged academic strength, and strength of character.

Judd's nickname for me was "Knoll," which was actually a bizarre contraction for "Know All," as in "Know-it-all." The interesting thing was that it wasn't assigned because I acted like I *thought* I knew it all; it was assigned, rather – in a jovial moment of reflection – because we realized how often I actually did (in terms of Sosai lauding some choice that I'd made or another). I was never the strongest, I ultimately failed to graduate, and, in doing so, I'm sure I disappointed Mas

Oyama to his core. I was, however, very often in very good sync with my teacher's expectations, and that fact has left me very confident in my ability to decide, later in life, what Mas Oyama would have approved of, and what he would not.

Mas Oyama ate with us in the dormitory every Saturday night, and stories of eating with him are nearly legend enough to be cliché, but the fact was I did share my Saturday evening meal with him nearly every week for 70 weeks while an uchi deshi, and the experience *was* a remarkable one. My first teacher, Mas Oyama's nephew Seong Soo Choi, had long since told me that his uncle came of age in Korea in an era when food was hard to come by, meat sometimes not even once per year, and this is the reason most often given for why consuming such incredible volumes of food was such a priority for him. As an uchi deshi, however, I came to understand a much more practical reason. We trained so hard that it was almost impossible, in the beginning, for us to maintain – let alone gain! – any body weight.

Ten weeks into our life in Japan there was one night at the public bath (Yui Sempai took us out weekly to the public bath to practice his English) when all three of us, Sandor, Judd, and I, all weighed in at exactly the same weight, 65 kg (143 pounds). The fact that all of us had entered the program at 70 kg (154 lbs) or more meant that we were all quite dismayed. Judd visited the hospital once that summer and took fluids intravenously when he developed a horrible heat rash, but all of us were in dire straits. Hashimoto Sempai, who, like Mocaram, had been condemned to sleep in the main bedroom-for-12 with all of the rest of us first-year students, took his revenge by sleeping in a corner and pointing the one oscillating fan towards himself as he slept, intentionally not allowing it to blow over any of the rest of us. It was 90 degrees at night that summer, and too hot to sleep on our futons. It was as if the fabric burned our skin. As a result I slept directly on the tatami, taking hourly trips to the sink to soak and wring out two hand towels, one that I laid on my forehead, the other on my chest. Judd toughed it out on his futon, and took fewer trips to the sink, and woke up, one morning, with these horrible red welts all over his body. It was that hot. Add to that the intensity of our training, the fact that we were only allowed 90 seconds to eat breakfast (always rice, raw egg, miso soup, and fermented beans), and the fact that lunch and dinner were fixed portions, and there was nothing to eat between meals, and it was next to impossible for us to gain weight. Sandor, who was only in Japan for three months, hit 65 kg for the first time since he was a teenager, and he actually became quite afraid that he had somehow become deathly ill.

Gaunt, like escapees from a prison camp, we would greet Sosai every Saturday night at 7 p.m. and absolutely bust our bellies with the sheer quantity of food we were compelled to eat. We didn't understand in the beginning, we had just been told by Mocaram that we were not allowed to pause in our eating until Sosai told us it was enough, and that "usually every time, someone will throw up."

Of course we were always excited to see Sosai; he was so famous and awe-inspiring that it was hard for us to behold him as human. But consider for a moment that at night, several times in those first several weeks, we foreigners were huddled in the night trying to sleep, armed beneath our blankets because we'd been told by Mocaram we'd have to fight for our lives when the Japanese came back from one of their nighttime sakadachi sessions. Or, later in the summer, we were sleeping without blankets in one-hour sets because the heat was so bad that we feared for our health. Meanwhile, our third-year sempais would threaten us with jumping squats or sakadachi should we ever fall out of every morning's six-kilometer run, which we ran, every single morning, at a virtual race pace. Imagine how we felt, therefore, to learn that now we'd potentially be compelled to eat until we threw up, and in front of Sosai, no less!

The truth was somewhat less extreme, although it took us some months to learn the routine enough to settle down and enjoy. We *did* find the Saturday evening table to be set with three times what a normal meal was: grilled fish (which we ate all of, including the head, bones, and tail), a fried pork cutlet, and hearty chicken soup – three entrées – which, along with an enormous bowl of white sticky rice, an enormous plate of salad, and various other side dishes, was already more than we felt like we could force into our reduced-capacity bellies; and soon afterwards, we *did* learn that that wasn't even nearly all of it, because in the middle of the table were these enormous washtub-size boiling pots of more chicken soup (more whole chicken parts and radish than broth) and these enormous wooden-lidded wooden bowls of more rice; and we *did* learn very quickly that we were, indeed, not allowed to pause in our eating, because anytime we did, Sosai would "encourage" us by calling us by name and telling us to help ourselves to more chicken and more rice from the communal bowls, which added fourth and fifth entrée-size portions to what we already had to eat of the individual portions already in front of us. We were not allowed to speak, or look right or left, as we ate, and we were not allowed to set down our bowl or chopsticks, and Sosai made sure that we never stopped chewing, or shoveling more vast quantities of food into our mouths. He looked at us disapprovingly if we took small bites, so we never did. Indeed, every once in a while – in my 18 months there – someone did have to excuse themselves to throw up, and once one of the Japanese even lost it right there at the table. Sosai laughed, and said, "Okay, okay, no problem! Clean it up, and let's give him some more food!"

"Osu!" we'd say, and go right on eating as if nothing had happened.

That's Sosai at the head of the table, and, starting on his left, Mocaram, Sandor, Judd, myself, and Ishida. That's Kato in the foreground. This roll of photographs was taken at the end of Sandor's 3 months in the dormitory, so I had only been in Japan for 3 months. You can see how skinny we all were then, Judd, Sandor and I, all 143 pounds.

But then, that really wasn't all of it, because once Sosai told us "It's enough!" we would clear the table, and the third-year uchi deshi who drove his car would produce cakes that Sosai brought, every Saturday, and hot tea would be served. Of course, with our bellies already splitting, we could barely even imagine drinking that hot tea, but we had no choice. Once that was done, Sosai would send one of the Japanese out for watermelon, and we'd each be apportioned our own third or half of a watermelon, and not only were we not allowed to stop until we'd eaten it all, but we would be "encouraged" by Sosai for leaving any red fruit whatsoever on the rind. Once again, I'm ashamed to write how eventually, once I learned the routine, I would scrape the rind deep into the green, and Sosai would say, "That's good Ligo! Great! Eat as much as you can!"

Aside from learning how to manage all of that food to the point where we could actually make it enjoyable – the secret was eating all the personal portions of food first, since they would not be replenished, before moving on to the chicken and rice, which would be – we came to know why Sosai was making us eat so much. It stretched the capacity of our stomachs to such an extent that we'd lie on the tatami upstairs in the dormitory and moan as if we were about to burst, and – the unexpected result! – we'd be ravenous all week long, trying to find every scrap of food available to fill that extra stomach capacity we'd formed on Saturday night. We trained so hard, and lost so much weight, and needed so much protein, and so many calories, to build the muscle necessary to carry us through the workouts we had that – Sosai knew! – we needed to eat like that to make us hungry enough so that we might come close to getting enough fuel into our bodies to keep us sustained.

"Judd!" Sosai would call out, and another time, "Ligo! What's your weight now?" (His most frequent question of us foreigners.)

"Osu!" we would reply, "It's 68 kilograms!"

"Very good!" Sosai would say, "Eat more! Get even stronger!"

"Osu!" we'd reply, filled with pride and ambition, deeply contemplating the trials and challenges of out next week of training. Finally, each Saturday night, Sosai would leave, and we were left hardly able to believe that we'd just eaten dinner with Mas Oyama, the founder of Kyokushin. Fate had smiled on us, after all! We'd just completed yet another evening meal with Mas Oyama, the god of modern karate, and we were at no loss to understand how great an honor that was.

Many years later in Korea with my first teacher, Master Seong Soo Choi,
the youngest son of Mas Oyama's oldest brother, at the gravesite of Mas
Oyama's parents (shown here) and older siblings. This small mountain,

owned by the Choi family, is the "sleeping dragon" mountain, for which the kata, Garyu, was named. As a boy, Mas Oyama, shouted on this spot, "One day my roar, will wake this dragon!"

One Boy's Flight to Mas Oyama's Japan

❧

THE NOVEL

Taking turns posing for photographs on the lawn of a Zen temple at this beautiful location atop a mountain overlooking the Pacific, Sandor snapped this photograph of me with my camera at Tateyama, the site of Honbu's annual summer camp, during my second month in Japan. My first teacher, Master Choi, had been passionate about developing my "jumping ability," as he put it, as he trained me to jump over obstacles (usually standing people's outstretched arms) and break boards in karate demonstrations. Of course I was very light then, and I was to learn that flashy demonstrations like this had very little to do with full-contact fighting.

Foreword

WHAT ENSUES HERE is Book One of the true story that was this author's uchi deshi experience, told to the absolute best of my recollection. More so than simply recalling the story, I have reconstructed, to the best of my ability, the voice of the 19-year-old version of me that lived it. I use his words, his thoughts, and his feelings to relay the experience as I experienced it, often in real time. The reader will find that 19-year-old's voice to encompass a 19-year-old's worldview. The reader will therefore encounter his naiveté, his virtue and vice, his bias and prejudice, his blind ambition – his lingering childhood belief in magic! – his human potential for misinterpreting the truths that he beholds.

In order to bring that voice to life, the story must, by necessity, be told through the lens of the whole life that that 19-year-old had lived up until each moment of experience. This portion of my story does take place exclusively in Japan, but conscious and subconscious recollection takes the reader frequently back in time to episodes of the whole, threatened existence that drove me to Japan in the first place. At 19, I was most definitely running away from a situation at home that I could no longer survive – I did, in fact, *flee to Mas Oyama's Japan* – and the character introduced here would make no sense without a thorough revelation of the situation that had made him what he was. We were not robots in Japan, after all. We were not carbon copies of each other. We were pseudo–adult individuals, each complete with our own strengths, our own histories, our own individual, and often private, flaws.

Accordingly, the reader will find this account to be one-third childhood and adolescent experience, one-third my history with Master Choi (my first teacher, the nephew of Mas Oyama who recommended me to him), and one-third my arrival at Mas Oyama's world headquarters dojo and my first encounters with the man himself. I have taken steps to conceal the actual identities of private individuals, although since my own name is mine to use, and others in the book that share my pre-Japan history also happen share my name, my efforts are, by definition, not perfect.

The entirety of this Book One takes place in my first two days in Japan. Subsequent parts will cover weeks instead of days, and finally months instead of weeks, and I will complete the story in *not too many more* future installments. I very strongly recommend the audiobook available at Amazon.com (or, if it's not yet available, see updates on the Ligo Ink page at ligodojo.com). The poetry side of this prose-poetry telling is subtle enough that even the infrequent poetry reader ought to be able to comfortably settle into the liberties I've taken throughout in terms of poetic license. Any reader, however, who wishes for either a fuller experience or easier access to the material should seriously consider listening to the book read aloud. It takes me just over five hours, on tape, to read all of the book's 31 chapters.

i.

An avalanche exploding through a gorge, we're charging through Tokyo streets.

A stampede!

Between two buildings, a narrow opening. Our ankles colliding, I'm one of thirteen.

My first morning, and we, Mas Oyama's head-shaved *uchi deshi*, the residents of his Young Lions' Dormitory.

Double-file at a breakneck pace, anyone seeing us would think we were terrified to be left behind, afraid of torture, our fingernails pulled out. The bottoms of my feet rub away, the sharp curves like bare feet on hot coals, I'm the only American, the only Caucasian, and my head spins.

I'm finally in Japan.

Maybe if I fall apart I can end the agony!

Such an unbelievable, sustained pace!

Lungs exploding. Hips, stretched.

Tearing.

Out of control like the 200-man stampede at the start of our state and regional cross-country races in high school.

Was that just two years ago? Was it *even* two?

There the pace eventually slowed, the mob dispersed.

Not here.

A suicide pace!

Like nothing I've ever seen.

Collapse, Nathan! Stay behind. Get better acquainted with the asphalt!

Shouted Japanese.

"*Osu! Kuruma desu!*" Someone at the back of the mob.

"Osu!" My voice with the rest, a car is coming up from behind.

"Osu!" Spelled O-S-U, but pronounced "osse!" with its long o and silent u, not taught in college Japanese. Means something like the "Yes, Sir!" we use with Master Choi in the training hall, except it's also different.

"I will press forward despite any hardship," Mocaram tries to explain it means, in his thick French accent.

Mocaram.

French Algerian in the dormitory from Nice.

Only English speaker in the dormitory.

One year in Japan already.

Younger, still, than me.

Clearly stronger.

Physically superior.

I'm nineteen, but still half a boy, I think. Always the late bloomer.

My column, closest to the traffic, leaps in behind the runners against the curb, merging so the car can pass.

Running.

Has never required so much of my strength.

Have to fight!

Not to land on the heels of the runner beside me, pulling ahead, in front of me now, sweat pooled in that pocket of his lower back.

Heaving muscle soaks through white cotton.

Dirt.

From yesterday's sit-ups on gravel, I think. Running shoe toes kick my heels, the runner behind me. Twice. Three times.

I just understood an actual Japanese sentence, spoken by an actual Japanese person, actually in Japan!

"Kuruma desu," he said. "It is a car!" A car is coming up from behind.

I've waited so long.

My freshman year at Templeton, and then Chapel Hill to study Japanese. The University of North Carolina at Chapel Hill. Master Choi's quaint little university city.

Spoiled, rich, conservative.

Basketball crazy.

College student Michael Jordan signing his autograph for me at the gas station, I'm 11. "Listen to your heart." That was Master Choi's voice, I'm barely 19. Their import – their echo! – takes my breath away. That day, the first of the rebirth that's become of me.

Those words, the catalyst.

"Listen to your heart," and I did, and that's why I'm here.

Jesus, was that just three months ago?

Was it only three?

I've lived a lifetime since then, and somehow that was just this spring.

But Tokyo summer now, and his thick Korean accent.

Echoes.

Eyes that burn into me.

Piercing.

Deep brown.

Now diverted.

Hurt.

Seong Soo, little Choi Seong Soo, shy Korean boy with a girl's nickname.

Trained.

Grown now into a titan.

Physics Professor and karate man.

For six years now, "Master Choi," we call him.

Sees through me, loves me like his son, torn between cultures. Lost, master, twisted, genius, savant, seer. More than father.

Family.

Who am I kidding?

Mom.

An echo merely of warmth and now mostly just that pang in my gut. Pang also of the Prescott family being gone. Left my stepfather Bob and all my stepsisters, and now she's single for the third time. Aging Chapel Hill therapist so desperate for therapy had to become one.

Lost in self-analysis.

Preoccupied, and tells me I'M the broken one?

Crazy, I think.

Definitely gone.

And Gatlin?

Mouthing the name as I run, my eyes itch, my throat tightens, and I laugh to myself.

Twin paths!

Parallel constant nagging wrecks.

Exceptional bitch of a stepmother, and nobody believes it because of the cliché.

And Dad?

There's a puzzle!

My father.

The would-be protector. The *should-be* protector.

But he's wounded, timid and weak. Templeton College Professor of Art History. Old now to have two new, young kids. Wife-eclipsed. Lost. Red mustache turning gray. So meek and fun-loving, people can't believe him guilty of the injury he causes. It's in him to reclaim himself.

Isn't it?

There's Martha.

Now that was family! Oh beautiful Martha! Love as it was meant to be, loves me!

Genuine.

Spineless, my father!

Lost her and then blocks me from her for six years. "Not giving your new stepmother a card on Mother's Day is not an option."

His voice.

Breathless.

Red-faced.

A shaken soda can getting ready to burst.

Mustache.

Quivering.

I'm thirteen and missing Martha, missing home, at the dining room table in the new house on Templeton's Main Street. There's a faint scent of paint stripper, the floors have not yet been done. My skin.

Burns.

From the purple spray as it lights on my skin. Both of them, my parents, Mom and my father, Dad and my mother, both of them need me gone to enact their fresh starts. Gracie's the third wife after Martha and my mom. "Gracie" for "Gatlin." What the fuck kind of name is Gracie, anyway? Gotta do something with Gatlin, I suppose.

Spoiler.

Bitch.

Purple paint stripper.

Car engine revving up from behind, lungs bursting. What would I do if I have to throw up?

I'd be lost.

Left behind.

Swallowed by Tokyo's streets.

Gotta run to keep up, Nathan.

Run!

ii.

Black plastic! – shiny glass blur and a swoosh roars into view.

Car side mirror passes. So close!

So close I can see - I can feel! - the breaking plastic, see it breaking my hip if it hits me.

"My 'hip' passes before my eyes?"

Ha! Humor, a healthy dose, at the irony!

Good, Nathan!

Do what it takes.

Persist.

We leap back beside the runners ahead of us, back into double file.

Too slow!

The Frenchman, my *sempai* Mocaram, shoves me, runs into me from behind. Sempai means "senior."

"Hurry up, Ligo!" he spits.

Morphing from the single-file thirteen back to the double-file seven. Formation constricts like an accordion. I must have lost a stride and wound up under Mocaram's feet.

They know already how to lunge forward like that, everyone ready for it except me.

The Japanese sempai are at the front, Iwaya Sempai leading the pack. Our job to alter *our* pace to keep up with his. Not his to adjust his own to make sure that we do.

What if I stumble?

Will I be in trouble?

Frenchman's dangerous.

Fighting here's the norm. Accuses me of not knowing anything about Kyokushin. Looks like he WANTS to be intimidating.

Six years!

Six years I was a student of Master Choi, Mas Oyama's nephew in Chapel Hill, and never even learned the word "osu," he accuses. Wide-eared Arab on the tatami.

The Young Lions' Dormitory.

Paper walls, a trace of Shinto incense from the open window yesterday evening. Ceiling-high stacked, tri-folded futons in the corner, stacked like *The Princess and the Pea*. A flickering fluorescent bulb hanging from fine chains in an aluminum fixture with a string. My home. A shared bedroom for twelve, all in one room, for 999 more nights. Tokyo's night, stunningly silent now that the training is through. Mas Oyama's karate, those non-stop karate shouts, *kiai* they're called in Japanese, from the world headquarters building just three feet away, through two walls shaking the earth, shaking the dormitory, echoing still in my brain, cracking Honbu's earthquake-cracked concrete back wall.

Master Choi, I try to explain, is Korean and can't use the Japanese of the Kyokushin dojo without being shunned by his expat Korean community in Chapel Hill. Their parents' generation, so mistreated by imperial Japan.

Enslaved.

Annexed.

Made sex slaves.

Forced to study Japanese, and to take Japanese names.

Bicycle lane ending ahead. Have to dodge through that gap in the railing in three, two … watch out! Just the right height to …

Ha! Not careful and I'll rack my balls!

That's it, Nathan. Revel in the comedy of being here in the first place!

Close! – but I managed it.

Kicked my trailing leg back behind, to keep from taking the corner of that stainless steel rail in the crease of my leg. How can they possibly charge through this obstacle course every morning, without ever slowing?

They ACCELERATE when they encounter cause for delay!

Fighting, always forward.

Wheezing.

Jesus, I'm wheezing!

Haven't felt like this since fifth grade. Chapel Hill, and *Pacers*, an after-school running club for kids. Racing in the woods, that long steep hill and rocks and roots to make sure I don't trip. Mom takes me and they test me for asthma. Blowing through that plastic tube. Clay roofing tiles, a bamboo screen, a miniature evergreen blurring by, splinted with rope and multiple wooden poles to force an ornamental shape. Bonsai trees on a ledge. So many suits on bicycles. Need to spit. Can't afford to break my rhythm.

Hold it.

Swallow.

Texture, the taste of phlegm.

Morning of my first full day in Japan, the first of a thousand.

French Mocaram, my sempai since he's been living in the dormitory for one year before me. "Yes, Ligo, I heard that Mas Oyama was born in Korea, but he – how do you say? – turned his back? – yes, he turned his back on his Korean family, Ligo, when he took his Japanese name.

"Anyway, Koreans are *orrible* at karate."

The French "horrible" without the h. I wonder why he has to be so condescending. Maybe French Algerians are like that. I have to answer him with "osu."

"OSU!" I shout, bringing it up from my low belly, standing there barefoot on the tatami.

Yesterday.

The jet lag–dark surreal of the dormitory.

He's so satisfied to hear me tell him "osu!" Makes him feel big.

Didn't he say he'd just turned eighteen?

"They are much weaker than the Japanese," he says, "as we can see. In the tournaments. Where they are every time beaten in the first round. Yes, beaten to death, Ligo. *Umiliated.*" That was "humiliated" without the h. "… I wouldn't want to be Korean. They are very weak."

Weak like my teacher, he means.

"Osu!" my voice. I have no choice but to answer "osu," like the "Yes, Sir" we used in the training hall at UNC. Forcing me to agree with him that my teacher and all Koreans who haven't renounced their heritage and become Japanese are weak. His faint smile, close-cropped black-African's hair, he nods to agree with my agreement.

Angriest my father ever was, was when, as a child, I used the word "nigger." Never uttered it since but thanks to my father at least now I know what it means.

The worst thing one can say about another, and I wonder why this guy's welcome has to be so hateful.

The emaciated Japanese buzz around.

Crashing in, out when the hollow door slams. Too busy for me, afraid maybe. I see it in their eyes. Like I'm the first white guy they've ever seen, and me.

To deny.

Left in the charge of this French guy, the dormitory's only other foreigner.

Martha was afraid when I first met *her*. Gracie stepped in and put on a front, condescending like she was supposed to be somebody.

Too insecure in her new role to share the truth of her with a child.

Coarse and cocky like this Frenchman.

And look where it got her.

Look where it got *me!*

Tokyo.

Standing at attention.

Fudo dachi, he tells me the stance is called. Next to my futon upstairs in the dormitory's "Big Room." Feet parallel, shoulder width apart, weight equal on both feet, fists clenched at my sides and in front of my hips. Mocaram sprawled out in the corner on the tatami with one leg outstretched, his elbow resting on his other knee.

I suppose the Japanese'll be better, kinder.

"Yes, but it's not true," I wish I'd said.

"Mas Oyama *didn't* turn his back on Korea. Master Choi's uncle, Choi Baedal, adopted the name 'Ma-su-ta-tsu O-yama' since Korean immigrants were forced to take Japanese names. 'O-yama' means 'great mountain.' I can't remember now how the Chinese characters of 'Ma-su-ta-tsu,' pronounced 'Mastats,' are a reference to 'the Korean people,' but they are."

A straightaway ahead.

How can these streets possibly be so quiet?

Two hundred more yards – we're at a flat-out sprint now! – and then which way? I'm gasping for air.

Small-town.

Miniature.

The city-set in a Godzilla movie.

But this is Tokyo, one of the biggest cities on the planet!

A huge thoroughfare like the one I came in on, on the airport bus. My late afternoon arrival at the Metropolitan Hotel where it drops off. They slice their way in through the city, somewhere over there, somehow completely separate from these tiny streets, lined by one- and two-story Japanese homes.

I know they're there, over there, but somehow even the sound of all that traffic's blocked out.

This whole, long row of homes.

One- or two-square-meter gardens, proudly displaying manicured miniature shrubs and trees, stainless mailboxes on their iron gates, yelping dogs on the concrete of the two-foot strips of would-be yard running up to fill the gaps in between. Old men and women and schoolboys and -girls in navy-blue uniforms, riding bicycles up and down as if the streets were theirs, so leisurely, as if believing the cars, which even now seem somehow to make no sound, couldn't possibly hurt them.

How can these possibly be two-way streets?

Another car ahead.

And "Osu! Kuruma desu!" one of the emaciated Japanese yells from behind.

Two cars this time!

One ahead, and also one behind.

"Osu!" My voice, and we all leap back into single file.

Perhaps the cars will pass each other as we approach!

Perhaps our path will be blocked!

Perhaps we'll have those eight or ten seconds to drop our pace down to jogging in place, so perhaps I can rest.

Maybe then I can breathe!

iii.

Honbu's basement showers.

A long slow exhale.

A moment of peace, my eyes closed, and for a moment even the sound's blocked out.

Hot water.

Gushing, cradles my skull. Embraces in the shape of honey from a spoon. Showering with my head shaved is different from any I've ever had.

A shower actually in Japan?

Different still.

Hot, rushing afterbirth!

My own. Spills outwards at the feet of a new man. I lift my chin.

Change how the sheets fall off my skull.

Those running off my brow separate and roll backwards off.

Comb past my ears.

A beautiful woman's cupped hands.

A massage with oil.

Blind, I reach out, feel for the shower knobs.

Corroded, and with sharp edges behind. Slippery like soap, and connected to wobbly pipes. I have one minute left to shower, dress, and join Mocaram.

Body's wrecked.

Numb.

That absence of sensation in my legs to prove that it's

done, this dubious-hilarious fact of such an incomprehensible, probably-was hallucinatory run.

The knob on the right.

Which way for more heat? and my brother in the States.

Can't slap me on the back and tell me I'm insane, so he laughs to himself and shakes his head. Celebrates! I'm in Japan and my parents don't even know. Only Martha so far. And her folks, and my dad's. Four in-laws of my father's long-dead marriage to Martha.

How come THEY still get to be friends?

My voice.

"Shall we sit down?"

Sounds timid even to me. A difficult conversation looming and "There's no turning back now, Nathan," I'd have muttered if I was alone. Four of my life's grandparents gather 'round a round kitchenette table, a rough underside where I could stick my gum if I were still in school, and I pull it two inches towards me and the wall, across the vinyl to make more room.

The condo itself, overpriced.

One that'll revert back to the home when they die, and with my heels, I scoot my chair farther 'round to make more room for a fifth. The Pines at Templeton, a lifetime's worth of trinkets saved up and squeezed into two-bedroom apartments with wheelchair-wide doors, grab bars in the bathrooms for ease, niceties exchanged, and, in the eyes of these four old people, I see.

They enjoy the days they have left, force it if they have to, and then they won't have to be aware, all the time, of how little time there really might be.

I brace myself, and tell them what I came to say.

The Ligos.

Joe and Dorothy Ligo, loving but stern. A funeral home owner/operator, lifelong undertaker, retired now and come south to be near his son. Every silver hair in place, and part of one finger and his thumb missing from the lawnmower that rolled. My grandmother Dotty who raised the kids, and Dad who adored her, making us laugh that time by imitating one of her expressions of stern disapproval. The funeral home in Slippery Rock, my father's childhood home through school, college, marriage, and beyond. Vague memories, but then they bought the place next door. The apple orchard, the basement I saw only once where the bodies were prepared, our red sleeping bags for kids in the living room with all the grandfather clocks, tock tock tick, tock tock tick, and then we went out and saw our first movie.

The Rescuers.

Was it Mom with us, or was that Martha? Must have been Mom, we were still that young. Joe and Dorothy Ligo. Bemused. I'm nineteen and in a millisecond I dash the Ligo grandchild generic, one propagated and protected by the stern part of their stern and closeted loving. In just four days I'll be off to Japan.

"Oh, look, Joe, this fourth grandchild of ours has a personality of his own!"

Home.

My nostrils fill with water and I breathe in steadily past my lips. I gulp down Tokyo tap water, like hot green tea with a trace of copper. Five days have passed since then, but still I can feel the corners of my mouth twitching into an impulse to laugh. I celebrate! – the rules I break in the name of my escape underway. I'm relieved that Martha's folks are here, to explain it once I'm gone. That, or Cliff'll change the subject and chuckle the bemusement away. Tall, lanky Cliff in his suspenders, a Tampa Nugget cigar noticeably absent today from his shirt pocket, and tiny little Mary. Hunched to even more tiny and peering, delightful, over the edge of the table.

Clifford and Marion Strawn, attorneys both from George Washington University in D.C., and Cliff became a Florida real estate developer.

Alabama hunter.

Cross-country storyteller.

Martha, the photographer. Only child, artist, professor.

And Dad's parents push my father toward the pulpit all his life, one arm twisted always behind his back. Cliff and Mary hold their breath and send Martha to Japan. She's twenty-one in the Tokyo fish market of 1964, and raised independent enough to not be afraid of Zen. "I'll be there for three years," I explain, and that part they get: any one of them might not be around when I get home.

But Calloway Peak, then.

Grandfather's highest peak!

That outcrop of stone between my feet, just two days before my grandparents at The Pines. It's barely dawn and a whitewater river of mist soars by, I see again that last look in Master Choi's eyes, and from that I know that so much more can be mine. "Listen to your heart," he says, and the world falls out from under me. I'm too worn out after seven years of all this crap at home to leap up and shout, but, like sugar the honesty of what I collaterally share with the oldest members of my clan coats my teeth, and I'm carried away.

Oh, the truth!

Duty to family, the most raw of any I've ever shared, gushes out in the resolute calm of a Nathan Ligo finally free.

My love for family!

Pent up and beaten down, deeper and deeper, and year after year. Whipping cords of white mist, and an acid-burned pine. It's Gatlin's words, the rolled-up newspaper's in her hand this time, and it's me, not our childhood dog Mina, that's supposed to learn obedience. It's *her* household already now for six long years, and Dad expects my spine always curved, my tail always between my knees.

But to sit these four down, together, and tell them?

Not that, because I can't, but at least Japan?

To explain Master Choi, to tell them from the heart, and try to explain what it's all about even though throat-tightening pity prevents me from telling them about Dad, and I know they lack the all-important context and likely won't get it?

The freedom!

Filial piety without rebuke! Honesty in the raw, the kind I learned from Master Choi.

Raw because I deliver it with my eyes. Raw like Master Choi delivered it. Telepathic. I *see-deliver* what I want to be seen, straight into the heart of those who'll let me. And this day, like Master Choi to me, my grandparents *do* let me.

So honest words aren't necessary.

Years! Wasted.

Neither of my parents can tolerate the truth of me. Seven long years Dad kept me from Martha, and in these new, second, separate lives of my parents without her, and without the Prescott family in Chapel Hill, there's no excuse for honesty. No excuse for truth. No excuse for Nathan Ligo. Their life with me. Their *lives!* – are lives passed already by.

Killers!

Killers of the connections we shared. Happy now that Mom's in Chapel Hill, her head spinning at my unexplained absence. My mom, the therapist and her endless circles. Happy that Dad and his family are in Princeton for the semester! Can't keep their act together anyway. We'll skip that generation for the time being, and celebrate this, one chance only for communication between me and my surviving grandparents.

One conversation.

A few words.

And soon they'll die.

And the crux of it? The great honesty that I share?

A morsel again of humor, tantalizing, tempting, gushing hot water from above, a second swallow to follow the first, and I know it.

The heart of it.

Is that *I* already have. Died, that is. Nathan Ligo has died and gone away. The Nathan Ligo they know, if they ever really tried, will never be back from Japan.

Nathan Ligo's gone to war.

And the Nathan Ligo they know will never come home.

iv.

"Succeed or die!"

Flesh, burning.

Throat, tightening.

Gasp for air!

Damn, two cars this time! And they're waiting for *us* to pass! They're stopped in their tracks, front bumper to front bumper, and Japanese streets so narrow, they can't pass without pulling out into the pedestrian lane.

No rest!

Not even now.

Of course they're waiting, I should already have known!

We are Kyokushin!

We are karate, Mas Oyama's uchi deshi, his live-in disciples. Mas Oyama's personal students, and they know it. The pride of Japan's martial tradition, actually conquering the world this time.

Kyokushin, Japan's strongest bare-knuckle karate. Sure, they can't tell from our T-shirts, but they must know the karate uniform pants. *Dogi* pants they're called in Japanese. They must know, no other *karateka* in Japan must run like this.

How can anyone in the world?

Such a breakneck pace.

A suicide pace!

A do-or-die pace.

A love-for-Japan's-military-past pace.

"We'll drop dead in our tracks before we sacrifice our speed" are the words this stampede, were it a beast, would speak.

"We are Mas Oyama's uchi deshi!

"The hopes and dreams of Japan.

"We are Kyokushin. We are *Budo*. We will not be stopped. We will never again surrender!"

Master Choi's eyes.

Deep brown.

Fixed on mine in a crowd of mostly clueless college students.

UNC.

The University of North Carolina at Chapel Hill.

A dozen, maybe fourteen, standing at attention.

Sweaty karate uniforms, the hardwood floor at UNC as Master Choi explains.

I can't recall the particulars, but in his eyes, I see.

Truth.

Mountains, for Koreans.

An image of unshakable strength.

O-yama.

His uncle.

"Great Mountain."

English.

Butchered.

Some of the others don't understand. Their bulky, deliberate word use. They complain after class. "What did he say? Was that English?" Yes, I know that it was, but I get every other word by context, read the rest, and more.

In his eyes.

Perhaps they can't see what I see.

In sixth grade I had a stone with which I could control the weather.

Will it to snow like the weatherman warned, they'll close

the school, and we can all go home. Home apart from this knot in my stomach, home where I'll be free.

Home, walled up in my room where it's safe.

Home, the five channels on my black-and-white TV.

Why don't they look at me, why don't they invite me like the rest? Is something wrong with me? Is my being so "cute," so "bright," like my parents always say, and so small really so ugly to them?

"Of course …"

Shy titan's words.

Continue.

"The ocean waves will eventually wear down the mountain, and one could argue which one is more powerful. The sea never stops attacking the mountain, but instead of diminishing its height, it merely exposes the harder and harder rock, at the beach before …"

Hilarious! – his mistaken word choice.

Since I understand, and can feel the others around me, confused. "Beach," he said, but he meant "coast." Crashing waves wearing down rocky cliffs, exposing harder and harder stone. I see Mas Oyama, his uncle, his two years of secluded mountain training, punching the trees around his cabin, thousands of times daily till the trees wither and die, and his fists!

Like a stonemason's hammers!

The student standing at attention to my right.

Literal.

Sightless.

He's counting on Master Choi's *words* to communicate.

Thinking about *our* beach in North Carolina. I can feel it, he's lost in sand, waves, bikinis, beach towels, an obese woman in a suit with flaps like a loincloth as if it might hide what a bathing suit couldn't possibly hide. His mind wanders. He's got an anthropology exam. Less than English, Master Choi's words, but more than just words.

Telepathic.

He continues.

Thick accent, shy titan, savant.

"… the mountain's height is never affected by the waves. This was how much my uncle loved Korea. The Japanese forced him to take a Japanese name, but he took this one, 'Great Mountain,' and lived a life that would show them all the strength of the Korean spirit. Like the mountain, Mas Oyama's spirit would never be broken.

"… of course I told you many times how when my uncle was a boy, he ran to the top of a mountain in Korea near his birthplace. The mountain was called "Sleeping Dragon," and he shouted when he was just nine years old, 'One day my roar will wake this sleeping dragon!'

"Even then he knew how powerful he would be. He became the strongest karate man in Japan, and, quite frankly, after that, the strongest karate man in the world!"

Master Choi.

Kind, warm.

Stern, insistent.

Love.

Power.

The answer for me.

Family.

What family?

Father?

Impotent.

Mother?

Pulling out.

Martha?

Robbed of Martha.

Love, comfort, warmth, stolen away. Wisps of white mist. Storm force gusts of wind blasting past in utter silence. An island, splitting whitewater torrents of cloud. A granite island.

Grandfather's peak. Natural bonsai with roots walking out from the crevices in the rock. Their branches burned by acid rain. Another gust, and all of us shiver. The top of the world, and, by God, the world is mine this time!

Here within my grasp.

"I know the answers already," I write at my desk at Templeton, alone on Third East, freshman Belk Dormitory.

I'm 17.

But Grandfather's peak again, a year later and a Japanese sword in my grasp this time. I'm barely 19, just seven days ago now, and two before my grandparents at The Pines. The sword's an imitation, but it's got a sharpened blade. Wouldn't stand up to another, but it would sure cut flesh. My flesh if I asked it to, and that's why I bought it. Just over a week ago, but passed now, like a dream.

Was I really there?

Had to have been.

In Martha's pickup truck to Grandfather Mountain in the night.

The climb.

A flashlight and the Milky Way through the trees, the ridge after dawn. A shiver, a cloud, mist eddying 'round my ankles and for a moment even the mountain is gone? The top of the world, it is mine this time, and I'm embarrassed to have a sword in my grasp since it's a fake. A wisp of white curls past its blade. A symbol merely. A symbol of my undoing. My belly slit. Entrails, if I chose, spilling outwards into the crevices in the stone.

The valley below.

Immaculate.

Not a single crack in these Japanese streets!

Dear God, when will it end?

How much farther can it be?

How will I possibly find my way back to the dormitory?

I'll trip and I'll stumble, and I'll be left behind, they'll make two more turns through this maze of tiny streets, and I'll be lost.

And I'll never meet the man after all.

Mas Oyama.

My teacher's uncle, the bare-handed bull killer.

His private students.

These stampeding, miniature Japanese monsters!

Badgers and bone breakers. Tiny little killers! Calloused knuckles that protrude into knots like ball-peen hammers.

Templeton wouldn't believe it if I told them.

Templeton.

Would have no clue.

"Oh, but the world is a lot bigger!"

I know that already. Bigger than just Japan. Light-years! "I know the answers already," I write alone at my desk on Third East.

Freshman year and me, the youngest on campus. Skipped twelfth grade. Barely pubescent, I think. My weight class in wrestling was 135 last year, 112 in tenth grade.

One-twelve!

How can anyone be so small?

Dillon, my lover, my first and so overdue.

Templeton and olive-tinted skin, half-Lebanese but American as Iowa and apple pie, senior French literature major, English minor, loved me, made love to me, heaven for me, read Chaucer and Shelley, warmth like what family was for me-the-child.

She and I.

Two of a miniscule, 1200-student student body where everybody knows everybody. And me, the faculty brat, that Art Historian's son. Grew up in Templeton. Threw snowballs at Templeton students passing on the way to the post office at noon when I was six. A decade later and I'm picking the lock to Perkins Auditorium exam week with a screwdriver. The cat burglar again, breaking in, this time to solve calculus problems on the chalkboard in the night, all night. Inside Chambers's dome, that highest temple over Templeton's academia.

It's *my* temple this time.

I'm less than the rest and I know it. The only way to keep up is to break in and find a high place and to worship. "Study animals, Templeton students!" Not a dumb one among them. Bliss, on one hand, but "I'm not where I'm supposed to be," I write.

I'm seventeen, and "I can feel it! It's all meant to be mine!" I look inward at the explosion that created all we know and I see Brook Farm's Transcendentalists, an eleventh-grade research paper for Mrs. May's English class. We read Ralph Waldo Emerson, and for the moment I've become.

His all-seeing!

His eye.

His part, or particle, of God.

North Mecklenburg Senior High and its library, glancing outside where everyone who fits in at lunch hour resides.

All so comfortable in their skin!

Zen Mind, Beginner's Mind.

Blissful learning, but still I'm not satisfied. Need more. "I'm meant to be somewhere else, somewhere beyond. I can see the answers already, can feel them just within. I know that they're there. Will have to fight all the harder to unlock them."

Careful, Nathan! You might get what you ask for.

Got Japan.

Master Choi's Japan.

Mas Oyama's.

Run!

V.

Steam in my nostrils thickens to moisture in my throat.

Dull green as I open my eyes.

Flickering fluorescent bulbs in the basement locker room outside. Stacks of square wooden lockers and punching bags hanging. A low cardboard-tiled ceiling. Three dark walls, and an inadequate glow struggles in through the wall behind me of opaque, waffled glass. Through mildew. Years of soap scum. This geometric cubish rectangle at last of blinding steam. And falls inertly on dull green. Was it always green?

Am I really in Japan?

Yes.

Honbu's basement showers. "Honbu" means "headquarters" in Japanese.

My body's wrecked and Mocaram gave me two minutes to shower. The basement of the dojo building, the "Kaikan" he called it. The "Kyokushin-kaikan," Mas Oyama's world headquarters, we're late, and Iwaya's a threat.

The third-year sempai who will beat me, Mocaram says, if I come back late from the run.

What does he mean, he'll beat me anyway?

Under the shower, but still I sweat, a wave of fear tightens into my throat. My legs, I can't feel enough to be concerned and I allow myself, once more, to roam. Forty-five more seconds of shower. Massaging warmth. More than a mother's embrace, I tell myself. The one I remember. Ten years back. What a mother's embrace is meant to be.

No, I need more!

Need to succumb – need to revel in more than simple bliss. Need to *create* a greater bliss still. A stone with which I could control the weather, a childhood magical power, and a simple shower becomes a rushing warmth like Dillon inside, something better even than *that kind* of comfort. One I permit – one I allow! – to come. One I celebrate and shout, to counterbalance and erase the suffering of the run.

Martha, massaging my back, I'm eight, rubbing my ears with the smell of cocoa butter, and my mother now, and this time with powder. It's Johnson and Johnson's baby powder I smell, and she pats my bottom as well. The elastic of my underwear snaps back into place, and she giggles. I'm five in the trailer by the lake, still that soon after the divorce. My brother shakes his head, he's thirteen months older than me, at home, and twice my size. Twenty. A U.S. Marine, there's WMD, and the whole world's now moving towards Iraq.

He drops out of Templeton my same freshman year, since I'm there a year early, and who can blame him? Without Japan, without Martha, and without the Prescott family in Chapel Hill, the U.S. Marine Corps, certainly, is the fastest route out of bitch Gracie's Templeton.

A family dog challenges him.

Broad daylight in quiet little Templeton, and Aaron on the tail end of a ten-mile road march with ROTC. He's pissed 'cause his own pack strap broke and he's also carrying the pack of another runner who fell out of the run. Dog's ears laid all the way back, bares his teeth and charges from the other side of the street, howling. Aaron smiles inwardly and turns, raises his rubber-coated, decommissioned M-16 high over his head by its barrel, and charges right back at the dog, howling right back.

Dog yelps, realizes he's bitten off more than he can chew,

and takes off around the house to scoot under the back porch, and my brother, twice my size in combat boots, stomping through daffodils and screeching to a halt in twin ruts of mulch at the shock in the face of the old man there, jaw dropped, innocently raking leaves in his own back yard, in innocent, "Never-saw-anything-like-the-Ligo-boys" Templeton.

Aaron.

Running all the way home from Templeton Elementary School to the Abbotts' house on the Green, I'm 5 and he's 6. Huge white house with columns and colonial steps. Gray painted porch floorboards that warp, and the Abbotts are on sabbatical this spring. Cashion's Gulf, Templeton's only gas station on the one side, and the Village Green, *all of our* communal front lawn on the other.

My mother and brother and me, fresh out of the Richies' house on Dogwood Lane while *they* were away. Their orange cat, the pillow room and Rin Tin Tin on the TV after we come home from the schoolhouse each day. Black and white TV left over from a childhood in the funeral home. German Shepherd named Rin Tin Tin. He leaps the gorge with a rope in his teeth so the cavalry can tie it off to a tree, cross, blow their bugles, and save the day.

The trailer at the lake with the dock. Mom rented it, while working at the bank just after the divorce, and Aaron and I are at home, only every *other* week with Dad in the country. I'm home for the day already at the Abbotts' house since the schoolhouse gets out at noon, some second graders teased Aaron in the stairwell and he ran all the way home, one long block, and halfway across all of Templeton so far as a first grader is concerned. Straight in, and straight up the Abbotts' giant sleeping-bag-sliding, smooth wooden stairs to hide in one of the bedrooms where we weren't supposed to go, with the older Abbott boys' toys we weren't supposed to play with, high up on those permanent, eggshell-white glossy shelves.

The babysitter's there, it's naptime, and I don't get much worked up about it, because I'm five and it's not clear to me that older brothers at the big elementary school don't just run home sometimes. The principal arrives on foot to bring Aaron, fists clenched, back to school, and what's the big deal about that? Mom's crying, too. Going nuts already, I suppose, in her room with the piano, and the door shut. "Sometimes adults cry," she says, and it's nothing to worry about, yet she sure seems to do it a lot, and I like to eat margarine and sugar sandwiches. Aaron prefers melted cheese with the top of it leathery and brown from too long on broil in our lives' first toaster oven, and maybe Dad'll get one soon. *Adam-12*'s on TV and Grandma's dying in DC although we barely know her and don't know what cancer is. I gave her that miniature ceramic Dalmatian I got at the Village Store for Christmas last year when we went up – I remember it with one leg off, after I got it back when she died.

Grandpa at their home in Laurel, that's Maryland, walks us to the Public Library one time to check out the two that we're allowed of those children's books that come in thick plastic bags, with straps, and plastic snaps because of the records or tapes that come with them for kids who can't yet read to listen to. Grandpa walks real slow and his nose drips, he's "too young," and I didn't know he was born and grew up in Japan. Mom says he barely speaks because of the blood vessel that broke in his brain, which she calls a *stroke*.

Japan.

Honbu's basement showers.

A roaring furnace audible, almost even above the shower's roar. That colorful steam shovel with a determined, kind face, like *The Little Engine that Could*. "I think I can, I think I can." Digs a massive basement for a skyscraper building, and becomes trapped in the hole he dug, panics momentarily and cries in the night, big-penned frowny-face tears straight from his primary colors. In the end, he becomes retired, celebrated, venerated finally, and then converted into the new building's furnace, with a grin that's content on his face because now he gets to keep everyone warm.

That children's book, again, at the Children's Schoolhouse where, above all, John Henry represents, for me, titanic strength.

Ezra Jack Keats.

A whisper through the hills.

Born with a hammer in his hand. The steel-driving man. Legs crushed by rock in a cave-in, and a blasting-fuse still burning. "Drop that hammer, John Henry! It's at the end of your reach, and you're the only one who can! Crush the fuse before it goes off or the men will be killed!"

Hero, John Henry!

Like a whisper, shhhhh, straight through into the hearts of man. A titan like Mas Oyama.

Japan.

vi.

Splashing heat.

Pale green.

Honbu's basement shower, and it all comes back. Did I die on that mountain already, or is this death, and am I dying it slowly on this run?

Halfway done, I'm passing through.

The other side.

I'm left to wonder if it's true.

It's gotta be a hallucination after all, a few more strides and I'll no longer have to feel.

Anything.

Iwaya Sempai.

The biggest among us, the dormitory's dangerous senior student's at the lead.

He's clearly the fastest. No taller, I see, than me. I'm gasping now even to breathe. The fibers of his thick black nylon tracksuit strain to contain the wall of lean muscle underneath.

He's running like a machine.

"Be careful of Iwaya Sempai," Mocaram says, and we're scurrying around, picking up cigarette butts and hard, discarded chewing gum from in among the gravel in the park at six, sweating already in the sticky dawn before training.

"He hates foreigners," the Frenchman says. "He will beat you if he can find the *chance* – how do you say? –opportunity?

He will beat you if he can find the opportunity. You must stay together with the runners, Ligo. You must not be left behind, or if you come back late, he will scold you, and maybe then he will beat you.

"Maybe then he will beat *me!*"

Iwaya Sempai.

The only one in a tracksuit.

An earned privilege.

Running.

Like a gangster's Cadillac, cruising.

And the rest of us bounce along like cans chained to the bumper. All but me in off-white, dirt-stained and sweat-soaked karate uniform pants, running shoes, socks and the soles of my feet rub away. All of our heads shaved but theirs grown back to mere stubble. They got here one month before me, their waterlogged white T-shirts tucked in at the waist.

My dogi came with me from America, it's whiter than theirs.

Lighter.

Not yet stained with dirt from their park.

And, earlier, that was Ishi …

Was it Ishi-*guro* Sempai?

The other third-year guy. A bit feminine maybe and making up for it, I think, like me. Dropped out early on to run at his own pace. Smaller. To Iwaya Sempai inferior. Free to drop out because he's the same level in the dormitory hierarchy, both of them starting their third and final year.

It's not that I can't breathe.

It's that my body's shutting down!

I never do, so I'm sure I won't throw up.

It's the dark that's closing in.

It's not like I haven't been here before.

For 30 strides?

For 100?

More?

But this is new! I've never been *forced* to maintain it before!

People get *beaten* here if they fall out of the run!

In cross-country season, we'd *celebrate* once the race was through. The brown vinyl of those school bus seats, and my sweat suit hood pulled down over my face. The laughing, my teammates' separate, celebrative chatter.

But here?

Mocaram said that after the run there were thirty more minutes of grueling exercises to do. Push-ups, pull-ups, sit-ups, and something, he said, called jumping squats, and I can see in his eyes that it's those that scare him the most.

Charge forward, Nathan!

Avoid being scolded – or worse! – by Iwaya Sempai.

He even looks mean, that leering eye, a scowl and a hooked nose, and the fact that everyone's afraid of him. And that's Mocaram's classmate, the second-year Hashi …

Hashi-*moto*, I think.

He was fat before, really fat. His extra skin ripples up and down on his triceps in spite of the elastic of his skin-tight, drenched T-shirt. The rest of us get smaller, and skinnier and …

Ha!

"More malnourished-looking," it occurs to me as we get closer and closer to the end of the line. Three of the first-year guys – is it four, maybe? – smaller even than me. I'm five foot nine, weigh only one fifty-five. Nineteen now for three months already.

Nineteen?

Jesus, what happened to 18?

Seems like I just started Templeton a few months ago and for the first half of the year I was just 17.

Kuruda.

Running two bodies ahead of me. Cattycorner I can read the *kanji* written in permanent ink on his dogi pants.

Kuro, black.

Da, rice field.

"Kuro-Da." I must have learned *at least something* before it all fell apart, last semester, sophomore year at UNC.

Is he really five whole inches shorter than me?

Really only five four or five five?

Doesn't seem so small.

Runs like a machine built for running. A tank, with a big-block Corvette engine. Back muscles.

Chiseled.

Almost too big for his frame. The other first-year guys, eight of them, seven Japanese and one Korean. Six weeks here already before me. Sweat splashes off the surface of his T-shirt.

Saturated.

So small!

A dwarf, maybe?

His capacity for building muscle so outclasses his frame. At home, I'M the smallest. Maybe here I'll be average.

Insane!

"How much farther can it be?"

Running so fast.

Can barely get enough air in past my throat. Need all my lungs to maintain. My ribcage.

Aches.

Master Choi's voice, I'm fifteen.

Chapel Hill in junior high and I'm running with him and seven-foot Dave Popson, a UNC center I see playing basketball on TV who joined us at the CMAC to improve his balance and jumping ability. The three of us, Master Choi, giant him, and tiny little me, and Master Choi's thick Korean accent.

"Man is the only animal on the planet that breathes with his chest.

"Look at the tiger. Look at the wildcat, and the gazelle and the horse. Look at how they run! Fill up your low belly first, and only after that, allow your chest to fill. It will increase the capacity of your lungs."

But Master Choi, it's not working!

I'm battling these miniature Japanese streets and it's not enough!

None of the training's been enough!

This is what you must have meant when you told me you'd recommend me to your uncle when I'm strong enough, and that furthermore I might not ever be!

Am I strong enough now?

How can I possibly maintain?

I can't possibly control my breathing at this pace.

Forget it!

It's all that I can do to choke down enough air to feed this nonstop, berserk sprint!

A boulder in an avalanche!

Yes, but *this* boulder wants to stop rolling!

How much farther can it be?

Dr. Choi.

Ph.D.

Physics at UNC.

Those eyes that burn into me.

Mas Oyama's nephew!

The CMAC, his Carolina Martial Arts Club.

Saved me.

My stomach, ooouch! Jesus, hurts even to remember! God, how did I endure it?

Relentless!

Those three years of shadowy fear.

Room-spinning, vague, pain in a place I can't pinpoint, can't explain. "It could undo you here, too, Nathan!" Japan and I've only got one prescription bottle left.

And then?

The acid burn.

Roll the dice! Succeed or die.

I missed forty days of school, my eighth-grade year in Chapel Hill.

And Master Choi.

Sleek. Powerful. Eyes.

Piercing.

Eyes.

Refuge.

Loves me.

"I wish I had a son like you," his voice, and my life's forever changed. Of course he means "a son my age," I'm thirteen. Fetzer Gym at UNC, the fencing room, four days a week and my second home for six more years. My life begins in that impromptu training hall of his, in Master Choi, his eyes, those windows through to strength, family again, in Chapel Hill, my mother's Chapel Hill.

Mom.

What mom?

Decided already how much I'll cost, and she whittles me away.

I'm 18 when I know it for sure but she'd decided already when I was 15, when she went nuts and left my stepfather Bob and my stepsisters. Screaming at him in the kitchen while the twins, Fran and Betsy, and Aaron and I listen in the next room. Her voice, shrieking, "Why can't you just say it?" over and over again, but "It's because he doesn't feel that way; do you want him to lie?" we all know in the next room's the answer.

She's lost her mind.

Buys me dinner, deducts it from her "Child-Rearing Account" subtitled "Nathan." Birthday presents, another deduction. It's painted across her face. I'm a liability like her taxes and her telephone bill. When the money is spent, so then will she be. Free of son. Free of responsibility. Finally. Free of Nathan. Free to start over. Single. Childless. She thinks she can't breathe till all the money is gone and my presence is erased. Analyzes and analyzes, rationalizing a way out.

Of her animal, motherly obligation to son.

What, does she think I won't take care of *her* someday?

Not like this, I suppose.

I'll be an orphan and she'll be free to be a lonely old maid. In a shoe with black laces. *An Old Woman in a Shoe.* A children's book at the Schoolhouse, I'm five. Thick cardboard pages a toddler can't tear.

To hell with her anyway!

Deserves what she got for dropping out of the Prescott family. Deserves what she got, again, three months ago. Me, halfway through second semester and I'd disappeared, run away in must have seemed, a lifetime long, but was that really just this spring?

From UNC?

Let her sweat!

For mountain training, I'd pulled up stakes.

"Listen to your heart," that was Master Choi's voice, I'd failed him. Those words. His eyes that cut through me.

The insanity.

The dream!

For a moment in time, uchi deshi, it seemed, had fallen though, and I'd decided to live on a mountain and train, 1000 days like Mas Oyama set out to do.

A lifetime since then! – but could it have only been these past three months I spent in Templeton?

No one knows I'm here.

My hometown the size of a pinhead, and I avoid my usual circles. My father's family's on sabbatical this time, in Princeton, and me, I live 100 percent off the grid. I borrow a room from the mom of a high school girlfriend my father never liked and my stepmother discriminated against, and I work, two full-time jobs to save up and outfit three years of mountain training.

But then!

Even that fell through.

A bomb!

Master Choi didn't tell his uncle I'd dropped out of school and run away, and the CMAC's, my friend Rob in Chapel Hill, wrote me a letter and told me Mas Oyama'd sent the plane ticket anyway?

Instead of just letting Mas Oyama forget me – as "just some American kid" he'd never seen – Master Choi kept the option open for me, and Mas Oyama was still expecting me to come to Japan! Master Choi would lose face, it occurs to me, I'm paralyzed and struck dumb, and like a zombie in the night I stumble up my mountain trail. Grandfather's peak at dawn and a Japanese sword in my grasp that would sure cut flesh, my flesh, if I asked it to.

Its blade.

That wisp of white mist.

An about-face!

No choice.

Can't take the plane ticket Mas Oyama sent me. Can't risk that Master Choi would misunderstand and stop me from going to see! I'll buy my own to Japan and ask Mas Oyama's advice.

For Master Choi.

I'll succeed or die!

Even without his blessing if necessary?

Fool!

Idiot of a boy!

It was a fantasy!

Mountain training like the titan, Mas Oyama?

What did you think you were, some kind of comicbook character? Come on, Nathan, grow up!

Get with the program!

Run!

vii.

Make a magnetic connection, Nathan!

Tether yourself to the spine of the runner in front of you.

Visualize the pull and make it real.

A magnetic pull.

Like gravity.

A constant. A physical law of nature, one that can't be broken.

"Even planets pull on each other."

My last year of high school, eleventh grade. Mr. Clayton's North Meck classroom of physics and chemistry. People don't know what to make of me because it's all so clear to me, I never miss an answer. "I know the answers already, you see." Can see it all right there in front of me.

Even without the chalkboard.

Hanging there in space between me and him, there's J. J. Thompson, the science fair looming, and his cathode ray tube. His discovery to measure e over m, the charge-mass ratio of an electron. I can't make it work at North Meck, but finally in UNC's cold-tiled physics building, I finish it there a year later, with their equipment, a glowing tungsten filament in an evacuated glass ball, and a blue stream of electrons curving, because of the magnetic field from the Helmholtz coils I made on my own, the particles reacting in a trace of mercury gas.

A *magnetic* pull, Nathan!

Just make one.

Now, like in sixth grade with a magic stone you once made it snow.

Ride it!

Like a water-skier behind a boat, connect yourself to the runners in front of you!

Lean into it!

Relax.

Drift, painlessly along.

Yes!

That's it.

The tether takes hold!

Ha! Look at that, I'll be damned, I'm here in Japan!

Uchi deshi. Live-in disciple. My teacher's uncle, the creator of Kyokushin. Is it really true? Will I meet him finally, today? A wave of fear masked by the numb. Maybe he won't let me stay once he hears how I've come.

I'm here without Master Choi's blessing.

After six years!

Japan.

Musashi's Japan.

Mas Oyama's.

Some kind of alternate dimension.

A *quantum* leap!

From my tiny little world at home.

Templeton and Chapel Hill, Chapel Hill and Templeton. Mom leaves Templeton before third grade. Three hours by car to Bob Prescott's big red house, with a *new* pillow room, on Cobb Terrace near UNC, and Jane's grown up already, and the first of my six blonde stepsisters I see. I'm seven and it's my first Chapel Hill and "We're going down to the courthouse to get married," Mom says, and Aaron and I are too young to understand or care and don't look up from the cartoons we're watching on TV.

"Okay, whatever," isn't that what mothers do, with twenty-years-senior, pipe-smoking psychiatrists with big houses; and six daughters; and a proud, remaining few, last blond hairs that are eight inches too long and he wraps them all the way around the top of his head so it'll be like he has some, and loud-barking schnauzers named Yavole? Mrs. Harrison's my teacher, the progressive Glenwood Elementary School, and finally I can get Erin Haze out of my head who was in my second grade in Charlotte, but now I've fallen in love with this little nerdy girl named Emily Newsome, who's got Barth Wilson in tow, all year long, playing Nancy Drew or some other mystery game I don't understand 'cause the game only has dialogue and doesn't have any parts, and I can't get close enough, and she doesn't even know I exist. Finally I give up, and love a teacher of mine for the first time. Nameless now 'cause I can't remember anything but her hair, our student teacher, and her deep brown eyes. Doesn't matter that I'm eight and she's all grown up, I love her anyway, she's from a place called Fuquay Varina, and came to UNC to study teaching. I send her an Eiffel Tower keychain I bring back from France and wrap it in newspaper, but never I hear from her again.

The next year I'm in Templeton.

Living with Dad and Martha at the log house again and it's Aaron's second time at Templeton Elementary School, a throwback to some kind of primitive dark age of public school education compared to Chapel Hill. The principal has a paddle to paddle the students who get out of line, and I bring a live bat in from the log house in a coffee can one time, for show and tell, and it gets out and flies around the classroom, or was it dead and was that Aaron, and am I remembering the one at the log house that flew around and around upstairs and that Dad finally killed with a badminton racquet?

And finally I'm shunned by my classmates who don't let me play their games at recess and Mrs. Kerry dismisses me to

the library every day, first during math and later during half of
the day because I know math better than her and never miss
an answer in most of the other subjects as well. Thank God I'm
the class's worst speller, because then at least the other kids
know I'm human enough to dislike, but this first black woman
I've ever known? She shakes her finger at me and tells me in
front of the class every day how I ought to be ashamed, for not
knowing how to read and write better, since I'm so smart, and
I wonder whether she still would if she knew how the other
kids wouldn't let me play because I'm the smallest. I wonder if
she'd still berate me like that if she knew it broke the heart of
the only truly race-blind child in the entire class, and left me
crushed, day after day so low I wished I could disappear and
fade away into the linoleum, and magically be out at the log
house where Martha could help me with the pinhole camera I
had to make for Cub Scouts in Chapel Hill, and feed me treats
from her pantry, fried green tomatoes even, and I could run in
the forest and chase our dog Mina, and play with salamanders
and crayfish in the creek, and Japan now for nearly sixteen
hours already.

In seconds, I'll have to shut down the shower and follow
Mocaram to the dormitory, to Iwaya Sempai's dormitory where
he might beat me. And I'll eat a breakfast that might burn my
stomach. I've only got one prescription bottle left to last me
somehow for three years, and if Mas Oyama doesn't send me
away, that alone could be my undoing.

No.

For Master Choi.

I'll succeed or die!

His voice, and me, a tiny thirteen.

His eyes.

"Okay, it's possible," he says. His English painful and
deliberate. "You want to go to Japan? You want to become my
uncle's student?

"Yes," he goes on, "even you can do it if you train hard. And study hard, and make yourself strong. Follow my advice, grow up a little bit, and when the time comes, I'll write to my uncle. I'll recommend you to him and he'll take you if I do. And then, of course, you won't have to pay for that. Since he's my uncle … if I recommend you, he'll send you a plane ticket, but," he raises a finger, and tilts his brow, and drills through me now with every bit of whatever it is I see in him that's more serious than any serious I've ever known. " … but you have to listen to my advice, Nathan! No American has ever made it there. Of course you could be the first … but first you have to become DAMN strong. And the chances of that, frankly speaking, are not too good. Perhaps if when you grow up, you get a little bit bigger."

"Yes, Sir!"

That's the CMAC's "Osu!" and my boy's voice.

Eager.

Naïve.

I'm the only child in the training hall. Thirteen, but my body's that of an eleven-year old, I know, since I'm still so small in my eighth grade, surrounded here by titans in the training hall. Brian Moran, giant, powerful jaw. Senior at Chapel Hill High. Wrestler. Kicks that reach the ceiling, and the only other of Master Choi's students unaffiliated with the university.

The only one other than me.

Hiawatha Benbee.

Black. African, I think. Somehow otherwise ethnic. Red belt like the rest, older. The heaviest of the six, his fists bigger than both of mine put together. Scott Horman, grad student, psychology major, fiery-eyed behind his glasses, every bit Hiawatha's equal in a fight. That blue bandana he folds into a strip and ties around his forehead to keep his long hair back. That much older than me, a product of his teens in the seventies.

Steve Hodson's number four, the awkward one. So happy if sweat were a measure of strength!

Master Choi told us he looked like an actor, but we laughed inwardly, because he didn't look like any actor we knew. Maybe an actor from the seventies movies that made it translated, a decade late, to Korea, with sideburns and a hairy back and arms. Certainly sweat IS a measure of effort. An A Steve gets, at least there, an A for effort.

Titans anyway.

Even David Toleman who's my size, and I'm only thirteen. Thick glasses and a handlebar mustache and a bird chest with the tiniest tuft of hair in the middle. A biochemist with an elastic band to keep his glasses from falling off, and the only one other than Master Choi in a black belt. Every day when I come in, his feet are up on the rail by the windows and he's doing push-ups on his knuckles. Fifty every day, a hundred sometimes, his fists threatening to slide out from under him in puddles, on the smooth concrete, of sweat. So much sweat! Requires so much work to keep my fists from sliding out from under me, in that position, and in that much sweat.

Leticia Hawn is the last. Asian somehow, American as me, though. Japanese, I think. Shorter than me, but heavier like my mother because of her bulges which aren't all that athletic. Red-faced Asian. Skin, blemished somehow. Nice woman, but we practice fighting and I always get paired up with the girl. Me, Nathan Ligo, always the smallest in my world, paired up with the girl who started late in life and can't kick higher than her waist. I long for Japan. Already, at least, I see myself in Japan, but then it's a Japan I can't possibly fathom.

Japan.

The promised land.

Where birds fly backwards and rain falls up, and where trees, as likely as not, grow side to side. I'm weaker than the rest, smaller, "shrimp" they call me in school, "cute" those who are trying to be nice, but if I can make it to Japan? I'll be the stronger one! Instead of beside David and Leticia, I'll stand shoulder to shoulder with Brian and Hiawatha.

I'll learn from the barehanded bull fighter, Master Choi's uncle.

Raw!

Epitome of power.

Crushed mountain stones with his bare hands.

I'll invite him to crush my world at home.

Nathan *the Shrimp's* world.

That icy, mountain mist.

That wisp of white that drifts, silently, split past the blade of my Japanese sword.

Those acid-burned pines.

A gust of wind, that maelstrom of white, and *all of us* shiver this time.

viii.

Not one week's passed, that mountain mist, my plane ticket to Japan.

Feels unreal in my hand.

The log house, too. Surreal to find myself again in my childhood home. Martha's upstairs and, in my original bedroom, I thumb past the slick of those carbon-copied pages, awkwardly, confirming once again the pertinent information, and not really believing that it's there. Red carbon lettering that looks like code. Nine hundred and eighty-five dollars was nearly all the money I'd saved for mountain training, after the stove, and the tent and the North Face bag, and the rest. The sword for my belly if I failed.

The travel agency on Main Street.

The same street where Mina died when I was fifteen. The family dog that came with us when Dad abandoned Martha out here at the log house and bought the brick one in town with the purple paint stripper. Hurricane Hugo's tornado-downed trees in my father's backyard.

Was that really just three months ago?

Christ, I've lived a lifetime since then!

My father's ax, rusty in the shed where the replacement dog lives, and, "Unbury the yard for your father," says that same, unadulterated love for family that's been so pent up and squashed down. That force that picks up that ax moments home from my moments-before-abandoned sophomore year at UNC. Dad's gone, so finally it can. He's at Princeton with *that woman* and the kids, and so many pecan limbs down I can see no grass in the whole long backyard except where it's thigh-high, and growing up past the leaves on all the dead trees which are already brown.

Just yesterday Master Choi's life-stopping "Listen to your heart" cut me in half like one of those stainless steel disks on a meat slicing machine, and I leave Chapel Hill for mountain training, run away, it must have seemed. My first stop, Templeton. My first act, my father's trees. Everyone must believe I've broken.

But I've only closed out the world!

Wood chips and sweat and hours into the dark, "Succeed or die" rings in my head like John Henry's hammer on steel, and I don't need anyone anymore. Don't need the CMAC, or UNC, not even Japan.

Master Choi, even, became redundant that day.

Nathan Ligo certainly did.

"Listen to your heart," he says and I do, and it says, "Shut it down!" End the life of Nathan Ligo! End Nathan Ligo and Nathan Ligo's every personal attachment to the world. Embody success. Live success. Merge heart, life force, and art. Bring honor to Master Choi. In life? Yes, but even in death, too, it doesn't matter.

After his death, even!

A lifetime for Master Choi. If it takes me a lifetime, I'll bring back to him what he's given to me. What he's made of me. Made me ME again. Made me vital.

I'll make him immortal!

Love for him, so thick it runs through the streets like lava and fills the world to waist level. Only one way to answer love like that.

Die for it!

My father's ax, and blood from the blisters on my hands.

Burn yourself up for it!

Do what no American's ever seen!

Work to save money and succeed at your mountain training. That deathly shriek in the night on Grandfather's peak on my eighteenth birthday, that maelstrom of white one week before Japan. That place where the world is mine, and all the world's answers are at my fingertips. Train one thousand days, bring honor to Master Choi that way.

"Listen to your heart," Master Choi's thick Korean accent yesterday, my last at UNC. Such finality in his voice, "I don't need you anymore," he tells me. He feels betrayed, and he throws me away. He's done it before.

His eyes.

Cut through me.

Ingenious, this man!

Savant!

Seer!

The last time I was 17, and "Fix your attitude or get out, and never come back to the training hall," he says. Those eyes that burn into me.

Such finality!

I wasn't humble enough for a 17-year-old black belt, directing college students who were older than me, and after class, that night, I walk 40 miles from Chapel Hill to his apartment in North Carolina's capital city Raleigh to apologize. The last three of the ten hours staggering, my feet bleeding, and my focus forever galvanized.

And he wrote to his uncle that day.

"I have a child student who wants to train in Japan. Just this week he walked 40 miles to apologize to me, and show his desire to train in Japan. With your permission, when he's a bit older, in a couple years, perhaps I'll send him to you."

Master Choi's eyes.

Piercing.

Now diverted.

Hurt.

The doorway to his Raleigh apartment. Did he underestimate my commitment?

His genius!

Is it genius of a kind that's so great he could have actually been surprised at all that he'd orchestrated?

A 40-mile walk, and in my mind, a totally new conception of what I, the youngest of his students, might one day realize!

But this time I'm 19, and he has to know! – I'm a student at UNC this time – that if he casts me aside my path'll be hardened in steel, and if success is possible at all in Japan, there'll be no breaking me?

A T-intersection.

The mob! Mas Oyama's uchi deshi. Our parallel lines, and we'll have no choice but to turn.

"Please left! Let it be left!"

Left, and I'll be on the *inside* of the curve and I'll have only to maintain. Right and I'll be on the outside, and it'll be my column that'll have to lengthen its strides to keep up!

Damnit, we're turning right, our back.

Bends!

A caterpillar on crack, clackety clack, a roller coaster around the bend, no choice, I've got to keep up! It's that or maybe a beating by the hook-nosed Iwaya.

Can that really be?

Would he really beat me just 'cause I couldn't keep up with the run?

I just got here yesterday!

My rib cage.

My shoulders.

My hips and ankles.

The flesh on the balls of my feet, for the first time in my life inadequate to running, even with shoes and socks on. All of them burn, tear, threaten to split open with the strain of the outside of the curve.

I can barely believe it!

It was a girl this time, Anne Dodson of all people, that was the catalyst for it all!

A senior at UNC, she was just a diversion really. My second lover only, and me, her youngest ever. Master Choi's voice as he throws me away. "I don't need you any more," he says. He feels betrayed.

Savant!

Seer!

Genius so raw it happens without him, I should have known! He knew about Dillon at Templeton, after all.

God, it's her I remember!

Kissing her breasts in the night, I'd laid claim. They were mine now more than hers. Her voice, half asleep. "Jesus, Nathan, you're really starting to make me appreciate that part of my body." The blue of the street lamp outside, Cannon Dorm. It fights its way in, through Dillon's tie-dyed curtain. Twenty-one, Dillon's coming from only that. I don't even have to touch her down there to make it happen. And I do, too, again. It gets a bit softer but if I keep it moving, comdomless that one time and wet, and well, there it is! I'm back in business, and I cum again too.

Sweet, injured Dillon.

What was it that high school teacher did to her?

What did *I*?

I was 17 then and I remember.

Pink Floyd, Doc Martins, the Dead, and the Doors, and I see her now, kneeling on the cold tiled floor of the old Infirmary bathroom, ten-foot ceilings, glass transoms over the doors, hundred-year-old tile. She's praying with her elbows on the toilet seat, praying on her twenty-first birthday that the test will come back negative. We never speak it, but we know already that she's pregnant.

"You murdered your child!"

That's Gracie's voice, riddled with hate, because she resents so much having to live with another woman's kids. Who the fuck does she think she is?

Deserves what she got, too. And my father on the sidelines. Silent, sad, and impotent.

To Master Choi, my voice, I've just turned eighteen.

"I have a problem." (Girlfriend's pregnant.) Master Choi, deadly serious, "What's she going to do?" (Abortion, her choice.) "Then you *have* no problem," his words, more than simple words. Telepathic.

Not advice.

An order that cuts.

Straight through to my soul.

"You HAVE no problem. Concentrate on school, concentrate on your training, concentrate on Japan. Don't be so stupid in the future. Hey, man, come on! There'll be plenty of time for girls later! You don't need that now!"

"Yes, Sir!" my voice, and I'm never so sure.

But Anne Dodson then.

The CMAC's Rob and Virginia's friend, I barely knew her. A diversion. Another senior to take care of her youngest lover ever.

Only my second?

She didn't believe it.

That before her there was only Dillon.

Second semester, that, my second year, this one at UNC to be with Master Choi and study Japanese. That final push for Japan. Training and waiting, day after day, for Mas Oyama's acceptance letter to arrive, I'm momentarily paralyzed, and I've stopped even going to class. Only my training. Eating ginseng, rice, gruel that Master Choi brings me from his Raleigh apartment in Tupperware, and suddenly I'm failing out of Japanese, Basic Mechanics and Multi-Variable Calculus, all at the same time. It doesn't even occur to me that Master Choi would feel betrayed … to find out I was sleeping with a girl?

It baffles me.

Anne Dodson, her blonde curls, and her too many cigarettes. The four of us are in her family's condo that weekend on Sugar Mountain, and how could Master Choi possibly know?

How I'd lean into those torrents of icy wind and sleet on the balcony and behold Grandfather's peaks across the valley below? How I'd drink it all in, the cold, studying, and buying in to what I knew would be mine without Japan?

How that helped me to know I'd never fail?

But the very next day at UNC!

Oh, how ironically!

Rob told Master Choi I was away with them for the weekend, and "I don't need you anymore," Master Choi says, and I'm stopped in my tracks.

"Yes Sir!" my voice.

"But, Sir," I'm shocked, "what do you mean?"

"Listen to your heart," he says, and he turns away.

With such finality!

Those eyes that cut into me.

Master Choi's words.

Those simple four, the last of his before Japan, the ones I keep with me.

The ones I'll always keep with me.

The ones I insist on keeping with me no matter the cost.

Words that cut through me.

A laser, a paper-cut big enough to rip me in half at the sternum, my life.

Is forever changed.

By that man?

One more time.

Uchi deshi.

"Live-in disciple," personal student of uncle, Mas Oyama in Tokyo. No foreigner's ever graduated, no American. "One hundred and twenty have tried and failed before you," Mas

Oyama wrote in his letter to my parents when it finally arrived. My abandoning mother in Chapel Hill, and, anyhow, any hell's better than cohabitation with my impotent father, and that cunt of a stepmother who'd do or say anything at all to make sure I'd not stay around.

Spoiler!

Bitch!

And me.

Charging still forward, the blood blisters on the soles of my feet.

Today'll be the day that I'll finally, after six years, lay eyes on the legend Mas Oyama, the founder of Kyokushin, "Sosai" as I'm told I'm supposed to address him. Master Choi's seventy-year-old uncle who emerged from the mountains four decades ago to kill bulls with his bare hands, who bent American quarters in half between his thumb and two fingers on one hand. Mas Oyama, who told the Japanese press in 1975 he would open his own belly with a sword, and take his own life if his fighters, at his First, World Open Karate Tournament didn't prove themselves to become the strongest fighters in the world.

Today'll be the day I'm to meet Mas Oyama, but now I'll fall out of line.

I'll trip and fall out!

I'll be left behind.

Lost.

Beaten before my training even ever starts. I'll never meet the man, after all.

What will I do if I get lost?

Do I have enough Japanese to ask my way back?

Will Iwaya Sempai beat me?

What does Mocaram mean by he'll beat me anyway?

How could that be?

I just got here yesterday!

ix.

Insane, stampeding beasts!
Badgers and bone breakers!
We must be getting close.

There are the train tracks we crossed at the beginning of our run! That droning alarm, *wom, wom, wom,* to warn motorists, pedestrians. The candy cane gates will come down. A train is coming, a train in Tokyo is always coming. Of course then, at the beginning of our run, we crossed a bridge that looked down on the tracks from above, and now we're winding through at street level. Maybe we'll finally get to rest when the train comes.

If we get caught by the gates.

Can't see the bridge we ran over.

If we're getting close, why don't these buildings look familiar?

Shocking me free, French Arab Mocaram grabs me, my elbow from behind, spins me off the road and into a tiny square park. He's running behind me on my first day.

Volunteered.

To run with the first-year guys and keep an eye on me.

Three runners behind us, and his sudden attack!

It throws me off balance and sends them into a stumbling frenzy, first to keep their footing, and then to pass us by, and regain their hard-fought-for positions in line.

"Wait here, Ligo!" he hisses, his chest heaving.

"We'll rest and have water. Don't worry, I told them that it's your first day and you can't possibly keep up."

What the hell?

Come on, don't stop me, we're almost there! I try to free my arm. "But I can still keep up!" my voice. "How much further can it be?"

"No, stop here, Ligo, and we won't have to do the other training. Stop and take water! Wait here with me!"

"Listen to your heart."

Master Choi's biggest, his last four words, and I do listen. That voice tells me go to the mountains. Follow Mas Oyama. Embody Mas Oyama's own history. Can't make it to Japan to honor Master Choi as an uchi deshi?

Then go to the mountains!

Train alone. More hours per day than you sleep. Run those rocky slopes.

Shivering.

Bleeding knuckles cold on mountain stone.

Join the mountain demons, Chozan Shissai's *tengu*. Let your hair grow long, your beard to cover your face and guard it from the cold.

So clearly!

I hear still today that beast in the night, that blood-curdling screech, and wing beats like pounding whoops in silent cold, cascading snow and ice from limbs of acid-burned pines. Stay there three years like Mas Oyama. Become champion that way. Japan, later. Honor Master Choi. There's no other choice. He saved my life. I love him like my father.

No, I never loved my father like this!

Now I need more, I suppose, to fill the space my father leaves. Impotent. Bitch, my stepmother! Fake, macho cunt, so weak and whiny yet puts on that front. "You murdered your child," she says and who the fuck is she? Fat and self-loathing after childbirth. Skin on her thighs that's dimpled like cauliflower and yelled at me for walking into what was supposed to be my home, too, just because her bedroom door was open and she was standing there, in front of her mirror modeling that ridiculous, fat-control suit.

"Wanna see something that'll turn your stomach?" My brother's voice. We're in high school.

Found a Polaroid of her naked, legs spread. A horrendous wad of pubic hair, and a hideous broad, toothy smile. Found it alone, in the leather wallet big enough for a passport Dad takes with him when he travels, but left in his desk drawer, right there, where he invites us to do our homework, so careless!

France.

Dad takes us.

Used to take his students there, every other year to see the cathedrals, the art, its history. We're there with Martha, I'm eight. Aaron's nine. Held my father's hand the whole time, afraid I'd be lost, left behind. So comfortable there, my hand in his hand. So safe.

God, I'll bet that hand of my father's aches!

Martha.

So beautiful!

Hugs me so warm and so safe. Dropping that mustard in the supermarket aisle, "God damnit!" her voice, and her face flushing red. Glass and green paste goes everywhere, and Dad, angry and embarrassed. "They all knew what you said. You don't have to speak English to understand God damnit," he says.

"But don't worry," Martha's voice, she says in response to the silence she perceives in the back seat. Loire Valley vineyards blurring by, geese force-fed with funnels to make the pâté we ate for lunch. I have mazes. Aaron, Mad Libs. Dad reads us Poe. "Number eight hat." Rats and string. A prison break. Maybe that was Sherlock Holmes? Some mystery story. *The Pit and the Pendulum*, at least.

"We're not going to do that to you again," Martha's voice,

"your mother and your father split, but you don't have to be afraid. We won't put you through that again." I wasn't afraid, but Martha's embarrassing me, and my father squirms in the front seat. She thinks I'm quiet 'cause they were arguing, but I was only daydreaming, not even paying attention.

Martha.

Laid out naked on a rock, sunbathing by the pool. Beautiful, glowing, oiled. Out of body, she's floating above, arms open wide in Dillon's meditative Jesus position. Breasts spread by gravity. Nipples centered, erect, a faint breeze. Hot sun, grasshoppers whirring by, clicking. Woman. I'm five years old, six and seven, but I know. That's woman. Like "mother." She loves me and with her I'm so safe. She holds me, like Dad does on his lap, and loves me. They love each other. Love by the fire and the black-and-white TV. Warm in a house with jeans that come in off the line, frozen solid before school, and have to be laid on the woodstove to thaw.

Icy.

Mountain.

Wind.

The sword.

The one for my belly if I fail. I can't believe Master Choi didn't tell his uncle I wasn't coming! Didn't tell him I'd run away, left Chapel Hill, and his uncle sent the plane ticket anyway!

Mocaram's trying to swindle me.

I see it in his eyes.

He's trying to convince me it's in my best interest to lie, to pretend I've fallen out of the run because I'm not strong enough. The mob's rounding the bend. The last runner disappears. "We can catch them!"

I protest, but I'm overcome.

My eyes fall out of focus, my brain.

Suddenly stupid.

Black spots in the middle of my vision, and suddenly I

can see only around the edges. My esophagus closing, the front wall of it falling in on the back. I stumble, drop my hands to my knees, and gasp. Ashamed, I fight myself up, demand control, but stumble towards a mostly concrete but slate-topped public drinking fountain built maybe only, I see, so that people who live nearby can stop in for water. There's a bench and a spigot half way down the thing one might use to fill up a bucket, a bucket to flush their toilets if their plumbing stops working. Mocaram, still speaking, but I'm surrounded by black. All I see is the largest, the blackest raven I've ever seen. On the tree limb above me, he spreads his wings with a loud reordering.

Of massive, black-velvet wing feathers.

Glares down at me, with the blackest of black eyes I've ever seen. Beak like lopping shear blades held open, he'll drop down and pluck the eyes from my skull. Even the inside of his mouth is all black. Eight-inch feathers on the tips of his wings, split and spread like fingers to grab me.

I'll be damned, I was just thinking of Grandfather!

The mountain demon that accosted me there, in the frozen February night. I wrote that letter to Master Choi, the next morning on the peak, that granite island in that whitewater river of mist on my 18th birthday, a freshman at Templeton, and Dillon back at school. I told her I wanted to be alone that night, the import of my 18th birthday, my destiny. My knowing already what my future would hold, and we were in denial she was pregnant. Master Choi in Chapel Hill, the summer before, and pooled blood under silver-dollar-size disks of callus on the soles of my feet.

Highway 40, from Chapel Hill to Raleigh, paved with hot coals.

"Okay, but first you must eat," his thick Korean accent. Didn't mean to take the wind out of him when I walked forty miles, Chapel Hill to Raleigh to apologize. I'm half seventeen and the training hall is my new home, the CMAC, my second chance at family.

And I'll not lose another.

Master Choi, not father. More than father, like Martha, more than just mother. A passionate love for mother, one that takes my breath away and makes my eyes fill with tears it takes to replace the loss of the real thing.

That same passion for father.

Master.

Father.

Creator.

Endless pools of strength, love, deep brown, in his eyes, I can see his soul when he lets me, and he DOES let me! I hear his thoughts, know his actions before he moves, didn't mean this time to take the wind out of him. How could he possibly have known I'd have done something so dumb? Didn't even matter Jen Efird was there when I arrived. His student, older than me but my junior in the training hall. His lover, I suppose, I see now since she's blushing and waking up there, but Master Choi's long taught me none of that's my business.

I'm too tired.

Too focused, really, to notice.

I wouldn't knock on his door to let him know I'd walked forty miles, to make up for my attitude, so I stood up and bowed deeply when he came out for breakfast. Didn't mean to show him the blood on my feet, didn't know it was there! Blood must have pooled during that hour I was on his front steps. Turned one foot up and inspected the sole since it felt funny when I took off my shoe. Korean apartment, shoes piled haphazardly on the parquet by the door. The smell of kimchee, ramen, my ginseng gruel he makes for me and carries in Tupperware to Chapel Hill. Blood blisters the size of silver dollars. Deep purple. "Okay, but first you must eat."

His words.

And that's when he recommended me to his uncle.

Wisps of smoke-like white, carried by an unrelenting mountain wind, wrapping themselves silently, violently, around both me and that all-too-familiar outcropping of rock. Calloway Peak between my feet, Grandfather Mountain at dawn. North Carolina's second-highest peak. Alone to face that ghostly icy cold silence just eight days before now.

"No, it has to be Japan.

"I have to go there now! I have to go there absolutely as soon as possible!

"There's no other way."

I'd climbed there for half the night, alone and by flashlight, slipping over intermittent patches of ice, in among the rocks. I'd climbed there alone, specifically in search of that answer. "It has to be Japan. There's no other choice. It has to be Japan and it has to be now! It's the only way for Master Choi to save face. Be the first foreigner to graduate from Mas Oyama's uchi deshi program after all! It's the only way to repay the debt. Even without his permission, even without his knowledge, for Master Choi I'll go to Japan!"

But am I ready?

A sword in my hand. It doesn't matter. Ready or not ready is irrelevant. I have no choice. There'll be no failure. Not now. It will be my dead body that they'll carry out of the dormitory before that last day. One thousand days to graduate. "The one thing that I can't overcome, is the one thing that I must, in order to make it in Japan." Whatever that turns out to be, bring it on! I'm not important. Nathan Ligo is irrelevant.

Only success is important.

And without Nathan Ligo to hold me back?

I will personify success!

I will live success.

I will breathe it.

I will be it.

Close your eyes, Nathan. A thousand days later, open them, and you'll be the first American, ever, to graduate, from Mas Oyama's 1000-day program. That raven refolding his wings, but in no apparent hurry to do so. Staring down. So low and so close I could leap up and touch him if I chose. Maybe that's what that beast was on Grandfather's ridge. I'd heard there are ravens nesting there.

Could it be?

No, whatever that was, was much bigger. If there's any relation at all, this must just be one of his envoys, one of his spies.

"I got it, I got it," I say, mouthing the words, and I laugh. Telepathically, I address the bird on the off chance I'm right. "Don't get yourself all bent out of shape! I'll fight on. I have no choice."

"See?" Mocaram's saying.

He's ignoring the raven completely, and referring to the fact that I'd stumbled and almost fallen out. "Better to rest here." If I hadn't disliked him already for telling me that neither I nor my teacher knew anything, I really hate him now, for making me quit so close to the end.

My balance, returned.

The vertigo, overcome.

I stand tall, force controlled low-belly inhales and exhales like Master Choi showed me.

"Anyway, you have to say 'Osu!' to me, Ligo!" Mocaram's standing too close, his index finger outstretched, he's exhausted too. It's HIM that didn't want to keep up with the run, *his* discomfort overcame his fear of Iwaya, and now he's just afraid. "Don't forget, Ligo. I've been here for one year already before you. I am your sempai. You have to do as I say, and you have to answer me with 'osu.'"

"Osu!" I say. He's threatening me again. He's a green belt already, and I'm in no condition to fight.

Who am I kidding? Have I ever been?

"That's okay, Ligo," he slaps me on the shoulder, staggering me, and winks reassuringly.

But he's a liar.

"Don't worry," he says, "you will be my friend. No one else here can speak English, just that Korean Furoyama speaks some. It will be nice to practice my English. We gaijin have to stick together since the Japanese hate us."

My first day and a lifetime ahead of me.

If not this guy, I wonder, who *are* my friends going to be?

X.

Twelve hours in the dormitory.

My first day of a thousand!

Dinner, a berating by the Frenchman, the trash in the park. My first morning training, and this shower, now nearly exhausted.

My towel, the dark.

Borrowed and hanging on a locker room door waiting for me. It's Mocaram's, half size, and still damp. And there's breakfast in the dormitory.

Looming.

Thank God for such great water pressure! The furnace's roar, and so silly!

The irony of thanking a god for something so silly, and is that the first, actual smile I've cracked since the shock of this morning's training?

"Idiot!" I laugh. My eyes close for the last time under my first shower in Japan, and I see.

Grandfather's peak.

That black, screeching raven with talons to grab me, stretching his wings, and glaring down at Mocaram and me in the park. The biggest of any I've ever seen! The vertigo after the run, and my heart nearly stops.

The screech of that winged monster in the night on *Grandfather's* ridge.

Cutting the dark outside my tent.

My eighteenth birthday, the dead of night, and in some mystical language it sounds like it's trying to get through. "You're getting close now," it says. "Finally, Nathan, this is the way! Fulfill your destiny!"

Master Choi's eyes, and that raven's in the park.

They speak the same tongue.

Fucking Hell! Do I really want Mas Oyama to tell me I can stay?

My god, they run like that every day!

Cascading, warmth off my skull.

The howl!

Of Grandfather's mountain wind, that eerily silent but unrelenting maelstrom of white that soared past the summit, one week before now like a freight train's ghost. And one year before that, my 18th birthday. I sleep there alone to commemorate the passing of my childhood, to stand apart – to stand aghast! – at the loss of my family.

Under the shower, I shiver to consider that earlier time.

Dillon's back at school, and such frigid cold!

February night, I'm exposed to the wind that whips the fabric of my tent like a sail torn free in a storm, I shake so hard in an effort to sleep, and in my North Face bag for hours, and hours, into the night.

And finally I sleep.

And it was then!

At some wee morning hour, I realize the wind's dropped off to nothing, and it's been replaced with utterly still, dead winter silence like nothing I've ever heard.

No sound.

Literally.

Nothing.

Terrifying!

Not a single creak, a crack, or a drip, and with it came welcome, welcome sleep.

But then, like an earthquake or an atom bomb!

Splitting that, a bloodcurdling screech of that winged mountain beast tearing me from a dream of somewhere warmer, it leaps! – out of the tree tops just over my tent, and I hear cracking twigs and falling ice and snow, and these aren't twigs cracking like a bird's nest! They're like a bull elephant charging through the snapping trunks of trees, and it's right over me! My tent is next, I fully expect to be crushed!

But stillness again.

Half a second.

A lifetime.

My heart beats once.

There's cascading powdery ice crystals and snow piling down with a thud, and then drifting like barely more than the faintest mountain mist falling on the outside of my tent.

And then.

Wing beats!

Loud like pounding whoops in the night!

A wingspan like Mas Oyama's sleeping dragon, and POW, POW, POW, POW through the air, it accelerates! It takes all that it has to gain the elevation it needs to clear the opposite tree line.

And dive.

Off into the valley below, and it's gone.

Disappeared.

And true silence then!

My heart pounding, it glides, and I growl to myself, momentarily safe and warm, and "Over my dead body!" I swear. My voice, so matter-of-factly aloud and alone in that last second of my first one-minute shower in Japan and like the mountain, there's nobody there to hear.

"*Normal people* just don't have eighteenth-birthdays like that, Nathan. It IS your destiny. Master Choi gave me life once it was lost to me, and don't you ever forget it! Be the first

American to complete his legend-uncle's 1000 days. Do it to bring honor to Master Choi who did so much for you.

"Do it because then you can rest."

I reach for the knobs, and see Bonnie's warm, smiling face.

The travel agent on Main Street, those slick, waxy pages of my plane ticket to Japan. Eddie's wife – Eddie drove the bus to Nova Scotia that summer with DCPC, the church in Templeton where we don't go. But Bonnie's eyes, and now they're concerned. Mine are changed, they're not like a boy's anymore. My requested departure date is "a.s.a.p." and ASAP's for emergencies. Sick relatives. Funerals. The Templeton of 1990 and it's unheard of for 19-year-olds who still look like they're 17 to make emergency trips to Japan.

Such a small town!

Everyone knows everyone and Bonnie most certainly knows my folks. She arranges their flights to Europe. The ticket purchase takes most of the money I've saved for mountain training.

Like Mas Oyama.

Fool!

Child!

Child with childhood dreams!

Save money, you think, and then three years? Mountain training like Mas Oyama's requires only the cost of food, you believe? Equipment to survive on the ridgeline, indeed, but in those icy torrents of mist I can see from Anne Dodson's condo on Sugar Mountain? – looking upwards towards Grandfather's peaks, across the valley in the driving sleet, and wind so strong, Rob and I try to sustain a straight-bodied lean into the breezeway downstairs and almost succeed. But other than that, only food? *Mas Oyama* had someone to bring him food at his cabin once a month, but I'll be there alone, and near enough the store that I need. North Carolina. The top of the world's a three-hour hike from the supermarket.

Mountain training.

Was it fake like the sword?

The money I saved was barely enough for $1500 worth of gear I'll now never use and this plane ticket to Japan.

Would it have been enough?

How many more months would I have saved before setting out?

Just a few dollars left, and that gray, pinstripe suit.

Some kind of wool blend, anyway? – an endless rack of suits in a Charlotte thrift shop, I'm rifling through suits discarded by the congregation of that little white church across the tracks. God-fearing men and gospel singers, and mine fits me poorly. I stitch up the pants legs, struggling with a needle and thread in the dark basement room of Martha's log house where I grew up, my childhood bedroom, my first time back to sleep in a decade away. Nathan in his own bedroom again, so excited by coming home, and by going to Japan, that I can't sleep but I fight to stay awake to listen to the constant click, whirr, and trickle of the nighttime forest outside.

Tempting like a lullaby.

Battling heavy starch, I fail, despite Martha's iron, to make the wool look like it was meant to be stitched that way.

But anyway, if I'm going to present myself to my teacher's uncle in Japan, it'll be over my dead body that it'll be in anything less than a jacket and tie!

Over my dead body, my flight, a direct night flight to Tokyo but touches down for fuel in Anchorage, of all scary places, to take on additional passengers. Pitch black and gusting snow and a giant, firetruck-like machine that sprays something on the plane to keep it from icing up.

Like a car wash.

I can barely stay awake and I haven't flown overseas since I was eight, and my brother and me in France and Spain with Dad and Martha, and me, already asleep on the ground in New York City. I'm small enough to lie down over sideways in a single airplane seat, and my pillow keeps falling off the armrest during taxi. The adult in the row behind me finally has to leave it where it falls when he can no longer lean forward during takeoff.

Those same, nameless passengers eleven years later.

Surprised, when I change out of my sweats and sneakers and into my suit in the last hour of the flight. Gray T-shirt reads "FG." That's Master Choi's "Fetzer Gym" at UNC, and I embarrass myself when I tell Martha that Aaron once joked he thought it stood for "faggot god" since Tom was there too, to see me off for Japan and I couldn't tell afterward if he'd thought I was making light of a word that had likely hurt him. Our uncle Tom, whom we can't call that, of course, because of the book, and he's not really our uncle anyway. Professor of sociology in Charlotte who introduced Dad to Martha when I was five. My gray suit, down from the overhead compartment on a hanger and in a tall, white plastic kitchen trash bag, folded over once, and I disappear, for thirty minutes into the bathroom to shave, and come back out wearing a jacket and tie, and two specks of white tissue stuck to two tiny spots of blood on my face where I cut myself, shaving.

747 bathroom sinks are no place for shaving with 99-cent razors, I learn. And I do look ridiculous, I think.

But I growl it away.

Already at nineteen I'm daring to go where no peer I've ever met, or likely ever will, will likely ever dare to go. Further, that is, into this storybook world than the rest of them can only hope one day they'll get to experience secondhand. I know the answers already, I'll just have to work a bit harder to unlock them. My boat across the sea. Ursula K. LeGuin and *The Wizard of Earthsea*. His new teacher's across the big water and the mists are gathering. Suits, anyway, are for church after my father married Gracie when I was twelve and started making me go.

Today, I wear one and feel proud.

My head's shaved, and I wish I could carve the tux I wore at Dad's wedding to Gracie from my body with a knife, since Mother's Day cards, scrapers, and purple paint stripper on flesh, and that woman's inability to say a single thing nice already seem to have done the job so nicely.

And now there's nothing but the burn.

xi.

Sharp-pointed scissors.

Straight razors.

Black plastic combs in glass jar of blue, disinfectant on a high mirrored shelf.

The barber shop on Main Street.

Ken Nortan's been giving me flattops and crew cuts for two years of high school already, and one year at Templeton. Two cycles of wrestling season, cross-country season, and track. He must be seventy-five years old, and he bends down, now, lanky like Martha's Dad I saw yesterday at The Pines, to show me the bill of sale from when his own grandfather bought himself out of slavery.

His own grandfather!

A slave and an adult alive before 1865, and here it is 1990!

"You can take it all off this time," I tell him, although my head was already shaved three months ago before leaving Chapel Hill, and his clippers only get so close because they're electric, and not, of course, a razor. My head looks bald, and the butterflies in my stomach are jumping now because I know I'm off to Japan. My plane ticket's bought, and my head's scratchy like a peach's skin on steroids, and rubbed the wrong way. I'm 19. Would pass for 17, though. Cursed.

Still!

With the rosy-cheeked baby face to end them all, always

the smallest in my world. Makes me look soft and I hate it since no one believes me a fighter.

"It's been longer than a year since anyone's mistaken me for a girl," occurs to me at 16.

My arms are massive though now at 19, considering how scrawny is the rest. So many pushups on my knuckles and a narrow stance beneath my shoulders, so my deltoids and my triceps tend to develop rather than my chest. Out of place on a boy who looks so young and pretty and "like a Greek statue," Dillon says, when I'm naked and standing in the light that falls through her tie-dyed curtain in the night, and I've barely got any body hair when I'm turning 18 back at Templeton. Wool scratchy suit doesn't fit now for the life of me, and for my funny shape, and for its own funny shape, and I really must look small, it occurs to me.

My reflection in the glass.

On solid ground again after eleven hours in flight, and I see.

Myself.

Drifting like a ghost down the hallway towards Immigration.

Pale.

Bald.

Afraid.

My eyelids are heavy. I close my eyes and see Calloway Peak between my feet, and my crystal ball, forming. The future already! "It's my birthright," I remind myself. Tokyo's streets! Airport, turns out, isn't even in Tokyo. It's two hours from the city and my rudimentary Japanese allows me to communicate.

Barely.

With two Japanese ladies at the tourist information desk by the gate. I take that bus over there, they say, out through those glass doors, and out into an early dusk because of the gray, sticky weather, and because Japan doesn't save daylight, and because I'm still so sleepy. They tell me where to buy a ticket, and how to get to the Metropolitan Hotel in Tokyo's Ikebukuro district.

Coil-bound.

An inch-thick city atlas that shows every address in Tokyo, and the important one's 3 dash 3 dash 9 Nishi, that's "west," Ikebukuro, and that means the ninth building, in the third block, of the third district in the west side of Ikebukuro. The bus, just under two hours, and 2,100 yen. That's nearly $20, and a fifth of all the money I have left to spend. Seats are scratchy like felt, and I sleep through blurring highway lights, my head against the seat bristles that are longer than the hair on my head, and I wonder how I'll survive on my own if Mas Oyama turns me away.

There are seven long days before my roundtrip ticket's scheduled return.

A tightening in my throat.

The start of a burn.

I swallow air to force a belch, and some relief. Would I even be able to reschedule the return if I have to, I wonder? Seven days! I don't even have enough money to eat for two, let alone sleep in a hotel room, I'd have to sleep in the street! What the hell am I doing?

"Nathan!"

That was Gatlin's voice, shaming. It'll be years before I get the sound of her voice out of my head. Condescending and critical as if she needs, even actually feeds on someone near her to tear down. But at least this time we agree.

I must be insane!

What'll I do if he sends me away?

"No, he'll take me in."

He's Master Choi's uncle. At the very least he'll see that I get home again.

What a disaster that would be!

The four-star Metropolitan.

Marble-floored lobby late afternoon, and I ask a staff person to point me in the direction of the address I show them on Mas Oyama's letterhead. His bold signature in ballpoint at the bottom of the letter his secretary typed to my parents to invite me to Japan. Outside in the taxi lane after dark, she turns a photocopied page of an atlas like the one they'd had at the airport around, and around again, to get her bearings, and points me up the street past the fire station in what looks like a dead-end direction.

"Asoko desu ka?"

Over there? I ask, and I barely believe her smiling-eyed *"Hai!"* she responds, "Yes, it's down that little street." I don't quite catch "down that little street" in Japanese but there IS a street there, and I see it now, it could be that little street that I see on the map she's handing me, with a fresh circle drawn in red ink on Mas Oyama's world headquarters dojo.

"The first right, the first left, and then the first left after that again," I tell myself, since my hands are gonna be full. "That's what it looks like it'll be, and then I should see it."

Mas Oyama's world headquarters dojo, his temple in the sky.

I struggle with the *gozaimashita* part of *arigato gozaimashita*, "thank you very much" in Japanese, and she bows deeply and smiles at me.

Tokyo's May.

Humid already.

Summer coming in fast, and the wool, and the too-much-starch of my suit sticks to my skin. I stop for the fourth time before my first turn to switch my bags, from my left hand to right. Five, with the wait at the crosswalk. My one bag's that heavy. Full of books, and I watch the red, L.E.D. crosswalk numbers count down till I can cross. The enormity of my arrival crashes down, and I've forgotten to regulate my breath.

The Nathan Ligo tennis ball finally lands in Japan, and in red L.E.D. numbers I'm counting its bounces.

Ten. I'm in Templeton.

Nine, Chapel Hill.

Eight, Templeton again.

Templeton to Chapel Hill, and Chapel Hill to Templeton. Mom's house to Dad's, Dad's house to Mom's. Every other week for those two years in Templeton between the log house and Mom's four successive temporary homes, and then every other year after that, every other weekend, and every summer spent with the other parent. Mom in Chapel Hill with Bob and then she left Bob. Dad in Templeton with Martha and then he left Martha. Then Seth and Cassie were born. I was 13 for Seth, and 15 for Cassie. Gatlin's kids, and my dad's. Eighteen eventually when I leave Templeton for UNC, and to hell with it!

I changed diapers even!

My stomach.

The burn will pass.

It always does, but Tokyo's street just then!

It tilts.

The whole world's next, I swallow hard to keep the crosswalk from turning.

Seth and Cassie.

My brother and sister in Templeton. Innocents that love me, look up to me, take for granted that I'm a member of their family. An infant sleeping in the crook of my arm, a toddler's hand in my hand, and a fifty-fifty chance.

I'll lose them, too, in the end.

My suitcase strap and the burn of my skin, I wipe the sweat off my brow. Six years now, and it's only getting worse. My father's not reclaiming himself, and it'll be me or them.

Fuck her, my stepmother!

It'll be me that'll have to do the abandoning this time, either that, or tolerate her abuse.

For the rest of my life!

My love for family.

Beaten down.

Squashed.

A teenager at North Meck after school and my dad. His shaken soda can getting ready to burst. His mustache.

Quivering.

The baby's crying and Gracie's telling me I should be ashamed.

For not wanting to change a diaper?

And my poor eclipsed father can't figure out that it's her agenda that's so foul, and his, and her guilt trip that is never going to let me in. I'd carry my brother and sister to the ends of the Earth, of course, if I had to, although mostly these days I'm afraid they'll grow up like him.

No thoughts of his own.

My father's wife.

Behind the steering wheel now of her brown Toyota Tercel, she flips off a motorist at Templeton's one stoplight by the Green. He's older than her, I'm a tiny twelve, and from the back seat I'm glancing over at the Abbotts' colonial steps, remembering my matchbox cars, and wondering what happened to them.

Poor guy's driven through a yellow light as it turns, and it riles her because she couldn't blast through her red the second it turned green, and "Up yours, man!" her four fingernails flip up from under her chin.

Poor guy's eyes.

Surprised and concerned. Some pretty young woman's just assaulted him, and my dad in the passenger seat.

Calls her "Grace," and interjects a mood-lightening reference to feminism.

Paternal, caring criticism since she's angry, and she often cites her decade-late brand of angry feminism as something to be proud of. Emboldened instead of ashamed, she boasts and laughs, and blames the macho attitude on the Italian ancestry on her mother's side.

And Aaron and I have never seen such a thing!

A step-parent who requires such self-maintenance and denial to feel good about herself. Her coarse, brunette down-falling moll's hair! A decade of her jeans she can never make fit. There's not enough respect in the world, it occurs to me finally, to make up for how much self-love she's lacking.

My heartbroken father.

So much in love with Martha when I was a child, so unmistakable since they loved me and my brother so completely.

But what is this thing, exactly?

Something forced!

A perversion.

And I'm supposed to lie, too?

To bite my lip and pretend? To prepare Mother's Day cards I don't feel, to protect the esteem of someone who needs to tear down other people, including me, to feel good about herself?

On my jacket I wipe the sweat from my brow, and bending down now, I reach out for my suitcase straps. Red counting-down crosswalk L.E.D.'s continue their count.

The Nathan Ligo tennis ball.

Five.

Is this real? Am I really here in Japan?

Four.

Can it really be down that little street, and then will I see it?

Three.

Mas Oyama's majestic mountain monastery.

Two.

I'm standing up now and dead-lifting my bags, my suitcase strap cuts into my hand.

One.

The Prescott family, I'm thirteen. Christmas morning to balance the rest.

Celebration so thick and giddy, and Nathan and Aaron, and there's the twins, Fran and Betsy. The older four sisters, Anna, Jane, Helen and Stuart, and their husbands John, Jay and Todd. My mother and Bob. The OPs over for brunch most times, that's the "other Prescotts," Dick and Jean, and their kids, the cousins Ida and Elizabeth, and my uncle Bill and even Aunt Kathy down from Maryland that time?

So many stockings across the mantel, and my stepfather Bob rigs a special board to hang them all from, and still we have to lie half a dozen of them on the sofa. I buy presents for all of them each year, and after a few bumpy years with the three-years-older twins, that's family for me, and I love them.

My mom.

"Give me a break!" I catch myself mouthing the words.

That was the sane part of my family after Dad threw Martha away. Parents divorce, and parents remarry. That's not Dad's fault, of course. Even twelve-year-olds understand that.

But Gracie's pleading eyes just then.

"Go away and leave us alone," they say. "I really, really wish you'd stay in Chapel Hill with your mom." Her voice then, saying, "Of course we want you to stay with us in Templeton! Of course, you're always welcome here!"

How's that for something to live with?

For years on end.

My mom.

Screaming at Bob in the kitchen.

"Why can't you just say it?" she shouts over and over again, and I can't remember what the fuck it was she wanted him to say, but I can't shake the looks of total agreement in the faces of my brother and my sisters, the twins Fran and Betsy and me in the next room listening to the meltdown.

She was insane, and what a shame!

That was family for me, and since then she's whittling down the "Child-Rearing Account," subtitled "Nathan" till

I'm all gone too. Rubbed my back with baby powder when I was five at the trailer by the lake, and crying so much at the Abbotts' on the Green, but she was lying to herself, and lying to me, 'cause kids were too much for her from the start.

Heartbreak again.

My suitcase strap cutting into my hand.

My one bag's full of books, there are bat-size butterflies in my stomach. My shirt will be soaked from the effort when I finally meet Mas Oyama.

I still did figure I would meet him last night as I arrived.

Oh, please!

As if the god of modern karate would be up waiting for me!

xii.

"Hurry up, Ligo!"

The Frenchman at the top of the stairs. "We'll be late for the dormitory!"

"Osu!"

My voice on the way up. The furnace's insistent growl.

"I think I can, I think I can."

My shower complete.

The billowing steam.

I break free of that sauna-like mist, and Tokyo's norm is actually hotter, it occurs to me. At least in there, in the steam, the condensation had a cooling effect. My T-shirt sticks to my flesh as I take to the forest green of Honbu's basement steps.

"Damnit!" to myself as I trip on the top one.

My brother Aaron, a chubby seven.

He tumbles down the steep, 200-year-old, loose-board stairwell of the log house. "DAMNIT!" His boy's voice as he bangs to a stop on his butt, the laundry basket rolls all the way down, and Grandma and Grandpa bite their lips not to laugh. Sounds in Martha's kitchen like a load of firewood crashing down, and we only know they were laughing when Dad tells us the next morning.

"They never would have let you known they were amused," his voice explains, "because they don't want you to think they'd approve of kids misbehaving," and it was the cursing, not *the fall*, that was "misbehaving," I suppose.

I should have figured out yesterday, I realize, how to navigate this place. These stairs in sandals, in the Japanese way, and at this constant, frenzied pace. Watched that Japanese guy do it, late yesterday for the four-o'clock class.

Forest green, marbled and cracked.

Linoleum.

Poorly lit, and I charge up.

The Frenchman's at the top near the bench, and beyond him a row.

Of soiled cleaning rags laid out, drying on the concrete of the sun-streaked building foundation across the street. Yesterday, fresh off the bus at the Metropolitan, I step in for the very first time. Behold this same, shadowy lobby, but from the other end looking back. Head shaved, awkward, staggered under the weight of my bags. Pale, frightened, "the American" glides in through the glass of a crystal ball no one else knows, and I see myself.

Standing there.

Peering in.

Inquisitively.

Afraid maybe.

Doubting to see if I've really found the right place. The Kaikan lobby. Mas Oyama's world headquarters, my suit and my suitcases, and a Japanese guy in a dogi at the far end of the hall.

Charges up the stairs now just beside me, denying the banister as he swings round the corner to the second-floor dojo I've now *heard* so much of through the dormitory wall, but haven't yet seen.

First Japanese karateka I see.

Middle-aged. A huge mop of coarse, jet-black hair. A green belt cinched tightly round his karate white, stocky, overweight, and late for class. His sandals smack, smack, smack up the stairs. Chop, chop, chop in Japanese. Hazardous, reporting, rattly metal strips on the front edge of each stair, and without skipping a step.

So foreign to me!

And my legs like jelly, silently, and on the balls of my feet, I take three at a time.

And trip!

Like an idiot, on the top one.

Master Choi, I'm fourteen.

"Hey man, come on! You walk on your heels like you think you're a giant! *Don! Don! Don!* all the time across the floor like you want everyone to know you've arrived!" But my stomach hurts, I'm dizzy and weak, and with my cheeks I reach for a gulp of air, swallow it, belch to myself, and "You have walk silently on the balls of your feet!" he says.

"Yes, Sir!" I manage, but it comes out weak. I'm embarrassed, and he's approaching me. I wasn't yet standing at attention or on two feet.

My balance.

Always bad when my stomach's burning, and "How many times do I have to tell you!" he scolds. (Does he not realize that I almost didn't come today, and that I've missed two days of school already this week?) His eyes smile but it won't work with me. "The strongest man," he goes on, "is the one who can walk into the room, and no one even knows he's come in. I told you! Nobody in life cares about a *tough guy.*" Yes, Sir! I shout because I have to, and I don't like him much today.

Maybe I shouldn't have come.

But then I made myself.

Can't let Aaron get too far ahead.

Alpha Aaron. Big for his age in Templeton, 'cause then I won't wind up like him, and being like Aaron, surely, is the one sure way, finally, one day to erase me, Nathan Ligo and all that in me's so unbelievably small and so unbelievably weak.

Aaron.

Living with Dad and Gracie in Templeton for the first time separate from me, his ninth grade to practice karate for one more year before Sampson Law, his teacher, Templeton senior, graduates and goes back to Hong Kong.

Titan!

Leaps over standing men to break boards in Tae Kwon Do demonstrations, presses the whole stack on the Universal bench press machine.

And Mom finds me this guy?

Master Choi in Chapel Hill, who can't kick higher than his waist. But he IS a graduate student in physics, and "that's cool," I suppose, alone to myself. His university-only club karate class in the fencing room at UNC, and "Yes, Sir!" anyway. My voice again, a bit stronger this time, and I do notice, I think, and lo and behold, that it is my heels that ache, ever so slightly, from their impact with the hardwood crossing the floor. My legs wrecked, I take three or four of Honbu's basement steps at a time, and on the balls of my feet. Silently, like Master Choi taught me, finally. Catlike, and "Damnit!" to myself as I nearly fall on the top one.

My legs from the run.

Weak like I remember them, and I underestimate. Got the toe-end of my foot over everything but that half-inch strip of rattly, grooved metal at the front edge of each step. Frenchman's impatient and annoyed, and the Kaikan's green lobby now, for only the third time. Two of my roommates on lobby-guard duty. Dressed already after training, and standing at attention at the gate.

Rigid.

Fists clenched.

Standing in fudo dachi between me and yesterday's lost-looking Nathan, flanking the light of the outside, where between them he stands, peering in through the darkness.

A silhouette.

Two different of my roommates then, and these two, this morning post-shower in clean T-shirts already transparent with sweat.

Tokyo summer.

So thick after training and a one-minute shower.

So hot I need a machete to breathe.

And the fabric of my sweatpants, as I leap.

Sticks to my knees.

xiii.

"Run, Ligo!" the Frenchman hisses, and I have no choice but to run.

He's already turned.

Rushes out past the display cases, Mas Oyama's trophies, the horn he smashed off the skull of a bull with the edge of his hand. The shattered halves of a massive flat river stone he broke. The black and white photograph of him shaking hands with the King of Spain.

Yesterday.

A lifetime already, my one suitcase full of books, and we pass each other at the door. Nathan of this morning running out with the Frenchman and some scrawny white stranger in an uncomfortable wool suit. Nathan of yesterday stepping in for the very first time, fumbling in broken Japanese, two soldiers at the gate as two ladies behind the now-dark, curtained window, labeled "Information" in English as well, try to sort out who the hell I am.

And we're out in the street.

Only eight feet wide to the blank, back wall of the highrise adjacent.

Mocaram leans right, sharp into his turn, the shattered-tile mosaic of Sosai fighting a bull through the waiting room windows on what once was the front wall of the building. The sweet, cold water spigot where we drank after the run. We soar up the block away from the park and up toward the turn, on our way all the way around the block to the dormitory for breakfast. Yesterday it's me, and Kuruda and Oshikiri carrying my heavier bag, and I pity them. I feel, as I come in from the Metropolitan, lingering still in my head, my brown leather suitcase strap cutting into my hand.

Just finished my shower, and already I'm running again!

The immense weight of my library within.

Musashi's *Book of Five Rings* and Yoshikawa's novel *Musashi*. Chozan Shissai's *Discourse on the Art of Mountain Demons.*

The Art of War and many more, I've brought them all to Japan.

A complete set of Japanese language books I opted *not* to return to the library at UNC, and a narrow pass in between two tall buildings and me, staggering in from the bus yesterday afternoon. Afraid, I *feel* my way in at dusk and up to the Kyokushinkaikan. It's for the very first time, and I catch a glimpse, way back behind past the entrance. The edge of that park, and me and my bags yesterday afternoon in the dark. Two, tall buildings and one narrow lane in between opens up, and I see now an old man pushing a bike at the edge of a clearing. It's the neighborhood park where we begin our training this morning, and there's a high fence, bright lights that face away from me, stockade-like, and a towel tied round his head in an impossible knot for terrycloth so thick. An adult-sized version of a kid's bike, it seems to me.

Heavy.

A cruiser.

Not like the ten-speed we'd have at home, and me on Franklin Street. Full speed down the hill from summer school at UNC. I'm seventeen, I've not yet walked to Raleigh this summer, and I have one math class to take to enter Templeton early, my chin near my handlebars and my butt off the seat. Rushing hot air, my scalp, more wet from sweat than the shower, and down the quick block parallel to the park. We blur past a house with high concrete walls, two-story apartments barely seen from the street, and I marvel, "Uchi deshis run everywhere they go!"

"You must never let your sempais see you walking, Ligo!" The Frenchman this morning before training, insisting.

"Dash! Dash! Dash! If Iwaya Sempai *ever* sees you walking to the dormitory, or to the Kaikan from the dormitory, he'll *bash* you, and then we'll see how long you can last!"

The park.

Big enough for the infield and a bit more of a baseball diamond. Yesterday it's dark and bordered outside by a tree-shaded walk. An imposing, eighteen-foot-high chain-link screen designed to stop baseballs. And other sports-related projectiles, I think. We're on the third side now, the *back* of the Kaikan's small block, and I catch a glimpse at a sprint of that same chain-link screen at the far end of this parallel street.

And I remember.

Yesterday.

Glass windows in the buildings on all sides, my bags down in the sand, I catch up with the man pushing the bike and show him. Extend boldly the photocopied map the lady at the Metropolitan gave me. Split-toed shoes. Black, gummy rubber soles like Hollywood's ninjas of my early teens, and, "Oh, *construction workers* in Japan must wear shoes like those!"

Helps them to hold on to their scaffoldings, I suppose.

Neck, chin.

Gray stubble.

Cigarettes in a shirt pocket, turns as I approach, fearful, and stumble. Been sitting for eighteen hours on an airplane already, and the bus, and I shuffle inadvertently, once, in that yellow sandy gravel, and catch myself. "Hai!" he responds, cheerful, to my "*Sumimasen.*"

"Excuse me, please," that was "sumimasen" in Japanese, and I wonder if he's been drinking. "He's so friendly! Is this the guy tasked," I wonder, "with welcoming lost-looking white guys to Ikebukuro after dark?"

But I'm so tired, too surreal, and too out of place to laugh. There's Grandfather's steep rocky trail in the night and the peak after dawn, the Frenchman's now approaching the alleyway turnoff to the dorm, and there's me of last night with my bags after dark, and tidbits of trash in among the gravel this morning at six. My small handful of cigarette butts, that psychotic, six-kilometer dash, and one piece of chewed gum. The wrapper from a set of disposable chopsticks, and "the cleanest park I've ever seen!" I marvel, my fingertips. Dry, and scraped by the sand. I'm scurrying around, bent over and searching for trash. "Every morning," says Mocaram, and for the rest of thee years, "we have to clean up the park before the sempai comes out for training."

Careful, Nathan!

You might get what you asked for.

Got Japan.

"Kyo-ku-shin-kai-kan wa do-ko desu ka?"

My voice in broken Japanese. I wonder if it sounds hollow, afraid, after dark, and "Where is the Kyokushinkaikan?" I ask.

Old man points me this way, towards me of this morning and Mocaram turning into the dormitory alleyway, over here in the direction I'm facing anyway.

"Well, I'll be damned!"

"KARATE," right there in front of me, but five stories up! Faded.

Badly chipped, poorly lit, and a painted sign like a bill-board. Big, bold, black Roman letters, "KARATE," flanked on each end by ... can barely make it out ... chipped red paint. The circle-enclosed, diamond-like insignia, the logo for Mas Oyama's Kyokushin.

Can that really be it?

That shadowy, cracked building over there?

Six years!

Opening and closing, martial arts classes in Master Choi's training hall at UNC. Bowing at the start and the finish of every class towards the flags, and a laminated photograph of his uncle, taped up to the thick blue paint on a borrowed, dojo basement-floor column with duct tape. The fencing room, and Master Choi's famous stories. Mas Oyama, his uncle for years on end, and those powerful Japanese documentaries.

The brutally powerful bare-knuckle Kyokushin.

Ninomiya on film, his spin kicks like Brian Moran, and that man-size punching bag. Cornrowed Willie Williams from New York in the seventies. Six-foot-six and fights that black bear, bare-handed in Pennsylvania, and on film for the whole world to see. Powerful, physically, because he's "damn stupid," says Master Choi who met him once, "does what he's told," fights a bear, 'cause who the hell else would fight a bear? And it's a big, threatened, wild black bear, and he beats it with his punches and his kicks when they let it out of a cage, and finally they shoot it when it wrestles him to the ground, and doesn't die, but tries its best to maul him.

Mas Oyama's confident stare.

Sheaths a sword with a hollow pop of metal on wood at the end of the film. The First World Open Karate Tournament, and his Japanese fighters won, and he'll not need it for his belly after all. Surely, all of that, Kyokushin, the world's strongest karate must occupy some kind of vast, holy temple in the sky!

Some majestic mountain monastery.

High walls, head-shaved monks and a gong, thousands of candles like TV's Kwai Chang Caine and his Shaolin meditation hall? "Snatch the pebble from my hand," the old master says.

But this place?

It's run-down.

Cracked.

Dark, and Mocaram and I lean right into the alleyway to

the dormitory, turning tight into our turn, and Luke Skywalker just then.

His X-wing fighter in the Death Star trench, and dead Obi-wan says, "Use the force, Luke!" and my father and brother with me at the theater opening, I'm six.

Alley so narrow I could reach out to both sides, scrape the flesh off my knuckles if I wanted to, and the dormitory!

Rising upwards before me.

Dilapidated.

Two-story structure, was once a traditional Japanese home, slap dab in the middle of the block. Just one yard of clearance, if that, between it and the taller buildings on all sides. The dormitory and the Kaikan, opposite sides of one block. Mas Oyama and his sword over there from the park, and me and my bags wrapped up in the dark, and so much more than just human.

Masutatsu Oyama.

The man and his Kyokushin "was never meant to occupy a structure like that!"

The Kaikan.

Somehow less than a building should be. But Master Choi's words, though, cut through me like a meat-slicer disk. Less than English, and yet, so much more than mere words.

Telepathic.

"Tell me, Grasshopper. Tell me what it is that you see!"

That's the old master on the Prescott house TV, I'm fourteen in Chapel Hill after school. My stomach, it burns, and "Use your eyes, Nathan," Master Choi says, "the answer's right there in front of you."

"Yes."

"Yes, I can see it now, Master," the small Kwai Chang's voice in his Hollywood China monastery.

xiv.

Nearly dark yesterday evening, that Japanese man and his bike. Those grimy five stories reaching up from the park.

The Kyokushinkaikan.

Sand-colored, earthquake-cracked stucco or concrete. A leafless vine that creeps all the way up, just over, in the foreground, I see.

Another two-story, clay tile-roofed home.

Half-smashed.

And surrounded now, as I pan down, by a high canvas barrier. Part of its roof already removed.

Dismantled, I see, and an inscription on the screen. "Marked for demolition," it must be, in Japanese, and it exposes a blank side wall of the Kaikan never meant to be seen.

"A building designed only," I think, and me at eighteen in my father's Modern Architecture class, "for three feet of clearance between it and that old house in front of it." Take that house away, though, and half exposed now, a blank, ugly wall of the Kaikan and a haphazard assortment of tiny, opaque, sliding glass windows, positioned maybe only in accordance to some inside required function unseen. My father's baritone at the front of the class:

"Never *was* any intent by the designer to render the outside of *this* wall aesthetically pleasing."

"*Doomo arigatoo.*" That's "Thank you so much," I respond to the drunk.

An afterthought.

I nearly forgot, and I struggle with the "gozaimashita" again.

Still smiling eyes, gray stubble, and he bows. Turns back to his bike, continues on his way, and I pick up my bags, turn back towards the Kaikan and look.

Hid halfway in shadows, and "it *IS* my destiny," I realize, even if Vader's my father and my mother's long gone. Building's been added onto, I see, and I shouldn't forget that it's partially thanks to him I can see.

Those two floors *used to be* stair-stepped back from the street, it occurs to me, each higher floor smaller and with a narrow balcony built, out on to the roof of each lower floor … of what used to be an apartment building, perhaps? "Of course! It's been added onto," I think, "to make it a dojo!" Its second and third floors, brought forward to swallow up their used-to-be balconies, and the result from the street?

One awkward indeed.

And everyone now sees five stories. A naked, exposed, lopsided profile, never meant to be seen.

Master Choi's gonna kill me!

I bend down.

See past my fists to the ground, to switch my bags, my left hand to right, heave them up, and trudge on towards the Kaikan.

And Mocaram just then!

It's breakfast time after the run, and he pulls up short from his run down the alley and steps over the high threshold to the dorm.

My roommates.

All of them, from the sound of it – except for the two in the lobby, I think – crowded into the kitchen, the dining room, the morning commotion, the scrape and metallic chink of light chairs. Metal legs sliding across the parquet wooden floor and bumping into each other. Hot water, streaming. Silverware banging into a stainless steel sink. A muffled, a miscellaneous, a shouted chorus of "Osu!"

My father's Modern Architecture course.

Not eighteen months ago.

My freshman year at Templeton.

The threshold of the dormitory, and I'm kicking off my gummy brown rubber slippers, and positioning them. The ones the one named Suzuki gave me. Yesterday. His old ones, his name if I understood correctly written on them in permanent marker and complex kanji. Too much for me to read, half rubbed off anyway, and inside it's dark. Our tiny classroom, and our professor, my dad, has not yet arrived.

It's a misty, cold, eight a.m. in Templeton College's Oak Row.

Tiny, ancient brick building across from the one we now call "*Elm* Row." Mom used to teach piano in there, it too's the last of a row of three, and both of them now are classrooms employed by the Department of Fine Arts. One-room dormitories once, way back when Woodrow Wilson was at Templeton in school, the main quad over here instead by the church, and two rows of these tiny, one-story, open-fireplace, brick dorms.

And Aaron and I watch.

Two tiny little brown-eyed boys. School's out today for the snow, and for us, so exciting!

A slide show!

Projections of classical structures, sculptures on a screen, and my father's voice. Red-bearded and droning, thick black-rimmed glasses, and the Temple of Venus. "Its columns are rows of identical marble statues of the goddess herself," he goes on. My brother and me, and out from crinkly white paper, we eat grilled-cheese sandwiches from the M&M Soda Shop across the street, back there *in the way back* of that little room by the projector that hums, and still hums a lifetime later. I'm fresh out of Dillon's warm bed every morning on my way to his class, and eleven years later I'm back to that same building. A student myself this time in my own father's Modern Architecture class, and New York City this time?

My dad's Modern Architecture trip.

He and I look up from the street and behold, a modern skyscraper building on Fifth Avenue. First one of its kind, its predecessors all set back from the street to let sunlight filter down, but this one, we laugh!

At the story!

Creativity was at war with a city ordinance and the building's twenty feet back from the street like it's required to be. But this one's the first building ever to be *cantilevered* out, its enormous, fifty-story glass bulk right back out to the street since the ordinance applied only to the building's street level façade and front door, and no one had ever heard of *cantilevering out* such an enormous weight before the invention of reinforced concrete.

A classic solution!

A comic, a musical rendition of *Conjunction, Junction, What's Your Function?* A Saturday morning cartoon short, and the other one with Ben Franklin. His kite and his key, and Susan B. Anthony teaches "Necessity IS the mother of invention."

But Mas Oyama's *temple* over there *in the sky?*

The Kyokushikaikan.

A silhouette from the park against the mist and the glow of the sky, peering out through the dark, and dilapidated?

Is that really it?

Should I really believe what I see?

Laundry?

Karate uniforms, dogis hanging to my right on the pieces of pipe of the canvas demolition screen?

Narrow street, past the entrance and high-rise concrete. The blank back wall of a building adjacent, eight feet from the Kaikan's façade, one better arranged than the side, and the Frenchman's now sliding open the rattly wooden door to the dormitory.

The Young Lion's Dormitory.

I'm wasted after the run, and the one from the Kaikan, and my first morning meal is inside.

XV.

Dormitory foyer. Tall mirror, umbrellas and a mountain of shoes. Paper-like wood sliding door that rattles noisily in its tracks. Mocaram slams it wide open to the commotion within, and "Nathan, relax," I appeal to myself.

My stomach!

"It's just anticipation. Knock on wood," these are just *echoes* of burns. Unfamiliar food I'll have no choice but to eat, my Zantac's running out, and our eyes and his meet.

The tall, rosy-faced first-year named Kato.

Boyish face in a crowd of tiny little monsters, badgers and bone-breakers, he's rushing to please, carrying two giant bowls of hot, steaming white rice. He turns away to continue his chores, and I'm outside in the street by the hanging laundry and the demolition screen.

It's yesterday evening.

The Kyokushinkaikan, the American Ligo's arriving with his bags, approaching the front entrance for the very first time, and my heart stops.

At the first of a BOOM! BOOM! BOOM! BOOM! from some kind of monstrous king drum.

It nearly knocks me off my feet!

Burning, the palm of my hand, my leather suitcase straps not yet to the door, I *feel* the Earth shudder from the heart of the building, perhaps from the depths of the second floor, an earthquake, the heartbeat, an explosion! Kyokushin. A moment then of silence, I stagger forward on in.

And then!

I'm slammed once again, smacked stopped in my tracks by a second barrage, a BOOM!

BOOM!

BOOM!

BOOM!

That monstrous king drum!

The North Carolina Symphony by bus, and my 6th grade class. I'm its smallest eleven-year-old, and that drum!

At the back rear corner of the stage that rarely gets struck, but drumbeats that *cut* to the heart of my soul when finally they come. Crescendo, finale, arrival, my destiny! Forward again, it's too late to turn, the orchestra's united and BOOM! BOOM! BOOM! BOOM! for yet a third time, I can *feel!*

The sound waves.

They hit me.

They travel up from the ground, I'm pushing forward in spite of my confusion and fear. "Some kind of mystical, Japanese, otherworldly drum from inside the Kaikan?" I'm smacked on the inside, I'm stopped in my tracks.

"Maybe those *aren't* earthquake cracks ..."

My last glimpse straight up through the mist to the yellowing sky.

My neck bent all the way back to see the second floor sliding glass windows are all open, the lights are all on, lots of people inside, and out from there's where the drum beats must've come. High school at North Meck, and the windows turn out from Bev Clayton's physics and chemistry room. We huddle in pairs over black plastic pans. Ripples in water, mechanical vibrating wands have frequencies we can set, and we study wave theory with waves we can see. Reflection, refraction, interference, subtraction, apply then to sound, added to light, the colors of sight, ultraviolet, the pitch and the tone, their wavelength and two point nine-nine-seven-nine, two-four-five-eight times ten to the eighth – that's meters per second – the velocity of light, the Doppler effect, and the pitch-changing howl of a fast moving train.

But *this drum's a monster!*

Bomb blasts that cut!

Straight through to my soul. And earthquakes as well, waves that travel through stone. A final barrage as I step up to the door. A final *ten* blasts? – this time in volume decreasing, down, down, down, and now gone like a train off into the distance but still *echoes* in my brain.

Mas Oyama's dojo's front doors!

The main doors to the Kyokushinkaikan.

Foreboding.

Open wide.

Thick, heavy metal frames and what's thick enough to be, it occurs to me, it's like bulletproof glass.

White t-shirts, two shaved, bald badgers inside, fists clenched and standing at attention. A narrow hallway reaching back to the shadows at the back of the building.

And its green-tiled stairs.

A second-floor landing.

And another leading down.

And just then!

The smack, smack, smack as a green belt and dogi spins round by the heavy oak railing, his sandals on the stairs like firecrackers. The rat-tat-tat of a machine gun, the drum, the start of the training, and "Oh, this guy is late for class!" it must be. Imposing, heavy iron bars, right here to the right of me, and something inside that's too dark to see – another flight of stairs, maybe, right here at the front of the building? "But going where?" I wonder. "That doesn't make any sense." Glass cases back there by the bench, a trophy and a bull horn. A reception window just here, through to a small office area out here by the door. A poster on the wall, "Kyokushin."

"Must be the right place after all!"

A middle-aged woman in a blue sailor's suit.

Two of them, no, three, peering outwards through the glass, eyes smiling at me. These two bald guys, heads shaved "like wrestlers!" serious and grim. Had their eyes not shifted, hungrily almost, in response to my staggering on in, I'd have thought that they were statues.

Lean. Muscle-bound midgets in sandals!

Knuckles like ball-peen hammers.

Crooked teeth, dirty white T-shirts and matching, sky-blue tracksuit pants.

Drumming's now matched as thirty adult males in unison shout "Osu! Osu! Osu! Osu!" upstairs, and over and over again in response to one baritone voice at the front of the room. The teacher's come in – could it be him? Mas Oyama? – is that *his* voice in front of the room?

And then.

BOOM!

BOOM!

BOOM!

The building *actually* shakes this time!

It's a different kind!

Physical tremors as thirty pairs of adult heels strike the floor up above simultaneously, a titanic metronome over and over again, and it occurs to me, it must be part of the warm-up routine.

Twin killers!

Stone-faced, they turn.

Gargoyles, their talons towards me!

For refuge I find the Japanese woman's eyes, still reaching outward warmly. She stands and she bows, a bit nervously, heavy makeup and curls that are "Hmmm, not Japanese," I think.

"Must be new to scrawny little white boys like me showing up at her desk." Three women total behind glass and one of them a teen, in navy blue uniforms that match, and a verbal greeting in Japanese I don't understand.

Something like maybe a "How can I help you?"

My voice.

Robotic as I hear it, fumbling today, echoing still in my brain, and "Osu! Osu!" so loud and confidently this morning, as the Frenchman and me at the top of our lungs, we step into the dormitory dining room.

"Say 'Osu!' twice, Ligo!" his voice yesterday, reminding me.

That's the dormitory *rule*, every time we enter or leave. It's something more than tradition, there's a true threat of violence since the sempais are there with the rest of the dorm. But yesterday afternoon as I step into the Kaikan for the very first time?

Carefully chosen words.

My very first, spoken in my brand-new Japanese home.

Words.

Japanese, rudimentary, and actually rehearsed. The bus ride, the flight, and all the week before. Down the mountain last week, that icy morning in fact, I rehearse and try to sort out exactly what I'd say to whoever I'd meet when I arrive in Japan. "Master Choi would kill me if he knew!" and Mas Oyama, even, wouldn't be expecting me.

"*Watashi ga*" ("I am," I begin.) ... I have to think still in English and translate. *Ligo Nay-ee-zan desu!* ("I came from") *Amerika kara kimashita!* ("I will be an") *Uchi deshi desu! Watashi no* ("my") *sensei* ("is") Choi Seong Soo, ("the nephew of") Mas Oyama *no ooi desu!*"

So painful for me!

Yesterday to speak, and today to remember, but this woman?

She's relieved and so pleased that I'm speaking some words in Japanese, and the back of my neck tickles like spiders.

These twin killers are crowding up curious behind me!

And *Sumisu* Sensei at UNC.

Our classroom one morning. Professor of linguistics and my Japanese teacher my sophomore year, she's white as me. Su-mi-su's for "Smith," like Nay-ee-zan's for Nathan. It's the very first week of Japanese 101 underway, and Nathan Ligo that day?

The late bloomer. The boy.

The Templeton student who finished freshman year a year early, I'm strikingly different from the rest of the class. There are giant butterflies in my throat, and I squirm in my seat. I'm smarter than them, I have real cause to learn since next year I'll be off to Japan, but Templeton ...

It shook me.

Gatlin was there, her voice in my head.

My father's head bowed, his tongue all torn out. His hands, like that, they're buried deep in his jeans.

xvi.

My freshman year at Templeton.
Bliss, on the one hand. It was Templeton, after all!
But Gatlin.
To me and my life, a total stranger.
Her voice. Condescending, berating, shaming, and for a lifetime of days for my father I bear.
The brunt of it.
Her voice in my head, my father's hands buried deep in his jeans. I'm 18, and for him I've come to the start of my sophomore year at UNC.
Afraid.
The end of my year at Templeton, just three months ago, and I'd "murdered my child," according to her.
But who the fuck is she?
Dillon had decided, she's three years older than me and off to graduate school. It was her call and not mine, and it was my job at that point to offer support to my friend. And then, the semester is over, and I pack up my bags, my entire *dorm room* in fact, my Volkswagen Bug's all filled to the seams. Gracie's irate, jealous with hate, two months have passed, and I'm off to the beach with Dillon, her friends Sheri and Sara, for their graduation week. Emboldened though, now, and finally I've had enough.
'Cause *enough is enough!*
I'm leaving town anyway.

For UNC and Japan, and from Dillon's dorm room where I've lived all semester, standing and balanced, I call *that woman* on the phone, her office across town, that unsightly wad of pubic hair in its Polaroid frame. Level-voiced and polite, I need to talk to her, I explain.

I tell her directly, without raising my voice, how inappropriate, how rude, and how out of line, and I couldn't believe it, so ashamed that I was *shocked* and struck dumb as my father at the time, that two nights earlier when Dillon and I had stopped in – at my own family home! – on a Friday night to check in, Gatlin'd *refused*, shut the door in our face, and not let us come in.

"I told you!" her voice on the phone, defensive, condescending, hateful, irate, "we had a Friday night planned to watch TV, and be alone!" Her empty excuse, her spit on the phone, my father's purple paint stripper burning still at my skin, and "Young Man!" her voice, finally, "You will NOT address me in that tone!"

But an inward smile this time, 'cause my tone is normal, and look who's talking about who's addressing who in what tone. My voice didn't crack, and I'm stronger now than I've ever been, and I hold my ground and point out the truth on the phone. Less than one month past her idiotic "You murdered your child!" and having not yet seen Dillon, that slamming that door in our face was in fact a slap in the face and they might well have called Dillon, my friend, a whore to her face.

"All you needed do was be civil and explain," I hold my ground, "let us in for five minutes ... even express a moment of warmth, civility or concern. But you didn't even look at her! – when you turned us away and slammed the door in our face."

And my father, of course.

Once again silent in the background, his hands thus

buried deep in his jeans. Sad-eyed and impotent when my stepmother, his wife, the door to my family home she slams shut in our face.

Walking dead.

Shell of a man!

So one month later don't even bother telling him. The semester is over and I pack up my bags on my way out of town. I'm on my way to UNC, and as far as I'm concerned, Japan.

And I'll not see him again. Not this Nathan Ligo, anyhow.

The Nathan Ligo tennis ball.

One more time through the air, from one more backhand, returning the serve back to Chapel Hill again. To UNC and my inconvenienced mom, an open-handed smack, from my father's third wife. Her "any length necessary," and her "to any degree," her "any personal sacrifice of even her own dignity," to see that I'd feel, and know that I'd been, *so soundly smacked,* and that I'd therefore think twice, the next time around, before choosing to live in Templeton, and with my father again.

Sure it felt good! – to tell her she was wrong, to watch her lose her cool while I tell her the truth. Happy indeed! to stand up to that woman, the source of six years of my brother's and my misery at home, the reason why we no longer have one.

Like my father should do.

Like my brother should have done.

Like all of us should have done all the way through.

But at least *I* spoke my mind and packed up my room.

My '63 Bug.

I shift down into second and let up the clutch, punch the gas to the floor and reach third in a flash. Same man who made Bugs also made Porsche, and I learned pedals from my mom who taught me to drive, and who learned pedals herself, where pedals are art, on grandma's piano long before she could drive. Concord Road out of town without further adieu, Highway 85 North, Master Choi's Chapel Hill, and onwards to my sophomore year of school. From the beginning my plan, since UNC, that larger, state school, had Japanese.

"Sure, Gracie'll label me 'angry,' in a bid for an excuse." One more bid to degrade me, since I'm the one *cursed,* the kink in their mail, the wrench in their works, the thorn in the side of a man … who's given himself over to the Dark Side. One where selfish concern, his new wife and new life, and their two new kids, are all somehow sacred enough to throw his first two away.

My half-brother Seth in first grade.

Me stooping down to reach for his hand before crossing the street. Warm tiny hand in my grip, and I'm ready to lift him right off his feet should a car come too close. My blood in his hand.

"Tainted by his mom and he doesn't even know it!"

Innocent and clueless.

His name.

The third son of Adam after Abel and Cain, given him by a man with a graduate degree from none other than Princeton Seminary. My father, the preacher, before studying art, Nathan and Aaron just 12 and 13, and he names his third son Seth?

As if to celebrate!

The loss of his first two. As if he'd decided already! - six years before that, that given enough time, he and his wife would finally be able to get rid of his first two.

Exterminate.

Humiliate.

Punish.

Abandon.

My dad!

My hand in his hand, I'm so safe and in France and in Spain. Martha is there, I'm eight and alive.

But by twelve?

He's married this staffer!

A one-term Templeton student from his very first year teaching. The year I was born and Templeton's co-ed for the very first time. Mom teaches piano still in Elm Row, and Gatlin, called "Gracie," whom he might not have known. She's a full decade younger. Insecure, weak-ankled, has oversized tits.

The worst kind of awkward.

Feels discriminated against, and *compensates!* Cocky and simple, but can never be wrong, certainly not in the face of anything *male.* Angry feminist spawn! And as a wedding present, Dad gives her heartbroken, shaky, passive himself, and two jerked-around boys she can bully.

Boys she can degrade.

But she needs boys she can *scar!*

To somehow work out how she, girl-child, awkward and fugly, was somehow left wounded, left behind as a child, I can only imagine, by somebody *male.*

Weak-ankled and top-heavy.

Self-fulfilling prophecy.

My dad.

Heartbroken.

Reduced.

Lost Martha, and his spine left permanently curved, his tongue all cut out. Abandoner, unleasher of passive-aggressive all-silent abuse.

But nonetheless …

My Bug on the road, on my way out of town, fourth gear, and a heavy sigh. I'm learning finally, and I'm on the right side this time.

But I too was reduced.

To yet another new school, in yet another new place, and my mother's still gone.

In Chapel Hill.

In that shell of herself.

Half of her still back in the Prescott home she lost, and I. For the first time since school, since ninth grade at Phillips Junior High, I'm back to the scene of the crime, where I'd been so sick in eighth grade. That entire year sick, from that very first year split from my brother, Aaron, who'd already moved to Templeton. My brother who's nearly my twin, for the very first time in my life separated from him, and now, here I am.

Entering the university.

Afraid.

Shaken again by the undeniable proof of the loss of my dad, and by what *should have been* that vital part of an over-and-over-again shaken eighteen-year-old's emotional support structure at home.

Silly, I suppose!

A karateka destined for Mas Oyama's Japan, and I'd come in afraid! Afraid that I'd be alone, not know anyone and be, one more time, ashamed, and embarrassed to sit down in the cafeteria alone.

Eighteen years old!

The youngest sophomore on campus, weak and off balance to UNC.

Awkward and beaten, an orphan hated by his mute father at home and his half-engaged mom. Not a peer that he knew, and Aaron was gone, this time for good, his life was signed over to the United States Marine Corps.

And Chapel Hill?

A town that's now hollow for the absence of my mom who I couldn't much stand to look at anymore, because she was whittling me away, and for the absence of the Prescott home, the one across town that was my last comfortable, my last warm family home.

But Master Choi!

His thick Korean accent.

Savant!

Seer!

The answer for me.

Eyes that still say, "I wish I had a son like you." Surrogate father, his CMAC, my surrogate family, and thanks to these two, I'm eighteen and alive. I stand on two feet, and I've learned to stand up in spite of it all. Won't sit there and stand for my stepmother's trash, but nevertheless.

I'm alone.

And Templeton!

It shook me.

And in the front row, I'm bright-eyed and eager in *Sumisu* Sensei's room, and nobody knows it, but the butterflies! They *howl* again in my throat like werewolves set free, I'm swallowing air, belching it back out in a bid for relief.

But now, something new!

Something exciting and powerful rings in my head, my heart beats like it hasn't before, and always I see.

Mas Oyama's Japan!

Japanese, and in a matter of months and I'll be off to Japan. Master Choi showed me how to stand up on two feet, and Mas Oyama, my teacher, the next one to come. The bare-handed bull fighter, his turn next time to teach, and I was sure then that I'd learn! Bring honor to Master Choi for saving my life, and with my bare knuckles I'd learn. I'd kill *even the werewolves* this time. I'd tear limb out from limb with my teeth and my claws, leave the butterflies, the Zantac, and all that weakness at home.

And "Oh, is that so?"

The kind Japanese woman asks.

But how could she possibly know?

Her smiling eyes behind glass, my crystal ball cracked.
Kind Japanese lady's eyes smiling at me.
She understood and I turn.

A death sentence handed down I can no longer deny, and that pair! Those miniature bald-headed lobby guards crowding upwards behind, their breath on my neck. The inevitable, I turn.

And face them.

Two new step*brothers* this time, the very first two of my new family in Japan.

xvii.

Late yesterday afternoon.

My first minute of what's to become a thousand days in my new Japanese home.

Twin gargoyles on lobby guard duty.

"*U ara* uchi deshi?" the skinny, gap-toothed one asks, wide-eyed, surprising me.

"Hai, uchi deshi desu," yes, I will be an uchi deshi. My voice, a bit steadier this time, and Oshikiri speaks back.

In a thick Japanese accent.

"Yoo-ah cone-tah-ree? Han-gah-ree? O-soo-toe-ray-ree-ah?"

My country Hungary? Australia?

What the hell is he talking about?

No, I came from America, I say again, "Amerika kara kimashita." My teacher is Mas Oyama's nephew in America.

"My name is Ligo. *Rah-ee-go Nay-ee-zan.*"

"Nay-ee-zan san?"

A sideways exchanged look with his friend, and his twin scurries off towards the stairs at the back of the building.

A glint in the eye of this Japanese.

I could have sworn that I'd seen. Hard as nails, emaciated, and standing at attention, a badger, a killer, a cannibal so hungry he'd eat *me* if he could.

But a glint underneath?

A friendly, a curious, a young man just like me?

"Hai, (yes)," I say, "*watashi-no namae-ga* (my name is) Ligo."

"Rah-ee-go."

Easy for me. Spent a whole week in first-year Japanese on "What is your name? What year are you in school? What is your hobby?" and "How old are you?" *Ligo-san's* my name for a year already in *Su-mi-su* Sensei's room.

"Oh, I see," Oshikiri reverts to stern Japanese, "it's 'Ligo-san,' then?"

Hai! "It's Ligo, that's correct," and taking a chance, "I would like to speak to Mas Oyama, please."

I cringe.

Embarrassed this morning at breakfast to remember. A man like Sosai's not going to drop whatever he's doing to welcome lost little me. My room-scanning gaze finds Oshikiri in the dining room commotion, rushing with the rest to finish setting the table for breakfast.

"All in good time, Grasshopper!" says the wise old Chinese philosopher.

Ignorant.

Stupid!

"Shrimp" like they called me in school!

Japanese 101 at the limits of what I actually *can* say, grammar tangles in my head, and I battle with what I really *want* to say. I battle with, "Please, there were some last-minute changes concerning my plans, and I'm not really sure whether Mas Oyama, my own teacher in North Carolina's uncle, or even my teacher himself, for that matter, Master Choi, is actually even aware that I've come."

Oshikiri, however, who I know now this morning would never once have spoken Mas Oyama's name without the honorific *Sosai* attached, fidgets, looks sideways, and ignores my request.

Did he not understand?

He's distracted, his friend's scurried up that one flight of stairs to the landing at the back of the building. I follow his eyes, his gap-toothed, youthful concern. He's stumped and concerned, worried and not knowing just what he should do. They weren't expecting me. Plainly visible there, from here with my bags at the door, and my eyes more and more used to the dark at the back of the building, his twin, in matching sky-blue tracksuit pants. Squatting in sandals on green linoleum, V-shaped corded back, muscles curved forward and reaching down at the back of the second-floor landing, and suddenly, then, LOUD! – against the background clamor of the training upstairs, sounds like an elephant skidding to a stop on a bag full of marbles! Metal scrapes metal as he slides open one of those low, opaque sliding-glass windows I can see from the park. And like a car crash, BOOM! its frame to the jamb, it slams all the way open.

Bizarre!

No, that's French, of all things, on the tip of my tongue. Funny that my *high school* language kicks in, my brain in foreign language mode and I don't yet know how to say to myself "strange" in Japanese.

It is strange, though.

This guy should have been off to tell Mas Oyama I've come, but instead he's opened a window on the first floor landing at the back of the building?

Opaque, sliding glass.

Out through to the dusk, and even in the daylight of this morning for breakfast I can't see out through the glaze, of those matching single, stairwell-wide window panes. He's leaning outside, out into two feet of clearing, into two feet of space between two buildings for air, and out towards the next building. This window, *at the back* of the Kaikan, one I know now's facing the back wall of dorm, and an echoing! – a loud sliding open of some other matching window outside?

And *two* uchi deshi this time!

Leaning outward toward one another, talking in hushed

tones, one building to the next, across an alley so narrow nobody walks it, and talking about me, "the unexpected American" in hurried, in hushed tones.

Oshikiri.

Standing beside me, he's straining to hear.

"Ingenious!" it occurs to me.

If I wasn't so tired, and it all so surreal, I'd sure have believed.

Hilarious!

The mother of invention!

One step up from two cans and a string!

Me.

The surreal dining room crowd and commotion of this morning, and still in my haze, dehydrated and wasted from the run, and dehydrated and wasted from the shower, finally I realize. They use that loud marbly scrape of an old aluminum-framed window in an old aluminum window track as a telephone ring!

There are two windows!

The only access between the back-to-back Kaikan and the front-to-back dorm, and if they'd oiled their tracks they'd have to knock each time with a handle of a broom to get each other's attention!

But that loud, marbly scrape! – as one of them opens either window to its jamb with a boom, alerts his counterpart, the one in the first-floor dormitory dining room, that two-foot pass-through, through two sliding-glass windows not even built to line up. From the Kaikan landing, one leans all the way out and down to reach and receive whatever it is his friend in the dormitory dining room's leaning all the way up and outwards to hand him!

And Mocaram with me.

Black Arab this morning.

My only friend here so far, and a dozen large, blue-rimmed bowls of hot sticky rice fall into line.

Ceramic, steaming, and heavy.
A dozen uchi deshi.
Their double-filed frenzy, finally trapped and penned in.
The Young Lion's Dormitory, my first breakfast in Japan!

xviii.

Dark.

Shokudo, in Japanese.

The traditional Japanese dining room. Low-ceilinged like the inside of a storm drain. A tunnel. A milk truck tank. An aluminum can. *A cardboard poster tube* perhaps? – since its paneling's all wood. Flickering fluorescent lights overhead, and just big enough for all of us to fit in.

Feels cylindrical, but why?

It's Mas Oyama's eyes!

He's staring inwards from fifty like-sized photographs circling the room. Two-foot square glass frames leaning in, looking down on all sides. Looming. Haunting. Challenging. The God of Modern Karate. In that one's he's punching, and in that one blocking. Here, he's cross-legged and bare-chested under an icy waterfall, meditating. And there's one complete set of four, I see now, that are an artist's renditions. He's battling a bull, and in that one a panther.

Good God, I know he fought bulls, but surely he never fought a lion!

There's even one, a photograph just here, the 60-year-old titan up high on the back of a massive white Clydesdale. An endless row of karateka in white, a double file line behind him off into the mist, trudging onward off towards the horizon, bleeding bare feet and knee-deep in snow.

"The March of Kyokushin."

Those bold English words printed across the bottom of one. Kyokushin's march across the globe.

One hundred thirty countries, and twelve million strong. His sword in its sheath at the end of that film, its loud pop of metal on wood. The energy, the sweat, the metal, the chink of the chairs, the stainless steel sink, all swirls together in one constant, frenzied motion. *Osu!'s* all tripping over too many cloth-slippererd feet. Thirteen big bowls of hot steaming rice, the table as long as the dormitory is long, and our double-filed frenzy. Same double-file running formation from the mad dash of this morning, our avalanche of boulders, finally trapped and penned in.

The *shokudo*, the dormitory dining room.

A box canyon.

We're stuck into a space too tight to escape, but the kinetic energy! I laugh to myself at the idea of an uchi deshi who knows physics and chemistry.

Our teacher, bald-headed Bev Clayton, is sunburnt and freckled and, in his southern accent, he explains. Like heat, kinetic energy is always retained. I see him high up on his tractor beyond the football field, the mob of us fall into parallel lines. Caged in like ions. Corn planted in rows that sway in the wind, his family field through the woods, and the cross-country trail. We're running! I'm nearly the slowest, and we're welcoming two teams to our first race at North Meck, a cross-country meet! We're proud to have the least well-maintained of the division's cross-country trails, and at least *we know* where to plant our feet to miss the roots and not fall on our faces. Light speed, in our pockets we hold all the aces. Charged, numbered particles, quivering. Ping-pong balls settling into a lottery jackpot machine. The dormitory dining room, a cardboard picture tube, my eyes and his meet.

The rosy-faced first-year named Kato.

And me.

The newcomer.

The only white guy.

And there's Oshikiri.

Ligo-san, "the American," legs like jelly, stomach remembering, on Mocaram's heels, weaving our way in through the dining room crowd.

We're nine of the thirteen now!

Standing at attention behind rows of low stools, and the last several of us racing to get to our places. Two or three over there in the kitchen and still working, and the rest of us are tucking in tighter.

Our dirt-stained Fruit of the Looms.

Everyone now turns, faces the far end of the room where the *sempais'* door is, where the window on the right passes through to Honbu's stairwell, where the door on the left leads last night to upstairs. The *obiya,* the dormitory "Big Room," where eight or nine of us slept, where in front of us there at the end of the room, beside the sempai's door, hang two daunting rectangles of Japanese text in black wooden frames.

Finely printed calligraphy.

Complex.

Kanji behind glass. "Could it be? the Training Hall Oath?" I wonder again as I wondered last night. No, but it's something like that. "Can't be. The Training Hall Oath has just seven lines, and this one's like twenty!"

David Toleman at UNC.

He's leading the oath. The subterranean windowless multipurpose room and "One! We will train our hearts and bodies, for a firm and unshaking spirit!" we echo his tone before moving on to the Oath's second line.

Hot pasty soup.

It looks like soup, at least, in thirteen small bowls, and something else brown.

In yet another size down, one more set of red plastic bowls.

These Japanese dishes.

Something sticky and brown, chopsticks at a glance in front of each person, and a short empty glass. An egg in its shell that I gather to be, from the one that I saw that started to roll, and was so gingerly caught and returned to its place, an egg that is raw.

"Cool," I think, "like Rocky." I used to eat them at school after weight training.

Perspiration.

A drop from Mocaram's hairline, getting ready to fall.

White eggshell sheen.

Condensation, the steam, and a thump through the door.

To the sempais' room!

The sempais are coming.

A French-accented hiss, whispered, and turning to me. "Bow and say 'Osu!' Ligo, when the sempai comes in!"

Brown, sticky beans.

Is that what I smell? If I wasn't so tired, I'd smile that I know. No matter what they are I'll eat them, and they'll probably be good.

I see just then in a blink.

Home.

Martha's long-handled kitchen tongs.

Some salt, and we fry green tomatoes we picked right off the vine, tomatoes I helped grow by tying them to their lines. Anyone would think we were insane! – but there were grasshoppers that year like a Biblical plague, and Martha had read you could make bug spray by grinding grasshoppers up, and pressing their juice out into a paste, and applying it by hand to the plants that they ate.

Aaron and I to the delight of small boys, that whole day on a mission!

Martha's voice.

Ringing of home, promising us pennies for every one we

could catch, and we watch! That day after dark from the French louvered doors of the pantry. As she braces herself.

And mashes down.

The power button.

On the first ever food processor we've known. The cream-colored Cuisinart she got from Dad's folks at Christmastime this year, and in a crunching hum WHIRRRR!

The blade spins all the way around like a weed-eater blade! – and four dollars and twenty-two cents' worth of Biblical plague, some of them alive and still squirming in place, are rendered in an instant into a green slimy paste, and the next day we help her to spray out that goop onto our tomato plants.

The log house.

My childhood home.

So hot in the sun, and North Carolina's red clay. August or July and the hillside haze. That grasshopper *whir!* as one of them flies by through heat waves so thick the sunlight ripples already so soon after it came up.

The furry, needly prick of the tomato vine!

Similar, but so much sharper than a peach's fuzz, just above the leaves at the top of the fruit. My tiny boy's fingers pull back, and "Ouch!" I exclaim. Tomatoes picked green, and those were the tomatoes we ate, ones we'd defended and grown when on my tiptoes I'd reach and couldn't even touch the top of the tomato stakes!

Couldn't even stand *catsup* before that, we hated tomatoes that bad.

But then!

Martha hatches a plan.

Knows the difference in taste between the red and the green, and suspects that our resistance might have had something to do with the color.

And so.

With long kitchen tongs, and Martha's stern "Watch out for

the grease!" I'm standing up high on a chair in the kitchen, and in one of her aprons, and my tiny boy's hands turn, carefully, first one, then the next, each battered green piece of tomatoes from our vines, with salt – and lo and behold! – and three blows in a row, since they're too hot to eat! – and I'm eating tomatoes!

And I like them!

A hiss.

"Ligo!"

The Arab's hissed English is calling me back.

The *shokudo*, the dormitory dining room after the run.

"Make sure that you bow, and say 'Osu!' Ligo. The sempai are coming!

"And when they tell us to sit, keep your eyes only forward, and don't speak! And make sure when you eat, you pick up your bowl, and you don't take your lips away from your bowl, and you don't stop until every … how do you say? Every piece? … every little white thing of rice is gone?"

Fuck, I can't believe it.

The *Young Lions' Home!*

Japan.

About to eat my first morning meal.

The hook-nosed Iwaya, and my stomach constricts.

He'll beat me if he finds an excuse. That last window's the one, the last one at the front.

Opaque.

Sliding glass.

Right-front of the room, opposite the door to the third-years' room. It slides noisily open, yesterday afternoon.

The Kaikan lobby.

The lost-looking Nathan's just stumbled in.

Echoing still in my brain.

There's yesterday's marbly, ball-bearing scrape.

Of metal on metal from the Kaikan stairwell, and looking upwards outside at a catty-corner, a complex angle, the uchi deshi in here on kitchen duty leans out, and up into the damp airway in between, looking upwards to see where Oshikiri's lobby guard buddy leans outwards and down to report, in hurried, in hushed tones, that a new uchi deshi's arrived. "An *American*, it seems," and "What do we do?" since we weren't expecting an American.

"Are you sure?" it would have been, asking up from the dining room, "an American? He's not Australian or Hungarian?"

"Yes, I'm sure, hurry up!

"We better report to Hashimoto Sempai, or there'll be hell to pay! – when the third-year find out we let someone come in who wasn't supposed to be here!"

Wakatta! Urusai, matte!

"I got it, wait just a freakin' second!" his voice.

And "Damn it!" to himself, as he faces the fact he'll have no choice but to disturb one of the ones he hates so much to disturb. "Wait just one second, and I'll run upstairs and check with the sempai!"

Oshikiri's concerned eyes.

They shift back into line, they focus on mine by the information window. A tired smile inside.

"Ja-su-to wan mo-men-to, plea-zu," he says, completing the list of his basic expressions in English. "*Chotto matte kudasai*," the same thing again in Japanese, and "*Arigatoo gozaimashita,*" in my voice I confirm that I did understand, and I pronounced the "gozaimashita" correctly this time.

Not Japanese, black curls behind me.

Her heavy makeup, her blue sailor's suit smiles behind the glass, and exclaims, "*Aa! nihon-go ga dekimasu ne!*" accusing me, it seems, the newcomer Ligo, of speaking some Japanese.

Oshikiri grunts something, agrees.

Bends down and reaches for the straps of my bags to move them from the middle of the hall, and a sharp, upwards glance of surprise!

I should have foreseen!

"Oh my God!" in his eyes, when he feels the weight of my one bag. "What's he got in here? Crazy *gaijin* arrives from America with concrete blocks in his bags!"

I jump forward and grab, reach down for its straps. "*Hon desu,*" they are books, I say, and clearly he must think I'm insane.

"Boo-ku," he reads back in his Japanese pronunciation of English, with its barely audible but should-be-silent "u," "man-ney, man-ney boo-ku." And his sidekick at the back of the building makes the butterflies jump up into my throat at his tone, so suddenly changed!

"Osu!" half-shouted, and again, *Osu! Amerikajin-da to omoimasu!*

"Yes, I think he's an American!" he said, and he's addressing someone else now, someone who makes him shout his answers in that military-like tone I've never heard so loud. Oh my god, I just realized now, these really ARE the uchi deshi I waited five years to become!

They're a lot smaller than I thought they'd be.

"Osu!" his voice shouted again, and I'd forgotten completely the training underway, the earth-shaking racket above me, the second floor of the building. "I understood!' he says, and "Osu! Please excuse me, I'll take care of it right away!"

And lo and behold!

I knew those two expressions already.

Wakarimashita, the past tense of "I understand."

And *Shitsurei-shimasu,* a super polite way of saying "Excuse me, please," that actually means, "I'm going to commit a great rudeness now, by turning my back on you, and taking my leave."

Crazy Japanese!

A screech and a BOOM! as he slams the window shut once again, its frame with a crash to its jamb, and he's running back down, smack, smack, smack, his sandals on the green linoleum – or is that called Formica? – the rattly metal strips on the front edge of each step, and not missing a step. He's reporting in a hoarse whisper something in Japanese, and before I can understand, both of them look up at the sound of a much duller, an approaching chop, chop, chop on the blacktop outside and behind me. Another set of sandals on the asphalt approaching, and this time it's Kuruda, roaring up at a sprint, and I see this third roommate of mine for the very first time.

He's so small, but built like a truck!

"Osu! Osu!" he announces as he comes in through the door and slides to a stop, and to no one, it seems! – he bows with tight fists, and crossing the threshold, his eyes into mine, and in a whirlwind! – I'm back outside. Kuruda's grabbed the heavier of my bags, but he wasn't prepared, and Oshikiri knowing already, snatches up my second. He swings it over his shoulder, and grabs one of the other's straps, and I'm ushered outside. Two of them now running, shuffling together, to share at a run the weight of my heavier bag.

It's my very first run this time around the Kaikan's small block, and "Where the Hell are we going?" I wonder.

Feels like a dream.

A fog or a haze.

It's so nearly dark, and it's only a little after, for God's sake, four o'clock in the afternoon?

Maybe birds really do fly backwards in Japan, and the trees, they grow down, and the *kiais!* "Kiops" in Korean Master Choi explains, the shouts of karate have started upstairs. "My god!" those windows, the class, shaking the glass, but the rate!

So little time between shouts, "It's so fast! How can they possibly complete the techniques at that pace?" It's dark in the street, and my leather bag drags, this Christmas in Princeton and Gatlin and Dad. *That woman*, my stepmother gave me this bag, knowing I was off to Japan. Nice thought, but knowing her affinity for me, it was probably planned.

Her celebration!

I'm going away again, and the bag's poorly conceived. Its straps are too short to wear on a shoulder, and at the same time too long to hang at the end of a normal man's reach or it drags on the street.

Bone breakers!

Miniature twin killers, shuffling down the street, turn to each other, and Kuruda exclaims. "What in God's name has he got in here?" it must be. His voice always calm, but their deltoids bulge halfway up to their elbows to pull the bag's straps all the way up to their armpits, and Oshikiri finally stops. The leather bag's dragged on the street for the second time already, and he grabs the whole thing and swings it up onto one shoulder, and only he now, alone!

Carrying it's weight.

Shuffling his sandals, staggering under a bag that's almost his size, and Kuruda's picked up the other, my bag full of clothes, my *dogi* from America that's whiter than theirs, my Fetzer Gym t-shirt, and the sweats I took off somewhere over the Aleutians.

In a whirlwind the alley so narrow, and the dormitory dining room for my very first time. These stairs that are more like a ladder than stairs. The *obiya* on the second floor and Mocaram, my sempai, for the very first time.

"Put that bag up above," the Frenchman's voice echoes, indicating with a nod the shelf that wraps all the way around the ceiling of the room, the *obiya*, the "Big Room" where nine or ten of us slept, and I lift my bag up and put it on the shelf next to Kuruda's. A cardboard box. "Kuro," it says.

Black.

"Da."

Rice field.

But there's no room for my second.

My books.

They're probably too heavy anyway, it occurs to me, and my library remains on the tatami next to my futon when I finally take one down two hours later, and pass out and sleep, and already!

Here I am.

The newcomer, the American.

My books next to me, and, because of them, already I've made myself an exception, an uchi deshi who can do physics and chemistry.

His silly, ridiculous, his suitcase full of books.

xix.

The dormitory.

My first morning meal rising upwards in steam.

The table's composed of a long row of two-tops, side by side in a line to make one long table as long as the dormitory is long, and me.

Tucking in my shirt and looking down past my hands to my parallel feet.

It's hard not to see.

In a blink.

My memory.

My own, my hazy reflection in the black Formica gloss of a Crook's Corner table.

My face.

A tired 18-year-old's eyes, just one year ago looking upwards at me.

I'm exhausted and failing.

I'm taking Multi-Variable Calculus with that grad student on Mars from Lithuania or Estonia, and in that tiny UNC classroom I can't understand, not his Arabic symbols in chalk that he writes, not the sounds in Martian he mocks me to make, and Basic Mechanics in Physics with Calculus this time? Both at the same time. One hundred and fifty students all in the same room, an auditorium for Physics with Calculus, not just a mere room like we would have had at Templeton.

At least second semester Japanese matters this time, since before the year's over I'll be off to Japan! With a little luck, that is, if Mas Oyama says I can come.

And "What the hell am I doing here?" I wonder.

"I should be studying, or back at the gym training, getting ready for Japan, but instead I'm bussing Crook's Corner tables?"

Wasting time!

My *mother's* voice this time.

Reminding me.

About her "Child Rearing" account, subtitled "Nathan," and the money she spends is fast running out. Her therapist and her analytical mind. The methodical assassination of intuitive thought, my mom has become blind.

To me!

To reality!

"I know the answers already," I write to myself at Templeton last year, and I see. Without reading, the answers in front of me. It's Physics and Chemistry, *Zen Mind, Beginner's Mind*, the transcendentalists at Brook Farm, and "I'm still not where I'm supposed to be!" My sophomore year at UNC, my own basement apartment across town and my inconvenienced mom. One of Crook's Corner's inside tables for two, weekend nights after school, and in Japan this morning like an echo I *feel*.

My hand if I try.

Making that same, time-practiced circular pass on a Crook's Corner table with a starched dry, white cloth napkin to dry it's reflective surface. Broad, focused, spiraling strokes till every trace of the moisture is gone, and with it, my reflection, I see.

Past the napkin.

My right hand working, the surgery I had on the back of my hand. The white of the cloth, the white of the splint, and in my left hand's balanced my tray. Half-full water glasses jingle, coffee cups, heavy. Stacked-up desert plates and what's left of a chocolate sponge cake, I can smell!

The chocolate.

A trace of whipped cream scraped off the plate in the lines of a slightly bent fork's tines, and two delicate, two furry leaves of mint.

And wet shiny black.

That Formica table top, I drift back.

And return.

My melted-ice-cold, terry-cloth towel to the back right pocket of my black formal slacks. That wet cold hanging down the back of my leg, and me. Drawing attention. A curious little girl, bored, her parents are lost in discussion, her blonde hair and her tiny white dress, looking over at me? I'm carrying a tray through the dining room crowd and she sees, plainly visible against the black of the table on the back of my hand, the white Velcro straps of a white plastic splint from the surgery I had?

My thumb and two fingers only maneuvering the rag, and the middle two are isolated, strapped to the white plastic out straight, just one weekend past and I came back in to work. The last traces of ache from the sutures in place, I can see.

The flesh opened wide.

Like an eyelid on a table.

Stretched open wide on the back of my hand, a spot of red light surrounded by white, I'm there, but out of my mind. An anesthesiologist that's too aggressive for me, and I'm fading away 'cause I wanted to see. A surgical assistant pulls the wound open wide so the doctor can see.

This reconstructive surgery.

It's cartilage that holds the tendon in place, and I'm punching and breaking so many white pine boards, practicing my punch till the last one I broke, and outside of class – and to show Dillon of course – it dropped me to my knees! The parking lot by Templeton's Richardson dorm, and its gravelly surface that cuts into my knees. At night in the dark and a searing pain like my hand in hot grease.

Each time that much worse!

I'd heal, not complain, and do it again. And tear it again.

The *speed break*.

Holding the board, my left arm out straight, suspended between my left thumb and one finger, it's flat surface facing towards me, and I'd drop it, and punch it at just the right time! My middle right knuckle and the board with a *Whack!* Two clean halves of wood sent off into space, but this last one?

My knuckle split too this time?

And I feel it today, still in my brain, an echo of burns like a hot poker jabbed into the back of my hand.

"But at least the board broke!" my voice another time, trying to regain face. My teacher's uncle, a Mas Oyama I haven't yet met.

His own famous words.

Ones I imagine, asserting, "Either the board will be broken or I'll shatter my hand. Either way, I'll strike the board with all that I have!" Or so it is written that he said. One of the well-known mottos of Mas Oyama, the man, and *Master Choi's* words this time?

Explaining.

The *Samurai Way* where Japanese Budo was born.

Swordplay.

"Sacrifice your one arm if necessary," he says, "to live long enough to deliver the last blow, the one that'll take your attacker down before your life slips away." Mas Oyama the man, his uncle, the living example of Japan's martial way, and I draw attention to myself. Again! The meek *Rah-ee-go-san* in my Japanese class, when one night in the first week of school I cut open my thumb, on a tin can lid in the trash, nine stitches and then home from the emergency room to that basement apartment I rent, and I come in to class!

With *both of my hands* wrapped up in white gauze this time!

And Smith Sensei says later, she thought with a laugh that I'd had my hands torn up, her smiling eyes and her voice, "in some kind of industrial accident."

These tables for two.

Japan, ten in a row and lined by low stools!

Badgers and bone-breakers.

Our movement all now drawn to a close.

Ten of us now face the far end of them room, that calligraphy behind glass, and "fudo dachi," Mocaram explains yesterday. Our feet parallel, and shoulder-width apart. Equal weight on both feet, fists clenched at our sides and in front of our hips. My head spins for a moment! I can't believe that I'm here, my life in Japan, out of the corner of my eyes, and I see!

The uchi deshi ahead and across the table from me.

He's got gravel!

He's already showered, and he's got pieces of sand!

They're stabbing out from the flesh on the back of his hand. From pushups on rock, like that dirt in the back of their Fruit of the Looms, his knuckles like ball peen hammers, and finally I realize!

How silly I'd seem.

To the rest of them, if they knew that I'd once had surgery.

Ignorant American!

And a doctor to repair cartilage they try, day in and day out, with punches and push-ups on gravel to tear, to make their fists tougher.

And silence then, now.

We're waiting.

Everyone's still.

A single drop of sweat on black Arab curl.

It rolls.

It lets go and it falls.

Through steam rising up from thirteen hot steaming rice bowls and filling the room.

XX.

"Make sure that you bow, and say 'Osu!' Ligo!" The Frechman's voice hisses, "The sempais are coming!"

"And when they tell us to sit, keep your eyes only forward, and don't speak! And make sure when you eat, you pick up your bowl, and you don't take your lips away from your bowl, and you don't stop until every … how do you say? Every piece? … every little white thing of rice is gone."

That drop of sweat at his hairline.

Falling drop reflects.

A wink of light through the air, as "Osu!" my voice responds to Mocaram, the Frenchman, and my stomach constricts.

At the thought.

Of a time limit to eat, and what it might do to my stomach, and in an instant I see.

A wave of grief that gnaws at me.

I'm fifteen years old on Main Street.

In Templeton, stepping into my father's red brick home, my stepmother, the kitchen, and a cautious hello gathers in my throat. I wipe the sweat from my brow. The Prescott house kitchen just one year before that, I'm fourteen and home from ninth grade. That taste in my throat, Chapel Hill.

But Templeton now?

There's canned tunafish meat, laid out before me, and split up squarely into two slimy heaps.

One of them.

The light meat half way down the counter in a puddle on the cutting board that's slipped sideways off, a trickle of Bumble Bee, the Chicken of the Sea's spring water. One of four of the cutting board's four tiny feet right up to the edge of the brown-tiled counter, and just then!

That tiny globe through the air.

One drop of tunafish juice separates, takes flight. Its darker striations.

Over there.

Pulled out and separated by hand and into a strainer in the sink. My stepmother's hands. Her caught-off-guard eyes dart over and then back from her tunafish cans. Something's wrong, and the scene!

Something about it strips away my impulse to say hello cheerfully in spite of it all. Just last week, and we had that discussion and I told them I can't eat tunafish, it makes me sick, I explained, and finally they promised, my stepmother reluctantly, "Don't worry," she said, "we'll have something else planned."

"For dinner."

But my stepmother's hands, I'm baffled!

She's leaning over her sink, dissecting the mess, she and her kitchen up to their elbows in green, cans with white labels and pried-open lids, and this time some salmon? Pictures of pink, filets on the labels of two full-sized cans, one of them upright and the other tipped over. Two years in this household already, and still it feels empty in my father's new home.

But this time it's different.

Worse!

Somehow I've screwed up her plans.

I've come in from mowing the lawn, and she's angry – is she humiliated? – to see me just then.

She's been caught.

She and her tunafish meat, my stomach locks, the hairs on the back of my neck, the itch of the sweat off my brow, and mechanically.

It dawns on me.

"It can't be!"

She's been hatching a plan, she's been going even so far as to separate, by hand, the darker striations out of the tunafish cans, mixing the light part with salmon so I'd then have to eat what she couldn't stand I was getting my way not to eat, and so she could tell me first it was salmon, and then afterwards like she planned the "I told you so!" that's like oxygen for her.

Since she's so desperate all the time.

To say it.

My eyes divert, I'm too stunned. I wipe the sweat off my hands on the thighs of my jeans, my right reaches out for the refrigerator door, and I see.

The way-back of the yard.

Back down by the tracks, I'm cutting the lawn, not yet, with that weekly task, halfway done. The green of that pulverized grass paints the cuffs of my jeans, their shins, and up to my knees, the palms of my hands.

Itch.

My stepmother's embarrassed eyes then, her anger.

Continues to burn.

From purple paint stripper fumes eating into my skin. The vibration of that aluminum rod in my grip, the lawnmower's handle, the refrigerator door, that smell of gas. Mixes in my nostrils with tunafish, with grass and with sweat. One whole afternoon each week, during the school week, is a step up at least from working with purple paint stripper fumes, and for the whole summer long when I was just thirteen.

My brother Aaron's voice rings.

Two years later he's sixteen.

"Kind of feels like we're the servants around here, doesn't

it," he says, sarcastically, and "Slaves, the Ligo boys!" his beautiful punk girlfriend Siouxsin with her egg-white-lifted Mohawk agrees, trying to make light. It's nearly dark over here, and she's sitting on the hood of the VW Bug that was his before mine.

Across town.

One block up from the Abbotts' house on the Green, outside the elementary school gym where the other fourth graders wouldn't let me play kickball with them. Our Tae Kwon Do class is getting ready to start, and I assert. Precociously. Clear-headed, correct. Grown up so quickly, the analytical one, the young one of the three but the steady voice of reason, and for it.

Gatlin calls me angry.

My voice to my brother.

"Yeah, and it probably wouldn't feel like that," I say, "if it wasn't all so dead-ended."

"I mean, it wouldn't feel that way probably if Gracie could possibly stand to say a single thing nice. Maybe just once out of every four or five times she opens her mouth to tell us something we have to do, or that we're not allowed to do, or that we did something wrong, or that we're inadequate at something." But at 13 and 14 we're too young to know, and perhaps it's normal, we think, for 13- and 14-year-olds to spend their whole summers stripping paint off the woodwork in their fathers' new homes, pulling up, from their hands and knees, the thousands upon thousands of staples from the floor when the house's urine-stained carpet comes up from its decade-old wall-to-wall. Like ammonia. Like all of that dust, that sweat, that chemical scent seeps back through my brain, through my sinuses it comes back, sweat trickles in tracks down yellow rubber gloves all the way to my elbows, and a chemical tingle in my nostrils, my throat.

Burns for a moment as I cough.

Once.

To clear my throat, I'm looking for words, it's pollen this

time, it's smashed-up green, it's what's become of me that crashes in, and in a glance my stepmother's tunafish meat, her condescension, her deceit, and like refuge, my fingers reach and I touch.

The cold.

And the slick of a diet root beer can. It draws out past the pickles, the mayonnaise from the second shelf down in the fridge, and I see.

The Ligo house lawnmower's one-stroke engine.

Grumbling angrily.

But "It's okay now," I suppose, and I tell myself as I sweat, and swallow hard past my dry cotton throat, and haul that damn grumbling machine up and down for the eighteenth week in a row. I look up towards the house and its diet root beer can in the fridge, "because all I need do is maintain, and anyhow pushing a lawnmower's not bad training, and in a couple years I'll be off to Japan … and maybe before then, Dad'll come 'round and get his feet under him again."

Japan.

So thirsty this morning after the run!

"How I can possibly force down so much hot steaming rice?" I wonder. A snap and a fizz, and that Ligo house can of root beer pops open. It lifts to my lips, and "Oh my god, how I'd kill for one now!" its fizz and its burn. I swallow and turn, Gatlin's there, and my two seconds into the kitchen have become three.

Voicelessly.

We're trying to recover, but my natural impulse, that cheerful hello in my throat that might have made a difference is gone.

Irretrievable.

Her sink.

Her amazing display.

"Seriously?" though.

My lips in Japan, all on their own, in that millisecond they twitch towards the position to utter the word, but I hear my voice echo, my teenaged one, the words I actually mustered that day, feebly. "What's the tuna fish for?" they say, my boy's voice breaking the silence of the room.

But even louder than that?

Today in Japan.

I hear what I *wished* I'd said.

I hear, "Seriously?

"What the hell is that! You can't possibly be doing what I think you're doing!" but "Oh, that," my stepmother's voice, weak and off balance anyway, her eyes darting back over from the tunafish cans. "That's for *my lunch* for tomorrow," she says. "We're going to have *salmon* salad for dinner."

Her words.

They echo.

Indeed, I turn them back over, the words that she used, but her eyes!

The truths not the lies are speaking so much louder than her. Martha's fried green tomatoes with salt, and with tongs, and straight off the vine. Martha, my stepmother so patient, so warm and complete, she shows me how to love the tomatoes I hate, shows me how a stepparent should be.

And Bob in Chapel Hill?

Stern when necessary, but otherwise friendly.

And here, now, this woman?

This supposed-to-be second adult role model in our midst!

With her fists on her hips and her boobs in my face who can't stand to be told, certainly not by a 15-year-old who looks like he's 13, what she is, and is not, allowed to do in her own home, 'cause that would ring too much like there might be something wrong.

With one of her decisions, and somehow some unspeakable harm might be done.

To her ego.

And my father's voice then, still tumbling down.

I'm 16.

Some other exchange, another in the endless string that makes me feel stung has pushed me to the point that I finally unbite my tongue and tell my father what happened. Besides, he's on his own today. Caught him outside at that rickety, deep-grooved picnic table by the driveway, and if I catch him alone he still tends to be the enlightened father from my childhood I remember him to be.

"Gatlin wouldn't lie to you," he says, as if she's some kind of saint and he's up at his pulpit, and like I'll somehow be compelled to believe what my eyes didn't see when he simply decrees, "If she told you it was salmon, it was salmon."

"But Dad," I protest, precociously aware, but tragically somehow, in my disadvantaged boy's voice, "That's simply not the case."

"I came back in after finishing the lawn, and went straight back in to the fridge. I spent that whole hour hoping beyond hope that what I'd seen was wrong, that maybe she *was* making tunafish salad for her lunch. So I came back in, and right in front of her! – she stood right there and watched me as I looked all through the fridge.

"But would you believe?

"There wasn't any in there!

"Dad, what am I supposed to believe? She made her lunch and hid it somewhere?

"And so I sit there.

"Dad!

"Silently, all dinner long and eat everything else, push the meat round my plate, and she proceeds to tease me! She makes fun of me and tells me I'm 'not brave enough' to eat the salmon on my plate?

"Is that supposed to somehow be friendly?

"Is that supposed to mend bridges? Is that what she thinks is going to make me respect her? It's as if she wants me to challenge her so she can call me 'angry' again, and further degrade me."

Oh, but the soda can then!

So suddenly!

My dad's face, apparently

I've gone just one word too far.

My dad's eyes are welling up, he's turned red. He's getting ready to burst, my voice is taken away again, and next time I'll think twice, hold my tongue even longer before speaking up, and revealing the truth that hurts him so much, because I don't want to hurt him, after all, he's my dad.

Smart guy that raised me, though!

He can see what I see, and he knows what I was about to say.

He knows what was coming and it was his welling up and getting ready to explode that stopped me from spelling it out.

I mean, Dad, how could *YOU*, after all?

You were right there!

You sat right there silently while she made fun of me at the table, and called me weak and small in the face of her lie! You sat right there while she made fun of me for my stomach being upset!

What the fuck is that?

What's happened to "provide for and protect"?

What on earth's going on?

What's happened to the world that's it's become one.

In which.

My dad thinks if he stays stern-faced like this, and pretends not to see, that my brother and I at 15 and 16 will stop seeing too? Almost as if he would be so much happier if I just shut my eyes, and allowed myself to be.

Degraded for his sake.

To be dumbed down and belittled as my new and improved stepmother Gracie clearly wants me to be?

"You murdered your child," she says two years later, I'm 18, and who the fuck is she? And how can it not be that it wears me down, how can it not make me feel like I'm insane, when the two adult people in my home are so completely united in their desire to see the world the way she's decided it should be?

Instead of the way that it really is, right there in front of me?

"Seriously?" though.

In Japan.

I catch myself positioning my lips for mouthing the word.

"… it can't be!"

And she's right there in front of me.

Still lingering today.

Her voice in my head.

The door to the sempai's room that sticks in its frame, he kicks it from the inside, and it's the effeminate Ishiguro who emerges this time.

With a crash!

And just then a splash, that drop of grease from Mocaram's hairline.

It hits the table and leaps back up like the crown I remember from the stop-action film we watched in Mr. Clayton's high school chemistry class. I open my eyes wide, to stretch out my face, to wake up from my dream. I chase away an impulse to cry, that certainly I suppose wouldn't serve me just now.

Since brutal reality this time!

I'm here in Japan where I still have a chance.

Where no foreigner's ever made it before. One hundred twenty of them tried, but they got beaten by their sempais, and they failed.

But where I, Nathan Ligo, just might be the one!

Because unlike the rest, I was made.

In my father's fire-hot forge.

Where there was never any choice but to learn how not to give up, 'cause giving up would be to abandon my dad, and I love him.

For God's sake, he's my dad!

Isn't he?

At the core?

The one I remember him to be?

xxi.

Thunk!

Hollow door hits the wall and I'm all the way back.

Mas Oyama's dorm, the Young Lions' Home. Ishiguro Sempai strolls in, one hand in his pants.

He takes one step wider than the rest to rearrange his underwear. Heavy heels on the stairs, and Iwaya thumps down, slides open that second door in the front-left corner of the room, and thirteen of us shout "OSU!"

That Japanese bow, we bend at the waist.

Forward to thirty degrees, fists crossed to our opposite ears and then down to fudo dachi, our forward facing fists to a stop in front of our hips like atoms breaking. And Iwaya Sempai this time?

Stepping in.

Tucking in his shirt, and taking his place at the head of our parallel lines, he looks up.

And all of us do.

And there before us?

That finely printed Japanese calligraphy on silk, in two frames behind glass.

"The Training Hall Oath? …

"It can't be. The Training Hall Oath has seven lines, and this one's like twenty!"

I'm dizzy from the run, thirsty, and struggling to see.

He wastes no time.

All of us in line, and Iwaya once more back at the front of our parallel lines. No longer in black, but still a gangster's Cadillac between us and the complex script ... of the *Dormitory Oath*, it must be?

"Shomen ni REI!" he shouts.

"Bow to the front!" he must have said, and such a command from the bottom of his gut that even I, who don't understand, have no choice but to bow. A thunderous "OSU!" along with the rest, all of us, our fists from our ears, and down to our hips. Opaque sliding glass windows shake in their frames, split the stillness of Tokyo's dawn. Block's real-estate value must truly be down, as such a sound spills from the heart of it all, I can't even imagine an equivalent!

Never heard anything like it!

And with that, at a shout, Iwaya reads the first line.

"Our home is the Young Lion's Dormitory!" I think he begins, but after that I'm lost and can't read. Can't follow the Japanese. It's more shouted than read. His first sentence is so unbelievably long, and I can see where he reads, but four whole lines! – of fine print in vertical Japanese, before ...

"Oh, I know the routine!"

Thirteen of us behind, in that same shouted guttural tone, echo back the same line, reading it back at the top of our lungs. I say "we," but my God, it's not that I speak, it's more that I'm caught up in the terror of the thing!

I thought *Iwaya's* voice had shaken the glass, but *thirteen* times that!

Same shouted Japanese.

It moves the city block, and oh my God! – these walls are virtually paper and wood, and it's only just past, Tokyo's raven-calling eight o'clock of the dawn!

Undaunted, they go on.

My roommates around me, completing the line, and I realize again, it's the first line of TWENTY!

Every single syllable read, and not a single one missed. They have to *gasp* for air where the commas occur to build up enough pressure behind their diaphragms! – and then they howl the next phrase, or succession of phrases, without their volume diminishing, the tone of their voices never once cracking.

Written Japanese, I see.

At least.

From my Japanese class I can read, is primarily composed of characters from two casks. Borrowed Chinese pictograms, *kanji* they're called, ten thousand strong, it takes just to read a Tokyo newspaper in basic Japanese. But happily for the American who reads, intermingled with these is a second set:

Hiragana.

A syllabary composed of just forty-six characters, each one of a very limited set that makes up every single sound in Japanese. The world's easiest language to pronounce, and the hardest one to read.

And there they are, I can see.

Intermingled with the rest.

Hiragana in script, and I'm relieved that in among the kanji I don't know at all, there's the syllabary I can read. Learned them last year at *Sumisu* Sensei's UNC. Intermingled as they are to complement, for punctuation, context, and conjugation, and at least I can follow where my roommates are in the thing? by skipping to the next string of hiragana, and sounding them out, and waiting for the rest, in turn, to catch up.

Of course I don't know the meaning.

Giant ceramic rice bowls steaming, thick purple veins in Kuruda's neck popping, and we haven't yet made it to the Oath's second line!

It takes me back.

To the Training Hall Oath, in English this time.

To Master Choi's UNC, I'm 14, and on campus early.

To run.

Master Choi's six-mile black belt run, the course that they run, in North Carolina's scorching hot sun, before even starting the three hours of the CMAC's black belt test for their first and second degrees. Of course, I'm only 14, and Master Choi's only child student. Brian Moran is a senior at Chapel Hill High.

But I.

Am just finishing eighth grade. I'm one school year past my paint-stripper summer, pulling endless staples up from my knees, my first summer with Gracie in Templeton.

But Master Choi's eyes then?

"I wish that I had a son like you," his broken English, and I knew what he meant, one my age, not actually a son just like me.

But nevertheless, he challenges me!

To join the next test, the black belt test along with the rest. There's no pressure, of course, 'cause I'll just advance from blue belt to yellow, just four steps out of the ten and less than half way through to black … but something I see.

In the eyes of that man?

I want him, you see, to want a son just like me. Not one just my age, like he probably means.

My own dad's at home in Templeton and, well, it's so much easier to think that that's just a different world altogether. Martha is gone, and Dad's living with Gatlin. I haven't yet felt home there, instead something bizarre, something I can't lay a finger on right now, why it all seems so off? – and I'm running alone before regular class, accepting the challenge, and believing.

"Someday, if I keep it up, I'll eventually be free, and maybe even eventually stronger than the rest?"

Funny.

At fourteen, I find running hurts less in North Carolina's hot sun than my stomach when sick. And I've spent so many weeks now sick in a row.

This year.

Just recently, in fact, I've finally gotten back to going to school, right here at the end of the year. Makeup coursework assignments at home, and I study alone from the edge of my bed. That chart that I follow. One box for each class, my eighth grade teachers' varied-ink chicken scratch, and my black and white TV, silent for now at the foot of the bed.

But this isn't home school.

It's doing eighth grade alone! Empty pink Pepto-Bismol bottles scatter the floor.

But the Training Hall Oath?

The answer for me.

So similar, at least in routine, to this Dormitory Oath today in Japan I can't read.

David Toleman mostly, the biochem grad, recites it out loud at the end of each class with Master Choi watching.

In *seiza*.

That kneeling position with our fists on our hips. "The Training Hall Oath!" he shouts from his place at the front of the class. And we shout it right back, repeating his words. "The Training Hall Oath!" we echo the title right back from our parallel lines. We're all looking up, and there on the wall is that laminated photo! Mas Oyama's picture, Master Choi's uncle, the bare-handed bull killer, held up each day to the fencing room's borrowed blue-painted wall with duct tape.

"One!" David shouts, to start the first line, and "One!" we all shout, preparing to recite.

"We will train our hearts and bodies ..." *bird*-chested, glasses, handlebar mustache, he shouts that prescribed, lung-sized portion of the first line. He's emphasizing the end, and deep from his gut in the tone of a Hollywood Marine Corps drill sergeant, mixed up at least with the tone of the Shaolin Monastery master wannabe? It's far more than just shouts, at least it's become so for me. Some of the others can't see, it's hard to believe, but it's magical! – it seems.

The answer for me.

The solution.

It's still some years before just this sophomore year's run-away-from-home, but it's at least a destination!

And we read it right back, echoing his words.

"We will train our hearts and bodies!" fifteen of us shout at UNC. Karate uniforms in sweat at the end of our training, mimicking his tone, the basement multipurpose room, the fencing team gone. And thus right back, handing him the reins, it's his turn to read, and he concludes the first line "… for a firm, and unshaking spirit!" the first line out of seven:

"We will train our hearts and bodies for a firm and unshaking spirit!"

And now it's our turn.

"… for a firm and unshaking spirit!" we shout, and that first line is complete, the next one to come. David begins by announcing the number "Two!"

And then we do, too, and then "we will pursue, the true meaning of the Martial Way!" he shouts.

And then "… so that in time … !"

And finally he concludes "our senses may be alert!"

"We will pursue the true meaning of the Martial Way, so that in time, our senses may be alert!" is the whole line.

And more than just that, the rest of the seven lines broken up into twos, and sometimes into threes. He's reading the lines in segments, and we're echoing them back, too, in a military-like tone.

Two lines from seven are now done, and I'm running alone, weekday afternoons after school. Pounding it home. Making it mine. My creed and my way, the *samurai* way! – sacrificing my one arm, even, if necessary, for just one more chance at life.

Iwaya Sempai today in Japan begins his second line of what must be the *Dormitory* Oath? I'm here in Japan. I scan ahead for the hiragana I can read, and these Japanese badgers proceed, these Japanese bone-breakers are doing something now at least that's familiar to me.

"It's about time!" it occurs to me.

I had to cross an ocean to find them, and not be alone, but now here I am, and it's hard not to be afraid.

For this is the real thing!

Like running down the hill from UNC to start that six-mile run on my own.

In North Carolina's hot sun.

"I!" I speak out loud.

Sometimes under my breath, and three strides. I chant the words of the *Training Hall Oath* for the entire run. One word, or one syllable, aloud for every four strides that I run, and for six miles! – without stopping, and then starting it all over again, and over and over again, I'm 14. And in the blinding hot sun, lumbering down the road from UNC.

"Will!" is the next word of "I will train my heart and body," and three lumbering strides as I continue to run.

"Train!" comes next, I force myself to concentrate on the words. Five miles to go!

"My!" comes next, the *Training Hall Oath*.

"Heart!" after that, and left, right, left, still on Laurel Hill Road.

"And!" and stride, stride, stride, from UNC down.

"Body!" and two, three, four.

"For!" I then shout, and two, three, four.

The next word is "A!" and stride, stride, stride.

I confirm to myself, "a firm and unshaking spirit," under my breath, and stride, stride, stride.

"I will train my heart and body for a firm and unshaking spirit!"

The Frenchman, Japan, he's kicking my heels, and stride, stride, stride. Two parallel lines, I'm still pushing on, we're finally trapped and penned in.

Iwaya reads the next line, and stride, stride, stride, five years later, Japan.

Mas Oyama's Japan, I can feel my legs ache ...

Dear God, this is Japan!

I'm here in Japan! Thirteen blue ceramic rice bowls steaming and Iwaya has begun.

His third line.

I scan ahead for any kanji I can read.

How can anyone possibly learn a complete set enough to read this entire Oath in Japanese?

"One! We will train our hearts and bodies for a firm and unshaking spirit!" It's the *Training Hall* Oath that I hear in my head.

My roommates read back. "Two! We will pursue the true meaning of the Martial Way, so that in time our senses may be alert!"

I know that it's not that, but in the absence of that said, no English I can read, I hear "Three!"

"With true vigor," it's *David Toleman's* voice instead, "we will seek to cultivate a spirit of self denial!"

And Iwaya again.

"Four!"

"We will observe the rules of courtesy, respect our sempais, and refrain from violence!

My roommates then read it right back.

David Toleman this time in my head. "Five! We will follow the way of Zen, and never forget the true virtue of humility," I'm 14.

At the top of our lungs, "Live it, Nathan!"

The slick gym floor of the fencing room at UNC. Our voices in English.

Shouting.

"Six! We will look upwards to wisdom and strength, not seeking other desires!"

"Never forget, Nathan!"

And my roommates again. They've begun their echo of the next line.

"Seven! All our lives," we begin at UNC.

And then, "through the discipline of Karate!"

And finally.

"We will seek to fulfill, the true meaning of the Way! All our lives, through the discipline of Karate, we will seek to fulfill the true meaning of the Way."

Yes, Nathan! - that's finally it.

Live it!

The Way.

Live it one day.

Go to Japan!

Master Choi's Japan.

Mas Oyama, his uncle.

His uchi deshi.

The answer.

Three years have passed, since that purple paint stripper became one with my skin, and week after week, I spend.

Two point five hours.

Outside in the sun, sweating, and pushing that grumbling machine up and down, hearing her words, listening to my dad, and asking myself.

What the hell am I doing here?

Still!

Cutting this *new and improved* Ligo house lawn!

My brother's doing his senior year in Hong Kong, and the two children inside.

I'm the last one at home, and I have *real work* to do upstairs in my room, work that Master Choi is expecting me to do.

The three point five.

The grade point average he requires to send me to Japan … but instead I'm cutting the lawn?

To keep up appearances?

And to hide for him, my father.

To conceal from this tiny enlightened college town the stink that resides here in my father's new home?

xxii.

Stomach full.

Dishes stacked.

I follow Mocaram's lead and put mine in the sink.

Chopsticks in a fist, I drop mine in my glass. Both of them now stacked, in the white plastic bowl where those awful sticky beans were. White bowl in the red one where the clear pasty soup was, and all of that now stacked in my largest, the ceramic blue-rimmed rice bowl, and that whole, tall double handful down in the stainless steel sink, with two hands and a chink, and my glass that falls over, and chopsticks that spill.

"I wash these, Ligo. You go upstairs."

The Frenchman's voice, always sideways at me, and picking up my chopsticks.

"I will go up after one minute. Make sure that you say 'Osu!' two times when you pass by the sempai."

Four bodies in an alcove kitchen too tight for just two. "Osu!" my voice, still learning its use. An older Japanese woman squeezing in, she's got vegetables in bags, and she's surprised to see me, too. Asking the others who I am, and I pass, and I think that I see. Is that Mocaram *not* washing his and my dishes but explaining to the Japanese why *they* should wash them for me?

An uneasy feeling.

Queasy.

Something like fear. For the absence of eyes watching

me as I pass through the room. Only three roommates remain, frantic and panicked, they don't even look up, and that scares me. We had less than two minutes to eat, and everyone rushed out, "Osu! Osu!" each, one by one, on their way out to the Kaikan. But after four minutes or five, I'm still not finished. I'm still choking down all this lukewarm rice gruel. They're hurrying to clean Honbu, all of its nooks and its crannies, but "It's your first day, Ligo," the Frenchman explains, "and I told them you will rest.

"After breakfast, you go up to the *obiya*, and wait."

I can feel, though, that it's him. It's *him* that doesn't want to clean Honbu, but "Osu!" my voice again, gagging on rice and raw egg. Bland miso-based gruel that's no longer hot. How is it possible that these Japanese are already finished like that, eating and stacking their dishes in just over a minute?

Ishiguro just there in front of me, still eating.

Leisurely.

Watching the TV they moved up from the chair at the head of the table, up on to the table and under the Oath. But he's ignoring me. *I'm* not even allowed to look sideways during breakfast. "The TV," Mocaram's whisper through his rice and his teeth, "is only for the sempai. Don't ever look to your left or to your right, Ligo. Only at your food, and hurry up, Ligo, eat!"

"Osu," my voice sounds distant, somehow separate from me. But I'm encouraged in spite of it all, gagging down this paste like papier-maché mealy white, stained yellow with yolk, and a fleeting moment of hope.

"I can handle this!"

My stomach's not the problem, after all ... it's gagging down all this gruel ... and that I can do! "Osu! Osu!" I shout, backing towards the door to the upstairs on my way out of the room. Oughtta know it by now. Watched already as half a dozen of my roommates bowed, once to the sempais, and once to the room, all on their way out of the dining room.

Ishiguro Sempai's looking up at me now, annoyed.

Sempai sidekick of Iwaya Sempai, a sinister, slight smile. One that's put on, I see, in response to my "Osu!" and over his rice held up to his chest. Something else on top of *his* rice, in the steam rising up, something that looks tasty and that we didn't have on our rice. A variety morning TV show, lots of color and an announcer overexcited to be describing the weather. The antics so loud in the bustle of the dormitory. Hair cut short, Ishiguro Sempai, but a crew cut that's longer than anyone else's in the room.

Smile betrays curiosity though.

At the Dormitory's first and only white guy.

Me, the American's arrived, and I slide open the door behind me. Light as paper, and I see a small plastic opaque window's set in. Door rattles in its tracks and I step backwards and down, to the taut scratchy felt carpet covering the con-crete four inches down. Opposite me – just as the door clicks flush to its jamb – there's the sliding opaque window passing through from the dorm, and yesterday, over there, all the way through, and past the Kaikan stairwell, there's the lost-looking Nathan come in for the very first time. I wonder which one's Iwaya Sempai's room? He's upstairs already. I heard someone thumping at the sempais' end of the dorm.

Means he's not in our room though, the *obiya*, and a sigh of relief. Turning in place, and closing the door, I shut myself off from the sempai, Ishiguro.

I pass a toilet room to the right, I take a deep breath.

Peace.

I'm alone for the moment, and I drift past that second sliding door, this one standing wide open to the toilet within. Inside as I pass, I glance in. It's closet sized. Tiles on the floor, and a pair of brown slippers with the toe ends marked in black magic marker katakana that read, "yes, it's *toe-ee-ray*, I think." That's "toilet" in Japanese, they're waiting just inside for someone to step into, and "Is that really a toilet?" I think.

It's not exactly, though.

Can't be.

It's little more than a porcelain trough!

A step up to a ledge, looks more like a urinal, but one set in the floor, and mounted horizontal. Surely that's not where we're supposed to crap? There's nothing to sit down on and no water for it to splash down into! A porcelain trough like an old-fashioned bedpan just set in the floor. What are we supposed to do, I wonder, straddle and squat?

The outhouse in the woods at the log house.

I'm five years old, there's already plumbing inside, but just barely since last week there wasn't and I know what it means to poop over a concrete hole and let drop, four feet down to the dark mud, paper, and pooled steaming piss at the bottom like a portapotty in the woods, claiming that land, my father carving out his line in the sand. Baby-faced, his long red beard, those thick, black plastic glasses, and only five years a professor at Templeton already. His office at the end of the hall, past Herb the painter's office door standing open and those metal blinds. Venetian beige from ceiling to floor, and me. Peering out to see if I can still see Elm Row from there where mom's teaching piano right now and can't be disturbed. It's Martha's log house after my father is gone. She's rebuilt the outhouse, carved out a star in the door and a moon, and Dillon with me, I'm seventeen. I haven't been home in five years, and we laugh and peer down into the dark at a cobweb and the hole's now only two feet deep. Dry for the most part now, unused, and a sliver of green. A tight beam of sunlight that fights its way down, though a gap in the boards and down through the trees, down into the hole to shine on the dirt, and a small incandescent garden of moss growing down there, rich and glowing in that human-fertilized peat. I hear myself laugh though, and Dillon. We laugh in spite of a reality, it occurs to me, that's not all that funny. Here I am, at the log house again, and now in Japan. In both cases for years I've been fighting to find home.

For years on end.

The dining room door, click to the jamb, and turning in place past the toilet room, I wonder how could it have evaded me that they don't even have real toilets in Japan?

Not ones I can sit down on.

Stairs again.

Opposite, at the end of the hall, and almost back to the alley that leads up to the dormitory, but the full length of the dining room at the other end of the dorm.

But these?

Again.

They're not stairs, exactly.

It's more like a ladder than stairs. Felt sky-blue carpet stretched over stairs so steep I have to climb. Gingerly, on all fours, the flight as tall as me, times two when I'm bent over to crawl, and up to the second floor. The area of a coat closet contains an entire flight of stairs, going up. A full story's height, and we have to climb, fourteen-inch stairs barely six inches wide. Stairs turn tight, and I scamper. Hollow thumps turning left to ninety degrees, and there's the second floor sink rising upwards in front of me.

Stainless steel basin in the second floor hall. Deep enough for a bucket, and a row of toothbrushes behind it, lined up in three plastic cups on the windowsill. If you knocked one off, it occurs to me, it would fall down into the alley below, and they'd spill like chopsticks into that pass-through alley for air in-between the dormitory and the Kaikan.

Two more toilet rooms.

These on the second floor for us to use?

Closet-sized behind me on my left, just there to the right when facing down the stairs. Yesterday I peer down the dimly lit stairs on my way, and pee in one for the very first time. Piss spatters off the one millimeter only of clear water left on the glossy horizontal surface after the last flush. Water's too shallow and yellow splashes out. I redirect, aim for the well at the far end. A four-inch-deep well where everything goes down, and it sounds, this time, more like peeing's supposed to sound, since pee's splashing down into deep water.

Five doors total.

Here at the top of the stairs, Iwaya Sempai must be in that one at the end past the bathrooms, and the *obiya* just here. the "Big Room" behind me, I've learned that's it's called. Nine of us, was it ten? Slept in there last night.

Where was my place, now that the futons are gone?

Oh, yes, over there.

I see it as I open the door, my futon over there in the far corner last night, when I stumbled in, half asleep, from the toilet in the middle of the night, past the wood-paneled column in the middle of the room, and the virtual sea of futons and blankets and snoring Japanese, but now they're all stacked in the back opposite corner. A dozen futons and folded in thirds. They're stacked six feet tall like *The Princess and the Pea*. A storybook played on a kid's record player, and me.

Six years old.

And in Mom's tiny house in Cornelius that soon after the divorce. The same flowered cushions we had in the pillow room on Lorimar Street. I was there till I was four, in Templeton, and we all moved out to the log house, and it occurs to me.

My childhood home, and Mom was only there for less than a year, and if I was still a little kid I'd climb up on top of the stacked futons in the corner, like I used to do, up onto those flowered foam cushions of my childhood.

I laugh at the irony.

Since now at nineteen, I'm so tired I wish I could climb in between, embody the pea, and maybe then, when I dreamed, it would be of my graduation and of the titan I'll be.

xxiii.

The soles of my feet, the slick of the tatami.

I'm just inside the doorway now, to the dormitory's second floor "Big Room," the *obiya*, and "Osu! Osu!" from a distance I hear.

A muffled, a distant, somebody's Japanese voice. Distant and echoing through Honbu's cracked wall, across those three feet of space, the wall with the vine.

One of my roommates stepping in to the front door of the Kaikan, it must be.

Nothing in here on the floor, not end to end, not wall to wall, just that one wardrobe, and an electric, oscillating fan that's unplugged. Our stack of futons in the corner, in the back corner of the room, and otherwise just straw.

Tightly woven.

"Cool floor," I think, *tatami*.

Traditional Japanese like the ones in the movies, and "Oh, that must be why the Japanese don't wear shoes inside," it occurs to me. "Tatami's rigid like wood, but too delicate for shoes."

Sliding, waist-high windows down both sides of the room, opening to the alleys on both sides, and stretching to the closets at the end, the entire windowless far end of the room. Bookshelves between windows on side walls in two places, and I've never seen so many issues of Mas Oyama's *Power Karate* magazine before!

That's *Pow-wa Ka-la-tay*, in Japanese, and I see one, one

time. At UNC, 'cause Master Choi brought it in, and another time, two. But I can't read Japanese, that fine print kanji in type, and the fighters inside are so much bigger than me! "Bigger and stronger than I'll ever be," I'm fifteen. I see them inside, and I know just how huge Kyokushin karate must be.

Big enough that it has its own magazine.

"Christ!" I laugh inwardly. "Where's the sofa?"

I wanna collapse! Should I crash on the floor? I wanna put my feet up! Training is through, my stomach is full, I wanna curl up and relax! But am I allowed? During breakfast I wasn't even permitted to *speak!* I wasn't allowed to look to my left or my right, or look at the TV. Mocaram's following me up, and there's nothing on the floor. Not end to end, not wall to wall. Not even a sock, or a book, or a gum wrapper. Should I make myself an exception, and flop down like a bum, while my roommates rushed off in a frenzy to clean the Kaikan?

No.

Not me, I think. Not yet. I'll wait and I'll see.

"Osu! Osu!" I hear.

That's Mocaram's voice downstairs passing Ishiguro Sempai, leaving the dining room like me a minute before, and following me up, bowing by the TV on his way out of the room. "I'll be up after one minute, Ligo," he says, and I wish that he'd stay away for a few more and then I could rest. Will I meet Mas Oyama today? And will he let me stay once he learns that I came all the way to Japan without Master Choi's blessing? And will there be training again later, and will I have to fight? And will Iwaya Sempai beat me?

Japan's waking hours.

All filled up, it seems, with the most terrifying of soul-stirring sound.

The panicked frenzy of the run, the hyperventilation itself! No less loud than the Kaikan's great drum.

The groaning furnace when the showers were on, and

the roaring, throat-popping recitations during the Dormitory Ceremony, the Rules and the Song. The ruffling! – of those oily, night-black feathers from above, the winged beast that came so close to stopping my heart in Tokyo's dawn.

Even that bird!

Larger and louder, than such a thing in my life has ever before seemed.

My first two hours in the dormitory.

Yesterday.

Upstairs in the dormitory's big room, the *obiya*, the awesome, unrelenting cadence of Honbu's afternoon training through the wall. And I'm left there to process.

All that I'm at the same time learning, the life I'll be expected to lead.

During three years of training.

Honbu's four o'clock training.

The drum, and that endless barrage of *kiais*. Thirty or forty adult males, as they issue, in unison, concentrated "spirit shouts," as Master Choi called them, with each and every rep of an endless stream of techniques.

The dormitory's second floor.

Just thirty-six inches from Honbu's back wall. Main dojo just there, straight across on the other building's second floor, and even if there weren't windows on both buildings' back walls to see through at those certain awkward angles, that perpetual, droning sound would fight its way through.

The Earth.

Shakes!

I can hear the sweat spray as "Ichi!" the instructor's voice counts and, "Yahhh!", thirty adult males shout in response, a roar that's brought up from their diaphragms, from their feet through the floor. Their voice. I know it to be the substance that connects the physical of the strike to the spiritual. The desire from within that renders them meaningful.

"Ni!"
Yahhh!
"San!"
Yahhh!
"Shi!"
Yahhh!
And onwards and on. The instructor counts ten and then over again – one shout per second! – thirty counts, and thirty kiai's, answering per minute. Uninterrupted for hundreds and hundreds of techniques, for the first, whole forty minutes of the two-hour training.

And we kiai, too.

In Chapel Hill, downstairs in Fetzer Gym's multipurpose room, filled end to end with karate students in white. Master Choi's gone to great pains "to develop your shouting ability," he says, in conjunction with and to complement our "self-defense ability," he would say, and our fight.

"Let your enemy know your ferocity!" he says. Those piercing eyes of his, explain more than just words, and now I know.

All of that intensity was nothing before!

Not compared to this.

"Dear God, here we go!"

Japan.

The promised land.

I've never heard shouts issued with such sustained and unrelenting frequency as these here in the dark. The *obiya*. Fluorescent lights hanging down from fine chains. First two hours in the dormitory, my first two in the Japan that's to be my new home. I speak in hurried, in hushed tones with the eighteen-year-old, the French Algerian from Nice. Mocaram Ahamed, into whose care Kuruda and Oshikiri delivered me. Delivered *by default*, it seems, before taking their leave and scampering back down to the first floor, and back around the block from the dormitory. So busy like bees, killer bees in a swarm. Mocaram, the dormitory's only other Westerner.

If he really could be called Western, that is!

And for two whole hours then!

His voice and the shouts. The thuds of that most intense karate workout I've ever been that close to. I can feel it in my bones! It's goes onward and on. Droning on and on, and I'm tuning it out, desensitizing to it, the dark. Surreal. And fading away into the background as Mocaram talks, my jet lag, the haze, the dark unreal and the quiet of the dorm in the middle of the night when I come in from peeing and try to figure out, in the street light filtering down the alley and in, just how I'm supposed to cross back over that sea of deep breathing Japanese, and get to my futon without stepping on one.

Mocaram's over there explaining to me just how to use "Osu!" and I'm wondering in the night if I'm really here after all.

I suppose it's all over now.

My futon in the night, and that bizarre beanbag pillow damp with my sweat.

Over for the time being, anyway.

Peace, that is.

Quiet.

The comfort and warmth that's been gone for some years.

The comfort of home.

My longing for rest.

A Christmas morning gathering with the Prescott family on Ridgecrest.

Chapel Hill, and I'm 10, 11, and 12. All the way up to 16 before it ended then. Suddenly. The year I followed Aaron to Templeton for tenth grade, and Mom drove down six months later to tell us she'd left Bob and my last family home.

Twelve of us each year on the stairs.

Twelve!

Year after year and lined up by age, from the bottom to

the top. Waiting like that, for Bob and my Mom to tell us to rush down, and see "what Santa Claus brought."

Year after year, and barely that many hard wooden stairs up to the second floor where my room's at the top across from the twins,' Aaron and I live here, with Betsy and Fran, the twins, and then finally me alone, now living with them. Three years older than me. Preppy, beautiful and blonde. "Insecure perhaps?" I wonder finally, but socially, they're succeeding, and "that's huge!" – here in Chapel Hill where I fail so miserably to fit in. And I don't like them at first 'cause they too condescend, like all Chapel Hill kids have been trained to do. But finally I'm so hungry for their approval, and finally I win it!

I *long* for it once they're gone, and now I just miss them.

Betsy and Fran, the youngest of six, my stepfather Bob's six beautiful blondes. We live there together, in that house on Ridgecrest. And me. Alone with them after Aaron is gone. But it's Christmastime now, and all of Bob's other kids've come home. Anna. The pinup-beautiful one, two years older than the twins, and back home. Like some other times from her UNC sorority room. Five-foot-tall Jane the backpacker I've known since third grade on Cobb Terrace, and her husband, Todd, are in from Colorado. Helen with John from just across town, and my oldest stepsister Stuart's arrived with her husband Jay. My mother's younger brother Bill this year, and with a beard that looks funny on him. "Uncle Bill" all my life, and Brandy. Gandma's still-surviving schnauzer that barks, and whose whiskers get wet, chasing that ragged yellow tennis ball. That soggy ball in my hand. Wet. Warm with a dog's slobber, and Uncle Bill's holding him still at the top of the stairs, laughing and trying to establish, again this year, who's older, and where he's supposed to line up, above Stuart and Jay, or after them, and just above Helen and John.

"We alternate *years*," my boy's voice explains, "lined up oldest to youngest, and then the next year, from youngest to oldest," as I boast to a classmate in Mrs. Wier's fifth grade class at Glenwood Elementary School, telling her how many brothers and sisters I have. And the steps in the middle always get stuck, it occurs to me, Anna and Jane always half way down.

"But this year it's my turn!"

I'm eleven, the youngest, and the first in the line at the bottom of the stairs. Twelve steps up to my uncle Bill, and my oldest sibs who must already be thirty! – old enough, now, to know it doesn't matter who gets to go first.

But, still! – it doesn't matter.

Jay's shouting down and complaining that they're at the top. He's playing the game, all in the name of holiday cheer so thick, I can't find my way through to my other life left behind, the awkwardness at school, my stomach, and how I don't feel the same as everyone else. Thirteen of us this year! Each of us buys presents for all thirteen others, and day by each December day, the living room fills up, and we have to lift the lower branches of the Christmas tree to squeeze all the presents in under and between, and then it becomes not even possible anymore, and they start to wrap around the room and cover the floor.

Cassie and Seth, the babies on their way in Templeton with Dad and Gracie, and Aaron and me there for our *second* Christmas.

But in Chapel Hill!

There's Fran and Betsy, and Anna and Jane, and Stuart and Helen. Bo and Susan over from California one time, and the husbands are there, John, Jay and Todd. A fire hazard, our Christmas tree lights! The ping-pong table downstairs, a wrapping paper *storm!* Twisted ribbon and bows, and so many stockings are hung across the fireplace that we have to lay the rest on the sofas in the den, and "Why even have breakfast?" I wonder. I'm still so full! For days in a row on Christmas cookies Mom's been making all week. Peanut Blossoms with Hershey's kisses that Aaron and I, as toddlers, called "Possum Blooms" and it stuck. Green Mint Meringues with chocolate chips that have to rise overnight with the oven door open.

And now the dog Brandy's escaped!

And he's scampering down the stairs since I'm holding his ball. My uncle Bill, the ultimate uncle! Plays with us, computer games, and takes us last year to the frozen, closed Christmas Day, small-plane airport on Airport Road, to launch the model rocket that Aaron got, and he helped him put together. And Stuart's husband Jay who turned me on to comic books, and Sergeant Rock. Had so many they filled up multiple rooms in that house by the pond, and red-haired John. Listens to STYX and teaches me to fish at Sunset beach for hours on end, days on end during the great Sunset Beach "August Gatherings." All of us there. Year after year, actually two times per year, for those massive, multi-clan beach gatherings with the Prescotts, and all of Bob Prescott's friends, and their extended families, and Fran and Betsy that year.

My sisters.

Driving.

Me, in the back seat of Feedy, their little yellow first-car car, a Toyota Corolla with FDY in the license plate, and hence Feedy. Stopped in traffic between the pier and the Sunset Beach one-lane swinging bridge that crosses the sound. A virtual sea of reeds on both sides, and oyster shells stuck, exposed, and reaching upwards out through all that black mud. A gray heron, and an osprey nest. The blood-red sun going down. We're waiting for the boat to pass so we can cross, on our way to the store across on the mainland. Steve Winwood's on the radio, his "Back in the High Life Again," and the twins. Singing at the top of their lungs, and dancing in the front seat, and giddy and smoking cigarettes, and taking me, they with their fake IDs, to buy me my tonight's six pack of Budweiser in cans, and their Natural Light. They laugh with me, approvingly then, since they understand I'm gearing up to spend my night out until one a.m.. My curfew. Drinking and making out in the dunes with that little girl named Kendra, who's my age, and I met this year. Somehow distantly connected to one of the others of the August gathering's families. A virgin like me, both of us fifteen, and for the first time I'm not so interested in fishing.

Me, alone with the twins.

Not a one of the three of us have a care in the world. At Sunset Beach. We *are* back in the high life again, and we have no clue that it's coming to an end.

For my part, I'm floating on air because I'm hooking up with a girl for the third night in a row, and it's so overdue. I've finally fought my way through, finally gotten to where the twins, my stepsisters finally approve of me. They'll drop me off near the pier, and I'll walk south on the beach toward Kendra and Mad Inlet. Half way down to the McCoys' robin's-egg-blue house held up high and on stilts, the gray-haired McCoys, Katherine and Don, who have their Easter egg hunts every year in the dunes. Bill and Mini Hunt who live here year round, and the OPs. The "Other Prescotts," that is, the Judge, my step-uncle Dick and his second wife Jean, and the cousins, Ida and Elizabeth, who are Prescotts too, but came out somehow dark-haired in spite of the rest, and who'll be over for brunch once these presents are through, and the older two. From Uncle Dick's first marriage, Dickson and Lyn, under their beach umbrellas, in beach chairs and in sunglasses and surrounded by sand, and the waves, and the pelicans that keep crashing in.

The stairs, twelve of us lined up on the stairs, I perk up my ears, it's Mocaram on the stairs.

No time to rest!

It is all over, of course.

The high life.

I won't have a girlfriend here for three years, and I don't have older sisters anymore, and even though they did finally approve of me, I wasn't ever really strong enough to stand on my own, without hungering for that kind of approval, and isn't that why I'm here?

In Japan.

Becoming strong enough to stand on my own.

Even without family!

Even without parents, 'cause even Mom is long gone off into her haze, and Dad's fallen silent in the face his wife.

Today I'll meet Master Choi's uncle.

The living comic-book character.

The bare-handed bull killer, who bends quarters in half between his thumb and two fingers.

Mocaram's coming in and I turn, and "You have to bow and say 'Osu!' to me, Ligo!" he says, and "I was about to," I think, but I say, "Osu!" The wide-eared Korean Furoyama's with him, glasses and skinny and stepping in, and both of them in that same kind of rush.

xxiv.

Wide-eared Korean.

Everyone seems somehow to be annoyed as if I'm in the way all the time.

"Osu! Osu!" Furuyama bows to the room, and uh-oh, I forgot! – I'm supposed to bow to all the rooms when I enter!

"Osu! Osu!" I'm supposed to say.

When I enter the dining room and when I leave, and when I enter the *obiya* and when I leave, and when I enter the Kaikan.

Even when there's nobody here, I'm supposed to bow to the empty room.

I believe.

But now he's ignoring me.

Furoyama who's smaller than me.

A head that's disproportionately large, and a face like it was shaped by the blade of a shovel.

Flat.

His glasses with hard, black plastic rims, and a T-shirt with sleeves he rolls up to expose muscles that he doesn't really have, and I think back and remember me.

Chapel Hill at fourteen, my first half of ninth grade.

That photograph Jessica Levitz took of me.

The smallest kid in my class up against that brick wall at Phillips Junior High, and asked me if she could take one day. Her blue eyes and her curls, her braces and me. Jessica's one of the beautiful people, outside the cafeteria and the open-air stairs that lead down to the seventh grade hall, because I had rattails, and two earrings in one ear, and parachute pants, and a T-shirt that showed muscles I didn't really have, of course, and she smiles and compliments me, and tells me it's "cute," and I want to believe it 'cause it seems so sincere, since she was alone.

And maybe it could be *because* she was alone, it occurs to me, like my father outside at the deeply-grooved picnic table when his wife wasn't around, and he still tried to be himself.

But Jessica.

In the end I wasn't sure if it wasn't all to make fun.

She was part of the *in-crowd,* with Marcie Hatch, such a bitch, like a twin when they run in their pack! And such a thing seemed so much more like something the in-crowd would do.

To make fun.

Since otherwise I'm mostly not welcome.

And at the other end of that wall, that long blank, two-story brick wall of the gym, and just around the bend, the basketball courts where the buses come in, and the *in-crowd?*

All of them there in a team.

A *mob.*

As in "mob violence," that is, at lunchtime, it seemed, playing basketball *so strong!*

They feel so entitled to be.

"They really must think they're UNC!"

Only two years before that and Michael Jordan led UNC, a whole Chapel Hill generation in fact, to a championship, *someday I'll be somebody* mentality.

Furoyama.

His T-shirt tucked in, and his Carolina-blue tracksuit pants. The same ones all the first-year guys wear, and almost as soon as he's come in, he's grabbing something, a garment or a towel, I think, from a box up above, and he's turning around to rush out again.

And back to the Kaikan.

"What did you think of the *miso*, Ligo?" the Frenchman asks about the soup that we ate. He's content. For now. That I'm still standing up, tired, and standing at attention in the middle of the room.

Furoyama.

A Japanese name, it occurs to me. Like *Masutatsu Oyama*. These Koreans in Japan take Japanese names, and I wonder if Furoyama took one to be like him.

Master Choi.

His broken English.

Describing how his uncle was forced by the Japanese to take a Japanese name. "Even in school," his accent, his eyes scanning the room, "the Japanese forbade Koreans even to teach the Korean language."

But *lang-gwa-gee* he says, 'cause he can't quite pronounce *language*, and he uses *prohibited* carefully and every single one of its syllables said instead of *forbade*, and his use of *the Korean people* rings, just like I hear *the Cherokee Nation* ring sometimes, to refer to a proud people defeated, and beaten down, and believing, in spite of it all, in their right to reclaim something *more*, perhaps, than what was lost the first time around.

"They had to study *Japanese* in school," his voice goes on, and now he's got my eyes, and that's me alone, the only one in the training hall overlooking the *Master Choi-ism* confusion, and the others are distracted and pretending. Of course Master Choi was referring to the Japanese occupation *before* the war, and surely none of that's true any more, yet Furoyama, it seems, has taken a Japanese name, and I wonder if it's to help him find.

Something lost.

A shred of pride.

That national pride. He's grabbed something inside, an article I didn't see from one of the cardboard boxes he's now putting back up, high up onto the shelves high up above head level that wrap their way all the way around the shadowy wood-paneled ceiling of the room.

Kuruda's is there.

Beside it, I see. On his box, the kanji. *Kuro* for "black." *Da* for "rice field." Written in permanent ink. I guess that they keep all of their personal belongings in there? A cardboard box or two for each uchi deshi to use, and his name is written in permanent ink.

"Osu! Osu!" Furoyama shouts as he bows, ignoring me on his way out of the room again. Mocaram ignores my question as "Miso?" I ask, and he turns away to tell Furoyama something in Japanese.

Something about my teacher being Korean, I think.

"I told him your teacher was Korean," Mocaram turns back to me. Boasting. Or so it seems, that he speaks some Japanese.

Furoyama answers him with "Osu!" and then something else, but it's a bit of a half-hearted "Osu!" I couldn't hear the rest, and he closes the door behind him on his way out. "Osu!" I bow, and my toes grip the floor when they curl. They slip on the gloss. The tightly-woven, waxy straw floor of the room.

"You don't have to say 'Osu!' to Furoyama, Ligo," says Mocaram's voice, his French accent, flopping down with a thud, his legs all stretched out in front of him. "He's a first-year just like you. They all just came here six weeks ago, Suzuki, Yamakage, Kamokai, and the rest. I am second year like Hashimoto. You have to remember that I've been here for one year already before you."

"Osu!" my voice, I answer, and "It's not *miso*," he says. "You say *Miso-shiro*, Ligo. That is its name. That small red bowl of soup that we put – how do you say, *poured*? – it's that soup that we poured on the rice. And what did you think of the *natto*, Ligo?"

"Natto?" my voice.

"You have to say, 'Osu! Natto?' Ligo."

"Osu!" my voice again, hollow and weak, I fear that it sounds. Light-headed, detached. My body. Worn out from the training, the shower, the food coma, and the longing to sit down.

"The beans, Ligo. *Natto*. Nobody likes the beans until after some weeks. I ate them for you today, but Ishiguro Sempai watched me eat them. He knew that you didn't eat your own, and he was angry. Remember what I told you, the sempai will beat you if they can find the *chance*." That was the French word *chance*, but I understood, of course.

I'm opening and finding one particular page I remember from my high school textbook in French.

Like it was yesterday.

The first of a chapter from fifth-year French. Mrs. Holtzclaw's up there at the board, and an introductory passage about Paris. *Chance,* the French word for chance sounds so much like *Champs* from *Champs-Élysées*, and Dad drives that little red Citroën around the NASCAR-like circle at the *Arc de Triomphe*. Martha's in the front seat, and Aaron and me, our necks craning at the same back side window and looking upwards to see the floodlights. How they fall. On that monument in the circle, it's long after our bedtime, to the delight of small boys!

My father's coarse, red, curly hair.

I'm hugging the back of his seat, and both of my eight-year-old boy's hands clutch, lovingly, two handfuls of his hair. Martha as well, she's leaning across from the passenger seat to see the monument, her one hand on his chest and the other on his knee.

And then we're all laughing!

Since in the centrifugal force, I'm pulling Dad's hair, and he's shrieking as a joke and pretending it hurts. We're all so happy!

But this particular day.

So distinctly!

I can see my high school textbook, it's eleventh grade at North Meck. It's eight years later, and I'm remembering exactly, my dad. Just yesterday it dawned on me. He's taken to using *his wife's voice*, her words and her tone, to tell me, like her, that, in general, I should be ashamed.

Of everything I do.

For simply being.

That there's no excuse for me.

Thanks to Master Choi I'd gotten all A's. Of course I've been behind one year in math since I missed so much of 8th grade, there's that. But the exception? The best I could do this time was a C+ in French, and my fathers' voice then?

Echoes in my brain.

That tone that he's learned from his wife.

"I don't know how you can possibly congratulate yourself for getting all A's," my dad's voice falls stone cold in the gravel parking lot of the restaurant where he takes us for lunch, and where he took us for lunch every day that summer when we stripped all the woodwork in my father's new home, and pulled up the staples from the floor. " ... when you couldn't even manage to get any better than a C+ in French."

The world churns to a stop, and "Wait a minute, really?" I hear my boy's voice say what I didn't really say that day, but I feel still today.

It's eighth grade then in Chapel Hill, and I take one more swig from the Pepto-Bismol bottle I had to find and untangle from the wet towel and the sheets crammed down between the bed and the wall, and two more empties over there in the trash. It's Mr. Torrington's second-year French, his ballpoint chicken scratch in the chart along with the rest. Mom picks it up from the school office each week, so that I'll know what make-up coursework to do, as I fight my way through, and struggle not have to do the whole school year again.

But my fifth year of French this time?

I'm the only eleventh grader in the room since I started French early, and at least I'm holding on. Yesterday I spent the afternoon cutting the grass at the new and improved Ligo home, and at night after training, I study, and do nothing but study, for Master Choi, and to make it to Japan. Mrs. Holtzclaw's up there at the board, and I fight my way through this passage on Paris and the *Champs-Élysées*. I can't read it like the rest, and the reality, not the grade, of that C+ screams in my head with my father's voice.

It's no longer his own.

It's her voice now coming out of his mouth?

Her topics, her expressions and tone, and especially, it seems, even more these days when any topic comes up on which she's confronted me before, and now, noticeably, especially when he and I are off on our own.

Like he's trying to show me?

Like he's trying to prove.

That she's *not* unreasonable, that he would in fact address me naturally in exactly the same way too? He's so desperate to prove it, and to himself, I presume, because he can't confront *her*, or stand to watch me be crushed, so instead from his pulpit he decrees, and lies to himself and condescends, and belittles, and attacks and contends that I'm the expendable one, and that I should be ashamed?

Of everything I do?

For not allowing myself to be erased, like he does?

It's not quite the Nathan Ligo tennis ball again, but a new, a particularly twisted, punishing sort of backhand.

Perhaps he wants me to stay away, too.

That's Erica West, a classmate in my French class.

Her desk beside me, her blonde hair. And her smiling blue eyes. A senior. We're in different social circles so not exactly my friend, but she smiles.

Reassuringly.

Like a long lost older sister it seems now, she can see.

Not the extent of my misery, not my stepmother's tuna fish meat, not my father's inadvertent efforts to erase me, but at least just then, the tiny hint of tears in my eyes, she can see my fatigue.

The lack of refuge.

The need.

She can see how hard I'm struggling.

She's can't be fully aware but her intuition must know that it's a breaking heart that she sees, and for a moment.

For me.

It looks like that refuge is there?

In those blue eyes for a second and then looked away.

Her compassion.

Their approval that suggests.

There must be some love left after all?

I must have some worth.

"Next time, you have to eat your own natto, Ligo," Mocaram's French accent explains, and my nostrils fill with the scent of those putrid, sticky beans.

"Osu," my voice, and my throat tightens to see.

How Mocaram offered and took my natto from me before I'd even had a chance to choke it down like the rest, swallowing them whole with the rice and the gruel, and probably I could have done it. I'm standing in fudo dachi in the middle of the room, I want to collapse, and I wonder when Mocaram's going to finally let me rest.

"Perhaps you should fold the futons, Ligo."

The hairs on the back of my neck stand up, electric, my lower back, and I shudder.

Mocaram drilling me yesterday on Master Choi, telling me how all Koreans are weak, and telling me why he and Hashimoto are the only remaining second-years. "Why is there only *one* Japanese in your class?" I ask, the newcomer Nathan, my voice, "while there are *seven* in mine?"

"Yes. Funny you would ask, Ligo."

"The others ran away," Mocaram says, nodding, and looking away with a smile, and a glint of fear in his eye. "The sempai beat them in the night with baseball bats and threw them in the street with their clothes, and their bags, and told them not to come back." A redirect of his gaze and he indicates the street I came in on, at the end of the alley so narrow, past those six stacked, white shoebox-sized apartments with drainpipes on the outside, and air conditioning window units in rows, and its opening at a run like the Death Star trench in sight of the park.

Our windows are open, but it's night and no light's coming in, and I imagine two guys, bleeding out there on the concrete in the dark. My head spins, and for a moment, I'm back. I tune in to the shouts, and the kiais of the four o'clock training, the most rigorous workout I've ever heard, it occurs to me! Through the dormitory windows behind me, facing the Kaikan's back wall, and I wonder, "Will I have to fight today, and will Iwaya Sempai beat me?"

"They tied them up *and beat them with baseball bats*?" I ask. Careful, my voice, so as not to show fear.

"Yes, Ligo, you have no idea! You can not *comprendre* – how do you say, com, pre …"

"Comprehend?" my voice, but the breathing is wrong. It's hollow and weak, and I fear that I've given myself away.

"Yes, Ligo you can not com-pre-hend – you can not understand dormitory life. They tied them here in the obiya with the belts from the dogi. Their hands to each other and their ankles together. They tied them on their knees, sitting in *seiza* and they beat them on their arms and their thighs with the bats, and then, when they threw them in the street in the night, they ran away and never came back … I think maybe you should fold the futons, Ligo."

"Motherfucker!" my voice in my head, past a hollow weak *Osu!* that doesn't even sound like it's mine. "They tied them up? With white belts and they beat them with baseball bats? And they took them out in the night, and chased them away? You've got to be fucking kidding me! Is this what uchi deshi life is like?

"So this is why no American has ever made it here before?"

I look towards the door, and sure enough!

Just there in a tin stand eight or ten baseball bats cut in half, the fat ends only, to where they taper down to a girth one could manage in a grip. I realized already they were leftover halves after somebody broke them in half with their shins in karate demonstrations, but I see now that each sixteen-inch bat has a hole drilled through its handle and a loop of cord tied in. A loop big enough for a wrist. Turn it tight with a twist, and you'd never drop the thing as you swung.

"They've been retained as weapons!" I realize, "They're billy clubs!" and in my head I can see.

So clearly!

Mas Oyama's letter to my parents when he said I could come, and the one, two, O. The typewriter-typed number 120. One hundred and twenty have come here before you, come from other countries and tried, he wrote, but none of them could manage to stay, for the period of time they'd promised to stay. None of them so far have succeeded.

"Osu!" I say, my feet curl, and my toes feel the slick and the texture of the floor again. I turn towards the futons, which are already stacked, and I wonder how the hell am I supposed to fold them again.

"Take them all down, Ligo," the Frenchman says, standing up with a grunt and a sigh and an expression like it's such a bother to show me the way.

"You can see how none of them are *pishitto*?" his voice. It's a word I don't know, perhaps it's Japanese, but he uses his hands to show me "off kilter," the opposite of *pishitto* in Japanese, and indeed I can see, like his hands, the stack of futons from *The Princess and the Pea* is not exactly as straight, and upright, as it ought to be.

The echo of this morning's alarm clock beeps.

The Japanese of this morning, a dozen bloodthirsty beasts as they leap to their feet with one single thud of tatami on wood, and somehow they fold their futons so fast, they're already stacked in one stack in the corner of the room.

And Mocaram on his feet in the Tokyo dawn.

"What's going on?" I ask, and "Osu, what should I do?"

"Training, Ligo! It's morning training," he says. "Hurry up! You need your dogi pants and a T-shirt and your running shoes, and hurry up, Ligo, fold up your futon, and your *kakebuton* (he points at my blanket as he says *kakebuton*) and throw your pillow on the top with the rest ..." But by the time I throw my futon up to head level, up onto the stack and folded in thirds, I'm second to last, and only Mocaram's left, and I do see now, after the run and the shower, breakfast and the Dormitory Oath, that a couple of the futons near the bottom of the stack aren't quite lined up like they ought to be. They're squishing out sideways under the weight of the rest, and the whole stack *is* off kilter, and threatening to fall.

"Damn, I'm going to have to restack them after all!"

"Here, take them down, Ligo," Mocaram pulls one of the lopsided ones out from the bottom, and the whole, head-level stack of a dozen and a half futons folded in thirds slips, and slides, and tumbles down, the springy ones leap out, and the floppy ones sag, they're all different colors, the one I slept on was plaid, and "Damn it!" I think, "there's no cause to do that!" Some were folded up nicely, and I could have taken them down, and kept them that way.

"Oh, so here I am," it occurs to me then.

Japan.

Exhausted and fucked. "I told them you will rest, Ligo," the Frenchman's voice rings in my head. I've not been allowed to sit down, and now?

Half the obiya's floor is covered, again, by a whirlwind, a destruction! – a sea of futons. My work's all cut out for me.

But happily then!

That old familiar friend, a growl rises up from within.

"No."

"For Master Choi.

"I'll do it.

"Get to it, Nathan, you're here!

"There'll be no stopping you now.

"That is," it comes with a shudder, "if Mas Oyama says I can stay."

"Jesus!" I exclaim, but under my breath.

"Master Choi would kill me if he knew I were here."

XXV.

Pishitto, not off-kilter.

I construct.

My inexperienced, but straight-up-and-down, fast-growing futon stack in the corner.

The occasional *Kaw! Kaw!* of a crow, or the "Osu! Osu!" of a roommate through Honbu's back wall. I'm to meet Mas Oyama within the hour, and my stomach churns. I swallow hard and hurl another futon up, folded into thirds.

They're much smaller, but they might as well be mattresses for how heavy they are! Certainly right now for how worn out I am.

And Master Choi would kill me if he knew.

Master Choi.

At fourteen, I stand knee-deep in surf, and see him over there, oiled and bronze, and built like a truck. And only someone built like that, eccentric, confident and so foreign, could get away with wearing a Speedo-tight bathing suit on a crowded North Carolina beach without drawing attention to himself. He's soaking in the sun like he owns it, like he could tell it, too, almost, just what it should do, and it would probably do it.

The ocean, I'm quite convinced.

Is *his* ocean too.

If I doused myself in baby oil like that and spent even fifteen minutes in this sun, I'd transcend lobster red and burn straight through to melanoma black. He bathes in the stuff like he's daring the sun to get him, but instead of burning up, he only turns browner and browner, and stays.

Impervious.

His Speedo, his muscular frame, his deep brown skin, and his dark mirrored shades.

A titan.

I've finished eighth grade, and I'm finally finding balance again. One year in to my life with Master Choi, and it's occurred to me.

Master Choi might be more than he seemed.

Originally.

It's July, and we're at Holden Beach early to be with his wife, and two Korean couples I don't know, who have kids a lot younger than me. Before yesterday I didn't even know he was married.

His wife's a scientist, apparently, a petite little Korean lady in graduate school, somewhere but not UNC, and they don't live together. The rest of the CMAC, those members attending the annual summer beach training, will all drive down the day after tomorrow, after the Koreans leave, and my belly's still so full of kimchee, rice and bulgogi – that's sweet broiled garlic and beef – that I can't even imagine it's ever been happier.

Hard to conceive!

In Japan I swallow hard, my stomach's bursting and those brown sticky beans.

"You must never ask me personal things," Master Choi's voice in the car when I ask him about his wife, "nor should you speak about the things that you see. When I'm at my father's table in Korea, I'm not even allowed to speak without being spoken to first. It's the strict, Korean way. Discipline yourself to think three times before you speak, and consider if what you want to say has any value or any meaning."

"Yes, sir," I say, tentatively. I'm still so young, that "Yes sir!"

is still among the first thousand of thousands upon thousands I'm to say to him.

"Your life with me is Martial Arts," his thick Korean accent goes on, "I bring you down to the beach early, because you're the only child student, and because I told your mom. But I don't mix martial arts with family and friends, and nor should you. Enjoy this time, my friends all like you. But don't speak about what you see, think three times before you speak, and don't ask any questions about personal things."

"Yes, sir!" I say again, that's the CMAC's "Osu!" and my futon stack's halfway done. Mocaram said Mas Oyama will be at the Morning Ceremony at the Kaikan at 9:30, and my head spins.

It's nearly nine o'clock already, and that's when I'll meet him!

My hand.

For a moment of rest, I reach out, and lean on the obiya's wood-paneled column in the middle of the room. Mocaram's over there by the fan, outstretched on the tatami with his eyes closed and his head on a pillow he's gotten back out from the closets at the far end of the room.

He's ignoring me.

Trying to sleep.

I bend down and heave, another futon goes up. Echoes of the Young Lions' Song ring in my ears.

An album on a record player.

Downstairs.

Drones its way around and around just twenty minutes ago, when we haven't yet eaten, and I'm at the point, I think, where nothing else can surprise me.

But a song here in karate land?

At first that *does* surprise me! The recitation of the Dormitory Oath is finally complete, "and now they're going to sing?!"

One of my roommates falls out of line to turn a record

player on with a click, and then drops a needle in the appropri-
ate track with a *crack* and then tic, tic, tic as a fleck of dust or
a scratch at the start of the song spits rhythmically out of the
speaker on the side of the thing.

The twenty lines of the Dormitory Oath, and on the adjacent
wall a second one, the complex script of the dormitory *Rules*.
Around us, thirteen steaming-hot rice bowls that somehow
keep steaming, and on now to the third one?

Could it be?

One final set of kanji behind glass, I hadn't paid attention,
since this one, its layout, could only have been a poem, I thought.

But, no, it's a song, and it dawns on me!

After all that, can they possibly be getting ready to sing?

I'm upstairs and the HOWL of the Young Lions' Song
echoes in my ears. I work in the big room, and more than the
Dormitory Oath, it doesn't simply shake, it breaks!

Apart.

The city block!

Like an earthquake.

My heart thumps to remember!

The first two lines out of thirty, dear God, at a shout!

Mas Oyama must really be about taking over this city block!
We'll have Ikebukuro all to ourselves! I've given up following
along, but my roommates sing along with the record player, it
sounds like a march, but it's so loud and so powerful that they
just HOWL the words of a song that's about them!

My God, not only does Kyokushin have its own magazine,
but Mas Oyama's uchi deshi have their own theme song!

The March of Kyokushin!

And finally I see.

Oh, but of course!

It's all training!

We're in the dormitory for breakfast, and these guys still
haven't yet finished their morning training!

They're beet-red and sweat pours down their faces, they're standing at attention and still in their parallel lines. They put forth such incredible effort from their diaphragms, to shout their way through the Oath and the Rules, and now it's the Song, that I can't even imagine the run, or even the sit-ups and the crunches in the first floor dojo, could have possibly held a candle.

To this strain on their diaphragms!

As they maintain.

This constant pressure and shout.

They spend a dozen minutes engaged in this incredible howl, and then have only one minute to eat before they rush off to go clean.

The Kaikan, before Mas Oyama comes in.

And, oh, finally I see …

They have to pick up every cigarette butt in the park, every gum wrapper, running around bent over like crabs in the sand. They have to run six kilometers at that god-awful sprint, until they're so skinny they look like escapees from a concentration camp. All the other exercises next, and then they have one minute to shower before putting back on the same clothes in which they slept, and then a dozen minutes of this city-block-shaking ROAR, of not only the Oath, and the Rules, but also the Song! Before they have just one minute to slurp down that yellow sticky gruel, and then they SPRINT back around the block, off to the Kaikan to clean all of its nooks and its crannies. And it's not even nine o'clock in the morning!

And what do I mean, "They"?

It's me!

Here I am in the dormitory, throwing another futon up, I wanna collapse!

I'm exhausted from the run, my stomach's bursting from all that raw egg miso white gruel, and my ears still ringing from the howl of that song. I'm exhausted and I want to collapse, but instead I'm stacking these futons up in the corner! And Mocaram and I skipped the sit-ups in the first floor dojo, the pushups in the park, and the squats. I skipped the natto, and didn't run off after breakfast like the rest to clean at the Kaikan?

"Son of a bitch, this life is intense!"

And Master Choi would kill me if he knew!

That I came all the way to Japan without his blessing. "I wish that I had a son just like you," he says, and I want him, it occurs to me, to want a son just like me.

And now he'll think I've betrayed him!

"Yet I'm here," I console myself, "exactly because I'd rather die first before I failed him!"

Nathan Ligo's going to Japan, I realize, Nathan Ligo's going to war, and the Nathan Ligo they know will never return.

Not the same one, anyhow.

"It will be over my dead body," I exclaim, and I see that blade that would certainly cut flesh, my flesh, if I asked it to. My entrails on stone.

"It'll be over my dead body that I'll leave the dormitory before that 1000th day. Drag me out in the night, and cast me down on the concrete, bleeding.

"Watch and see!

"I'll be me that you'll see crawling back in!"

xxvi.

Master Choi.

Teaching now.

His dark brown muscular frame.

Holden Beach, Holden Beach, Emerald Isle, and then Sunset. Four different years and four different beaches. We're practicing kicking, and stances, in sand that's so hot it's easier to keep kicking like that, high over our heads, that or get our bare feet up onto those razor-sharp beds of sun-bleached shells as soon as we can, and Master Choi over there!

Impervious!

We're shouting as loud as we can, and still it's not loud enough for him? It's my fourth annual CMAC summer beach training, this time I'm eighteen, and it was just last week that I cranked up my VW Bug and moved out of my Templeton dorm room, last week that I was at Myrtle Beach with Dillon, and Sheri and Sara celebrating their graduation week.

And Master Choi's taken us all back.

To Sunset Beach.

My old haunt.

The site of the great Prescott family August and Easter clan gatherings that continue without me since now, after the divorce, I'm no longer invited.

I skipped twelfth grade at North Meck, and one year at Templeton is through, there was Gatlin, and I've packed up my room. This year at UNC likely won't even be a full year before I'll be off to Japan.

Finally.

To Mas Oyama's dormitory.

Where only by succeeding can I bring to Master Choi a shred of all that he's given me.

A place to be.

A sense that I have some value.

That I can be somebody!

Can't be to my dad. Don't wanna' be for my mom. So I'll be for the world!

For Master Choi!

The Student Union lobby at UNC.

He's walking up the stairs with his back to me.

I've spoken to him but something's wrong, he's not stopping. I've turned nineteen, first semester is done. My head is shaved, and I'm eating his ginseng, his rice gruel that he makes for me and brings home from Raleigh in Tupperware. My hands are finally now healed from the surgery and the tin can lid, and I'm still working at Crook's Corner weekend nights after school.

But I'm failing.

Multi-variable Calculus with that grad student on Mars from Lithuania or Estonia I can't understand. Second semester Japanese with Kanji this time, and Basic Mechanics with Calculus for the very first time.

And I'm training like a machine.

Fingertip pushups on the slick gym floor, and I'm jumping and clearing 200 times each day, from a standing position, a track and field hurdle set to the height of my chest. Feet together I stand and look down at the rail, twelve inches down from my chin. A slight exhale. And then like a bomb! I leap straight up and tuck, the soles of my feet reach so high, the tops of my thighs slam into my chest. And kipped into a ball like that in the air, I throw my hips forward and reach my spine into a backwards curve, reaching for the floor on the other side.

And I land.

A perfect plant, my feet together to stand with perfect balance like a gymnast would from his parallel bars, and my back just a millimeter from the bar.

And I turn around to face the bar.

I take just one breath and BOOM! I do it again!

Other people jump rope, but like Mas Oyama I'm learning to leap my body height!

From a standstill.

I'm lean, and hungry, my head is shaved.

But I've blown it this time?

Mas Oyama's written to tell us I could come, but I don't yet know when. He's told us how much my uchi deshi tuition will cost, and we've written back again to ask if he'd shoulder the cost, since I don't have any money, like his nephew always promised he would.

But by then I'm not going to class.

My apartment's off campus, and my bike my only way in to school, and instead of my Calculus and my Basic Mechanics, I'm waiting for the mail to come at the mailbox each day. Virtually paralyzed with fear that what Master Choi always told me, that his uncle would admit me without charging me, could possibly be wrong.

And yet that letter doesn't come.

Day after day, becomes week after week, and I'm training, and Master Choi doesn't know that I'm failing in school.

But then.

Finally!

The letter comes, and Mas Oyama's written to say he'd send me a plane ticket anyway, and support my whole way, and for a moment I'm relieved, 'cause finally!

I'll be off to Japan.

Rescued, it seems, from having to finish the semester,

since now there's no way I could catch up anyhow.

Of course I probably should have known.

That Master Choi would have other plans for me.

"After the semester is done," he says. "After you finish your classes, you can go. I'll write to my uncle, and tell him you'll come at the end of the school year."

And my planet stops spinning.

And I have no choice.

And like a teenager caught breaking the rules, I have to tell him I've not been to class, and I'm failing. And then my head is shaved, and I'm told I have no choice, I have to reclaim my grades and finish the school year successfully or he'll cancel the whole thing.

He feels betrayed.

And weeks pass, and I'm training like a machine, it's second semester and I'm doing all that.

Successfully.

But Anne Dodson then.

The CMAC's Rob and Virginia's friend. I'm still fighting, I'm back going to class, but then I'm also making up for lost ground again. The Nathan Ligo tennis ball finally trapped and penned in – but Templeton!

It shook me, and I've come in to UNC.

Afraid.

A karateka was destined for Mas Oyama's Japan, and I came in like a grade school kid. I'm afraid that I'd be alone, not know anyone and be, one more time ashamed. Embarrassed to sit down in the cafeteria alone.

Eighteen. Weak and off balance to UNC. And thanks to my dad's inadvertent erasing me, my stepmother's backhand, and my loss of the Prescott family.

Anne Dodson.

Rob and Virginia's friend. A chance to drown that out in the bedroom once again?

There's Master Choi on the stairs.

One day home from her condo on Sugar Mountain that time, the lobby of the Student Union, I address him, and he just keeps right on walking.

I catch up with him, and he stops and he turns.

His eyes.

Tired.

Concerned.

"I don't need you anymore," his words.

Like a knife.

Such finality!

"Yes sir!" I stammer in spite of myself, "… but what do you mean?"

"Listen to your heart," he says, stone cold.

Like a meat slicer disk.

Intuitive monster!

Creative like a machine!

He's trained me to see, to think three times before I speak, and most of all!

He's trained me to use my eyes.

To see.

The truth behind the surface, the sometimes lies of the rational.

And he knows!

Master Choi.

The last time he threatened to throw me away, I walked forty miles to his apartment to apologize, and he'd never seen such commitment in an American before! It floored him, coming out of meek little me. "Okay, first you must eat," his words, the blood blisters on my feet, and he recommended me to his uncle.

But now at UNC, "I have to be sure," I can see it in his eyes. "You're not ready."

"I don't need you any more."

Like a meat slicer disk.

Cuts through me.

"Listen to your heart," he says.

And I did. An intuitive command that cut straight to my soul.

"Go to the mountains!" it said.

For Master Choi.

Your entrails on stone.

Transcend all the rest!

You don't need Japan.

For the time being, you don't even need Master Choi.

Give your life over!

Who needs the grade after all?

When all there is, is success or failure. Only black and white, training and study. Japan, later.

College, later.

Three years on Grandfather's ridge.

That night of my eighteenth birthday, shivering. Cascading ice. The shriek of the mountain demon that accosted me there. Wing beats like drum beats, hollow whoops like the beats of that drum.

Like Mas Oyama, his two years alone.

Burn all the rest!

Only karate.

Nothing else.

And so.

One hundred days pass, and no one knows where I've gone. I've been in Templeton, to live and work and prepare for mountain training.

But then I find out, just one week ago, one week before Japan.

Mas Oyama sent the plane ticket anyhow!

Master Choi didn't tell him I'd run away!

I had no choice.

It had to be Japan!

Or Master Choi would lose face.

Intuitive machine!

Heart so thick, it cuts through sight.

And moves!

Beyond even the rational of the choice.

Such is Master Choi!

His genius!

Genius the others don't see. Master Choi's bizarre insanity is his all-loving creative intuitive monster set free, cut loose by a certain dangerous ability, a willingness to fall into it almost like immaturity, like a crash, and wind up making choices beyond what even the maddest benevolent among us can see.

And like proof?

I'm here in Japan.

I've seen that icy mist. I've seen my entrails on stone. It's Japan, and I'm far more ready than I ever possibly could have been before.

Master Choi would kill me if he knew!

But frankly.

If he was here with me?

And if he could see my run, and if he saw my heart? If he saw all that I'd seen, he'd know also that now, at least, he actually *does* have a son just like me.

Thanks to him, I'm as ready as I'll ever be!

XXVii.

Forest green, marbled and cracked.

I'm on the way up this time, and Mas Oyama's at the top. The second floor dojo, I'll see him, and my head spins.

At the terror.

The smack, smack, smack, as my sandals work their way up. Chop, chop, chop in Japanese, and this time I'm aware.

Of everything.

The world drones by, and in slow motion I see.

Every instant.

Every.

Step.

The fact. Master Choi doesn't know that I've come, and Mas Oyama might send me away.

And he sent the plane ticket anyway?

I can't understand.

My toes, and Suzuki's faux leather sandals, clear the front edge of each step.

Those rattly.

Metal strips at the front edge of each stair.

I follow yesterday's green belt on up, that mop of coarse, jet-black Japanese hair. My life passes before me, I'm hyper-aware, utterly careful, and perfectly sure to clear each deeply-grooved stainless steel strip at the front edge of each step. Conscious and as sure as I can be not to trip, I charge upwards again after Mocaram, my legs just as tired this time, but I'm floating on air, watching even every screw head that's set every ten inches across each rattly metal strip, I'm hyper-aware.

Of everything.

My breathing, my pulse, my balance and how much oxygen, in fact, is reaching my brain, that ultimate measure of whether I'm charging up right, whether I'll move too fast and stumble, breathe too little and fall once again.

On this landing.

As we turn.

At the back of the building, one hundred and eighty degrees, and switch back toward the street at the front of the Kaikan. I swing in the direction of the second-floor windows I know to be at the front of the building.

A thick, polished hardwood banister.

Slick in my grip, and I'm glad for a moment I'm holding on. For that one moment secure, and I'm sure I'll not fall, and finally this time.

I am gonna meet the man.

After all.

He's gotta let me stay!

I came all the way to Japan!

"Has it been only three months?" I wonder, "since 'listen to your heart,'" I hear, in Master Choi's voice, and I did.

Exactly that.

Like a heart attack.

Listened and saw it all again, the world at my fingertips. My options were never so clear.

From the corner of my eye and above, and backwards and down, I see, for a moment it occurs to me, the windowsill there. The one where Yamakage squatted down yesterday, his V-shaped back, and leaned outwards and down to notify the dorm that I'd come.

That sempai's annoyed tone.

Echoes from the dormitory in my brain. Dull gray aluminum

tracks with dust in their grooves, and I see for the first time from above the source of that marbly scrape they use as a telephone ring.

On up ahead of me, a silhouette, Mocaram backlit.

Natural light filters down.

Two steps this time, the back of his thighs at eye level. They're thick like tree trunks. So thick, it occurs to me, from this angle it seems like their girth is as wide as his waist coming down to his hips. There's no fat there. His muscles through his sweats, those red-white-and-blue work the dimly lit steps like that's what they were designed to do. Mocaram's sweats, red, white, and blue, and his t-shirt sky blue, not red, white, and blue like America's colors, but a twisted variation of European tones, worn down with grime, and hand washed, it seems, time after time.

The Frenchman.

My only friend here so far, condescending, charging on up beyond Yamakage's green-tiled landing. Indeed, there's the light from the second-floor windows, reaching in at the front of the building and peering out through the doorway up there. "That must be the doorway to the second floor dojo!" it occurs to me, its deep-brown dark wooden frame. Saw those windows from below in the street yesterday evening, my head rocked all the way back, and the yellowing sky. I heard Honbu's great drum, shaking the Earth, and those nonstop karate shouts continued in the dormitory through the back wall of the building.

And now?

But a murmur within?

The others are congregating there, my roommates settling in, where I can't yet see, there's another flight of stairs switching back at a hundred and eighty degrees behind me, just opposite the door and leading up to yet another green-tiled landing. Another one above me, switching back with an identical row of low landing windows, and "Oh, I see now!"

"Those are the ones just higher than the obiya's windows on the second floor of the dorm," it occurs to me, the ones I can see at an awkward cattycorner, a complex angle through the window over the deep, stainless sink where I'm brushing my teeth yesterday evening, standing on wobbly legs in a jet-lag haze and not believing I've come, finally, all the way to Japan, and on up to the third floor of the Kaikan, where they lead …

To Mas Oyama's offices, I think!

And to his apartment on the third and fourth floors of the building.

"Put your slippers here, Ligo," Mocaram's voice hisses, as we reach the second floor, and his eyes dart sideways before looking down, kicking off his own and positioning them side by side on the green linoleum.

They're parallel.

Two crowded rows, totaling sixteen pairs of shoes, facing out just beside the door. Except for several women's pairs, it's the same gathering of shoes, it occurs to me, that appears outside the dormitory's rattly sliding door to the dining room, when all my roommates were there, and Mocaram and I were late, and everyone'd gathered there for breakfast. Except that then they were parallel, and facing out, and in one single line that wrapped all the way around the vestibule, below that first step and up onto the barefoot-smooth hardwood floor of the dormitory.

But here.

There's no room for a single file line, and here there are sixteen pairs of assorted, molded-rubber, imitation leather open-toed shoes in two parallel lines, so perfectly ordered that it could only be Mas Oyama that they're expecting to see coming down, from the third floor, and into the dojo behind them this time?

Could Mas Oyama already be in there?

My teacher's uncle, the bare-handed bull slayer? His voice

already inside, I struggle my hearing inward to find a titan's voice as a part of that murmur?

Could it be?

Am I finally to meet the man, after all, will he send me away?

Mocaram stepping in ahead of me.

"Osu! Osu!" he shouts, and bows twice, and twice this salute louder than I've ever heard it before, he looks right.

To where the others are.

I can't yet see, I cross the threshold, and turn, expecting to see.

My destiny.

Standing there before me, in a dimly lit room, and a jet-lag haze.

My reflection, nearly, in the highly polished hardwood smooth floor, where the filtered-in afterthought light of the dawn is somehow more substantial, even, than the insufficient fluorescent tubes on the ceiling above me.

Their reflections in the floor.

Zigzag.

Like black and white television static, I scan the faces within, and my stomach.

It burns.

I'm looking for Mas Oyama.

The cave of my eighth grade bedroom in Chapel Hill.

The flickering light of my black and white TV set at the foot of my bed. Eighth grade that moment again, I'm alone, and home sick from school.

xxviii.

Time stops now.

Two days later, I bow.

My first two days in Japan have passed in a blur. This threshold again, the second floor dojo on Mocaram's heels.

We bow, "Osu! Osu!"

Those two times on the way in, it's my voice again just as loud as his, and it's the second floor dojo for only my fourth time. I've just waded through what must be *100 pairs of slippers* this time. The whole landing in fact, and up and down the stairs, the commotion inside is a roar.

All day yesterday in the dormitory after my second morning training, finally they've let me out of the dormitory, and the second floor dojo again!

For just my fourth time. My third morning ceremony this morning, and now this grading?

Apparently.

I'm told.

I'll have to wait before I begin karate training, and for me.

It's excruciating!

A day after day, endless wait in the dorm, and it'll be *morning* training for me.

The run, the push-ups and the squats. The sit-ups in the first floor dojo, and "all the first year," Mocaram explains, "don't do *ipponbu* – that's training in the dojo, Ligo – until after some weeks. You have to stay in the dormitory, and stay here and clean. Clean the tatami like I showed you, and stack the futons again, and wait. Wait till the sempai tells you to train."

At lunch yesterday.

Ryobo-san.

The Japanese woman in the dormitory that cooks all our meals.

She's grinning and looking at me.

And "You're lucky, Ligo," Mocaram explains.

"Tomorrow there's a *shokyu shinsa.* That's a grading for the colored belts – where everyone fights, and does all their kata, and shows their technique, and tries to – how do you say? – tries to go up in their belt color?

"You're lucky, Ligo, because for another day you don't have to train, just do morning training, and cleaning the park, stack the futons up, and you can watch all the fights."

But this morning?

My third in Japan.

And Mocaram.

"You have to stay behind in the dormitory, Ligo," he says, "for the sempais to tell us you can come."

And so like torture!

All morning long I'm disappointed, it's Honbu's great drum through the wall of the dorm, the shouts of the grading, the training, the fights, but now finally I've been called "to help out," he tells me, and I step in.

For only my second time.

To the second floor dojo in the main Honbu Dojo building.

The Kyokushinkaikan.

Mas Oyama's over there in a shirt and a tie at a table they've brought in, opposite the windows lining the front of the room – My god, that's really the man! – only the fourth time I've seen him, but I still can't believe it, I'm in Japan after all – but before him this time!

A hundred karateka in white!

Squeezed into a room one third the size of the fencing room at UNC where we've only ever seen thirty, and these two guys!

Two karateka in white, in the middle of the room, and they're killing each other!

My God, it's a fight!

The rest are circled around, shouting and cheering in a circle around the entire perimeter of the room, they're sitting and standing, and these two guys!

They're white belts, for god's sake!

They're punching each other with all of their might, and a sweeping shin kick to the legs just then! His feet skip out from under him and he almost goes down, and *whack!* he punches the other, straight to the jaw, and that one stumbles back to the wall. His eyes roll up for a second, and he nearly goes down, but two guys catch him, prop him up from the ground, where they're sitting cross-legged around the perimeter of the room and waiting their turn.

To fight.

They're behind him and can't see his face, I wonder if they knew he was knocked out for that moment on his feet when they caught him.

And Mas Oyama's laughing!

He slaps his one knee, and I know it was an illegal technique, since in kumite.

While practicing Kyokushin, we don't punch to the face, but he's laughing anyway and slapping his knee, and so are the others following suit at the head table, two or three others in suits, see him and are starting to laugh too.

I suppose I see why.

It's the guy who's throwing the punches!

He looks like he's insane! Is he forty years old? He's apologizing profusely, bowing, and Shitsurei-shimashita! "I was very rude," he exclaims. One more time, and then without missing a beat he throws another wild punch, and kicks his friend again full power with his shin and straight to the front of his knee, and the other one's eyes come back into line, and he kiais at the top of his lungs, and comes back and punches his friend.

It's a feeding frenzy!

Like sharks, hyenas, a pack of wild dogs all barking around, a circle of a hundred sets of gnashing teeth in white, all hungry and waiting their turn to fight, I can see.

Two by two, they're all gonna fight!

And I'm kinda detached, and in a separated timestop-like way, I marvel that I can see past the butterflies, the shock and my wobbly knees, shocked that I can see what's so funny. After all, that fighter apologized for punching his friend in the teeth, and then he hauled off and punched him again!

But my knees like jelly, and Mas Oyama then?

Leans forward in his chair, pulls his chin to his chest and looks forward over his glasses. "Daijoubu ka?" he asks in Japanese, his amazing boulder-rolling baritone. "Are you okay?" it must have been.

And the two fighters hear him!

Lo and behold, in the middle of their fight – and they're fighting like beasts! – and yet somehow they have the where-withal to hear. I'm shocked once again that they're that much aware, they hear their teacher's voice against the shouts of a hundred!

They pause for a second and "Osu!" the one shouts, the one that got punched in the teeth.

"I'm okay!" he indicates, and Mas Oyama wrinkles his brow, turns the corners of his mouth down in a frown of God-like determination and nods, and a brief wave of his hand. He conveys, "Carry on," and it was a gesture of telepathic command. More than just encouragement, it was *demanded empowerment*, it was *decreed*, it occurs to me. And "Osu!" they both hear it and obey and both shout, turn their eyes

THE NOVEL | Chapter xxviii

away from humility and love and back to ferocity again, and once again they tear in.

To each other.

My god, these are white belts, and they're killing each other!

The butterflies in my stomach, their claws, it's a brawl!

Each one refusing to go down, they don't seem to know karate too well, but they're adult men, and there's no stopping them. They're fighting with all that they have. We're allowed to kick to the head, but "my uncle doesn't let them punch to the face in the dojo," Master Choi's voice in my brain, because "it would be too bloody," he explains.

And this was an accident.

That punch to the jaw, but that's why my knees went momentarily weak.

I've never seen anything like it.

At the CMAC Master Choi would have stopped *everything*.

I never saw anyone there fight so hard in the training hall as these two white belts are fighting. The thumps! – as their fists fall, like bludgeons to the drums of their chests, and God forbid! – if there was ever an accident and someone at the CMAC.

Got punched in the face.

At UNC everything would scream to a stop and there'd be all this concern, but Mas Oyama!

He laughed?

Master Choi's uncle.

The man.

The seventy-year-old titan, the barehanded bull killer.

The founder of Kyokushin.

And two mornings ago?

The first time I saw him.

The second floor dojo and my first morning ceremony.

"Who's that?" he asks, looking at me, the mountain the man.

I can't breathe. In terror. He's been standing there where he's been lecturing us, at the front of the room for what seems like an eternity, but now, all of a sudden, he's looking at me and asking the uchi deshi where we stand in three parallel lines of four. I'm in the last row, and Mas Oyama knew, of course!

I shouldn't have been surprised.

The moment he stepped in, he knew I was there.

Three minutes but a lifetime after Mocaram and I came in and lined up in our three parallel lines, and everyone bowed "Osu!" at the top of our lungs, he sees me, and he knows I don't belong, but he's got business first to perform.

The tradition, the routine, the morning ceremony.

The drum and the bows, eyes closed for a moment, and we stand there and listen. The minutes tick by as he lectures in Japanese I can't understand, in shock that that's the man, and everyone says "Osu!" every time he pauses for a moment or catches his breath, but now that he's done?

He's turned and he's asking about me, the newcomer Nathan.

The American?

"Who is *he*?" it must have been.

And "Oh hell, here goes." They'll tell him. I'm Master Choi's student who's AWOL after all, he'll find out, or he'll know already, and he'll send me away, all the way back to the States, a failure.

"Osu!" they say.

"He's the uchi deshi from America!" Iwaya Sempai responds from his place in the first line, and Mas Oyama wrinkles his brow, "From America?" he asks, "Who is his teacher?" and just then!

A courage that shouldn't have been mine overwells. I jump in, and overstep my bounds once again.

"Osu!"

In Japanese, I pipe up.

"Watashi no sensei ga," my teacher is, "Choi Seong Soo," Mas Oyama's nephew, I proclaim.

"Ah so," Mas Oyama's responds, taken aback, I'd addressed him myself, and he looks at me with Master Choi's warm eyes. "Seong Soo!" he chuckles, "welcome. Welcome. *Gambatte kudasai.*"

A Japanese woman I've not seen, up from the back of the room, and suddenly she's sanding there, outside the formation beside me. "Sosai says 'welcome'," she says, "and to … hmm. How does one say? Persevere? Fight on. Train hard," she says. "Sosai says, 'You must train hard.'"

"Osu!" I respond to Mas Oyama, he nods ever so briefly in approval, and looks away, and could that really be all?

Mas Oyama was clearly surprised, as much as a titan like him might be over lost little me, but his answer.

So clearly!

He doesn't know yet, I think, that I'm here without Master Choi's blessing, but as far as he's concerned I'm supposed to be there, and I'm staying in Japan.

I'm baffled again … speechless.

Somehow I'll have to tell him.

Explain.

It would be dishonest to withhold the truth.

I have to tell him, and maybe then he'll send me away.

I hadn't anticipated this separation. More than just language, it's like there's a force field around him, apparently I can't just walk up to him, and initiate conversation like I could with Master Choi. All I can say is "Osu!" But I've got no choice, so perhaps after the ceremony I can talk to this woman?

His interpreter.

I can't understand.

Master Choi must not have told his uncle I'd disappeared, run away as far as everyone there is concerned.

xxix.

BOOM!

Just once, the Earth shakes!

That was Honbu's great drum, the left front corner of the room, it's the day of the grading. Hashimoto Sempai, and a hundred hungry white belt fighters in the room. He's got a fourteen-inch striker, it's wood, and an inch and a half around.

And like a billy club!

He swings it with all of his might, like a 110-mile-per-hour baseball pitch, and strikes its whittled rounded end to the waxed, stretched-tight rawhide of Honbu's great drum. Crisp leather stretched across a three-foot barrel of wood reverberates like sound waves I can see.

Springing out through the room.

The beige waxy surface vibrates at the speed of sound, its surface detail *oozes*. Its applied, finger-painted circles of conditioning wax vanish, it's impossible to focus on a surface that's vibrating like that, and the fight stops.

And everyone's clapping, and the two seem relieved.

And "Oh, so the drum signals the end of the fight," I see now, and the two guys are returning to their starting places in the middle of the room, both panting and one limping, and the other one rocking his jaw back and forth to see if it's broken, and tasting his lip to see if there's blood. They come back to face off on Mas Oyama's right and his left, and this referee? That older black belt in the middle of the floor, he's standing off-center and between, and facing Mas Oyama, and he has them first bow to each other and then to the man.

The bare-handed bull slayer.

The teacher of all of us, the founder of Kyokushin.

His cauliflower ear, his gold-rimmed glasses, his serious as a heart attack. His samurai sword against the flesh of his belly, and the corners of his mouth turn down, in nodding determined approval, and two mornings ago?

The first time I saw him.

The anticipation!

Burns.

I'm stepping out now of Suzuki's molded rubber sandals outside in the stairwell on the green linoleum, and positioning them in their parallel lines.

I follow Mocaram in.

It's my first morning ceremony, my first second floor dojo.

Two days before now.

"Osu! Osu!" It's *my* voice this time, stepping in.

Sheepishly.

I follow Mocaram's gaze.

To my right.

The butterflies – their claws! – my eyes scan the room.

That hint of my reflection in the floor, hazy like sleep in my eyes, the light is low, and it falls on deep-brown hardwood paneled walls, I can't see Mas Oyama – he's not yet arrived – but a raven just then, its caws!

Kaw, kaw, kaw!

That black-winged screech through the open window from the park where we trained, and over the roof of the marked-for-demolition, clay-tile-roofed home between us and the park. His beak like lopping shear blades, the feathers on the ends of his wings like fingers to grab me, that old man with his bicycle in the park, and those cigarette butts in the sand. A chopsticks wrapper, and that piece of chewed gum.

I peer in, scan the faces in the room.

The second floor dojo, its light-colored hardwood floor, and my roommates are there, lining up again. The Frenchman and I are the last to arrive, and there's only a little more than a dozen in the dojo this time?

One old man with gray hair in a tweed jacket and tie, not a karateka, I'm quite sure, and four or five ladies in blue sailor suits from the office upstairs, and from the *uketsuke*, that's the reception window downstairs at the front behind glass.

Several of them watch me come in, inquisitively. The one that spoke to me yesterday with curls that are, hmmm, not Japanese, I think, and they're smiling warmly with their eyes as they gather by the windows in the back of the room, and against the side wall by the widow near Honbu's great drum. "You stand here, Ligo," Mocaram's French-accented tone, as he condescends and indicates a space in the back row. The staff is against the walls, but the karateka, my roommates, the uchi deshi are gathering in three four-person parallel rows, a grid with five feet in between each person filling the whole room, and one by one we're turning back to face.

The deep-brown hardwood-framed door, the stairwell where I came in. Mas Oyama must be coming down.

I glance left to the front of the room, that must be Kawaminami Sempai?

And beholding the altar, is this really the Kyokushinkaikan? Could it be?

He barely even notices me.

In the front of the room, closest to where Mas Oyama's head table will stand two days later on the day of the grading, a starched white shirt and a tie, Kawaminami Sempai. It's the first time I've seen this sempai of mine, but Mocaram mentioned there was one more third-year guy, the oldest and therefore the senior – he's Sosai's driver, and according to Master Choi, a bodyguard? "The oldest guy gets to drive Mas Oyama's car,"

Mocaram says, wear a shirt and a tie, and live offsite at the driver's quarters at Sosai's house. Mas Oyama no longer lives on the third and fourth floors of the Kaikan, he explains.

My mind.

Touches momentarily, and remembers that second stairwell leading up from the first-floor lobby, there just inside, and locked in behind bars at the front of the building, a building that used to be something else, a stack of flats perhaps?

And now.

Mas Oyama's world headquarters dojo!

Am I really here in Japan? I turn my attention and consider once again.

The stairwell and the door, where Mas Oyama will come down and emerge into the second floor dojo. I turn my ear towards the stairs, my breath stops.

The butterflies, and I hear.

But still!

It's premature.

Mas Oyama's not there, it's Tokyo, the windows are open and I can't hear a single car. It's 9:30 in the morning in the heart of one of the biggest cities on the planet, and *kaw, kaw, kaw!* I hear once again, this time further away as if the city is empty, and as if he's perched up high on the hillside of bamboo, in the eaves of that samurai castle where the Zen monk Takuan locked the unruly Musashi for a thousand days with nothing but *The Art of War*.

To read.

The attic and the birds for company.

The pigeons and the crows, and God only knows how I've found myself here!

The Kyokushinkaikan, and that must be Kawaminami Sempai?

He seems so much more kind than the other third-year guys. Relaxed. He's looked up at the clock, it's 9:30 on the dot, and now he's leaving his place at the front right side of the dojo, the front right of the line, his seniority over Iwaya Sempai who's next to him in the front line. Iwaya Sempai even looks mean, his hooked Japanese nose, and Ishiguro, the slight, effeminate one next to him, and then, in the fourth place, there's their koohai Hashimoto, Mocaram's classmate nearest the drum. Kawaminami in socks, across the front of the room, back across in front of us all, a second line of four that's three of my Japanese classmates and the Korean Furoyama, and then the third and final line at the back, two Japanese, and Mocaram and me.

Kawaminami.

He strolls.

Past the Shinto hardwood, complex altar occupying the whole front wall of the room, he's taller and bigger than Iwaya Sempai by twenty pounds. He flips his tie over the shoulder of his starched white shirt, and from the windowsill behind Honbu's great drum, in the left front corner of the room, that left end of Mas Oyama's head table-to-be, he takes up Hashimoto's billy club, that rod of thick wood, from the windowsill beneath. Its opaque, waffled glass window slides sideways to open, and it stands six inches open to a sooty drainpipe outside. A drip, drip, drip, and he turns back to face.

The waxy bear hide.

The face of Honbu's great drum, one massive barrel-shaped cylinder of wood, it's four feet around, and four feet long.

Twin sheets of rawhide.

Stretched across both ends and nailed every inch by quadruple, parallel rows of brass-headed nails.

Honbu's great drum.

Taiko in Japanese.

Horizontal, and resting on a man-height rack of parallel wood beams. Kawaminami hauls back and swings, a baseball pitch again, and BOOM! BOOM! BOOM! BOOM!

Four times he swings and, involuntarily, I jump at the first, it's so loud!

He swings and he strikes as if he were summoning a demon! The booms are like explosions! They reverberate out into space not with the tone, but with the *sensation* of the vibrating *boooingg* of a snow shovel struck like a gong.

And then he waits, a long pause.

My stomach flips over, I anticipate.

Not sure if I should breathe, their echo subsides, and then four more times!

BOOM! BOOM! BOOM! BOOM!

Everyone's standing at attention and facing the front right side of the room where the door to the stairwell is, dawn's glowing in, its green linoleum, and its hardwood door frame. He's announcing Mas Oyama, beginning the ceremony.

BOOM! BOOM! BOOM! BOOM! for the third time then, and Master Choi in my mind.

His eyes.

Deep brown disks, twin pools that shine through to the core of his being. His suntan-oiled muscular bronze, he loves me like his son, "I wish I had a son like you" I hear, his Korean-accented tone, and I know that he does. I see his uncle in my mind's eye, Mas Oyama the man, the one from the photographs and the films, the founder of Kyokushin, and I know that he'd kill me, Master Choi, if he knew that I'd come.

Finally, in the end, without his blessing.

Yet I'm living the dream!

Japan.

Mas Oyama's Japan.

Master Choi's!

My own.

The one thing.

That I must overcome, is the thing that I can't, and I'll overcome it all! It all will be mine.

My birthright, after all!

Kawaminami's fourth barrage is different, but I've heard it before. It's the same one that starts each dojo training. One BOOM! by itself, and then a diminishing sequence of accelerating strikes. The first like that 110-mile-per-hour baseball pitch, and the next one a bit less, the next one less still and closer together, they cascade, until once at the end, they're so quiet and so rapid that he no longer swings his whole arm. No longer his elbow, his wrist is enough at that point, and he's tapping it down, like a stone skipping down into the depths of a well.

So hard to tell.

Am I really here?

The white smoke of the dawn on Grandfather's peak, just one week before now, and then Bonnie Keach, her smile, and my ticket to Japan from the travel agent on Main Street, and Ken Norton.

That letter from Master Choi's student Rob in Chapel Hill. I'd run away as far as everyone there was concerned. Three months ago, their misconceptions were bound to grow, and I let them!

I'm not important anymore, Nathan Ligo's irrelevant, let them believe what they will.

A breakdown, probably, they think?

But no.

It was a buckling down.

And mountain training for me?

One step shy of a life plan that's all in my head, a fantasy!

The wise old Chinese philosopher, the Zen monk Takuan, Mas Oyama, the man, the seventy-year-old titan, it was part of *his* legend. Like Musashi before him, a thousand days locked in a tower by Takuan, Mas Oyama spent two years of his youth on a mountaintop. A lonely cabin where he'd beaten to death the trees that surrounded his cabin, with punch after punch they'd withered and died beneath the weight of his strikes. Day after day, he'd lifted two times his body weight five hundred times over his head, and trained the edges of his hands like knives that could cut through mountain stones like they were butter, and his fists like the steel of a stonemason's hammer.

And deep in the night.

He'd read Yoshikawa's novel *Musashi* for comfort, and then fight, the fight of his life, against the demons that came, night after night, in the howl and the scream, and the utter silence in between, as the mountain, its spirits, did their damndest to beat him.

And *kaw, kaw, kaw*!

That black-winged beast of this morning, and the eve of my eighteenth birthday. Cascading ice through the silence of that February frozen night, and shivering in the night I was connected! My soul and my psyche joined to that mountain forever, that screech, that otherworldly beast, a cry that suggested I'd finally find my answers there?

"My God, it's so beautiful!"

I'm knocked off my feet! One week ago on Grandfather's peak, I collapse to my knees.

Like the breastbone of a bird, not split open, but caved in, I can stand but a minute! – I've fallen to the stone, and the sword clatters to my feet. It's the billion-year-old granite of Calloway Peak. It's dawn, and a whitewater river of mist blasts by like tubular white, the top of the world, and I'm encased all in white, enveloped in snow, my feet and the stone disappear beneath me. This is May, it's too warm for snow, but like a dead of night frozen in snow it's that silent!

And in the eddying wake of my body.

Where I, all alone, block that would-be howling maelstrom of white, I can see!

In that silence, uncanny for such terrible motion, for there's nothing, you see! – at that highest point of the world, for miles around, there's no obstacle! No higher outcropping of stone, only me for the wind to blast past, and so there's no howl, no scream, or no whoosh. Only as whitewater torrents of mist rush by, I'm surrounded, I'm encased, I'm cradled, I'm owned, I'm one with the stone, and I know in my bones, and in the samurai sword held tight in my grip, its blade clattered down onto the stone in front of me, there's no choice.

It's Japan!

It can only be Mas Oyama's Japan.

There's no other way!

My God, Nathan!

You've thrown so much away already!

Your family, your education, even your most valuable, you were willing even to let Master Choi believe that you'd thrown *him* away, everything you loved and everything you owned, your blank slate. Give it all away, Nathan, and live!

For Master Choi.

Die on that mountain before giving up, caving in, and running away. It is your destiny!

Live it!

Breathe it!

Embody success and it all will be yours. Become champion *that* way. Japan, later. Emerge after a thousand days and show them.

All.

The truth of what's inside you.

In a matter of moments, Mas Oyama will come down, the barehanded bull killer. After the ceremony, I'll have no choice. I have to find a way to tell him and he might send me away.

But don't worry, Nathan!

If anyone can understand, if anyone can see, it'll be him, Mas Oyama, the mountain, the man.

XXX.

BOOM! one final time.

That was Kawaminami this time, his 110-mile-per-hour baseball pitch. This one, full power and like an exclamation point after the cascading down.

And now.

A clatter of hardwood as wood bounces on wood, he's tossed his striker up onto the teak, or maybe it's oak, or some similar indestructible hardwood of the window still.

And he turns.

In one practiced motion.

An index finger hooked behind the knot of his tie, he turns and takes that first stride back towards his place in line, and slides his hand down so his navy, gold-striped necktie snakes, suavely, back down into place from over his shoulder. And now he's back over and assumed his position, and we're standing in fudo dachi to face the front right side of the room. Over there is the door to the stairwell where Mas Oyama will come down, and then all of a sudden!

Silence.

Everyone's perfectly still, you could hear a pin drop.

It's that quiet.

But the butterflies, their claws!

They scrape.

My insides like fingernails on slate.

"What the fuck, am I insane?" I wonder, and I hear my stepmother's voice, shaming.

"He's quick!" she says.

I've just turned eleven, and we're in Martha's and my father's bedroom upstairs at the log house. I don't know it yet, but I'm meeting my future stepmother for the very first time, I'm home in Templeton for the weekend from sixth grade in Chapel Hill, the Nathan Ligo tennis ball. I've got a Greek and Roman architecture project to do. Martha's away on business, I think, and I'm upstairs in the bedroom doing my chores, and my brother and I don't think it's at all strange that this other woman is here.

Martha and my father have plenty of friends.

But I'm vacuuming this weekend, and Aaron's downstairs doing the commodes, and here's this woman with my dad, and he's brought her upstairs to introduce her.

And "Ask yourself, Dad?"

I'm facing Mas Oyama's door in Japan, and nearly mouthing the words as I ask in my head, "How else could I possibly remember? Your life has become all about forgetting, but mine?

"How does a eleven-year-old *even remember* the very first time, the look that he saw in the eyes of a woman he was still months away from seeing again, or having any idea that she was to become someone important?"

I'm vacuuming *around a chair* as they come up, my father introduces her, and I smile and "Nice to meet you," I say, because I was raised, after all, to get along well with adults.

That voice of mine.

Innocent, trusting, friendly, unknowing.

Sure, that fourth grade teacher of mine at Templeton Elementary School had shown me that an adult could be abusive.

But in my own family home?

There's no precedent for an adult even being unfriendly!

They turn around to go back down, and my father's voice

just then, "Did you vacuum under the chair?" he asks.

My 11-year-old boy's voice responds, but I look like I'm nine. "Yes, I was about to do it, Dad," I say, as I had indeed intended to do.

But Gatlin.

The very first time I've met her.

Our very first minute together.

She winks and smiles at me, and "He's quick!" she asserts about me, like it's flirtatious or friendly to call me a good liar, and like she thinks she can cast that editorial comment out about me for her own gain in the eyes of my father, and like I would hear it somehow as an overture.

Perhaps she thinks kids are that dumb.

They've gone back down, and I've decided to hell with the chair, why should I move it anyway? – and for that one moment I stand there.

Wondering.

"That woman was just trying to be friendly, right? She was trying to impress my dad? Maybe she's just a bit awkward?"

And I'm sure I wouldn't have remembered.

Dad.

If that kind of wink, and belittling assertion, wasn't to be at the core of her character for all of the rest of the next eight years of my life. I wouldn't have remembered; if feeling good about herself?

For that woman?

Wasn't to be about establishing the negative in somebody else.

"Nathan!"

That was Gatlin's voice, shaming. I'm here in Japan without Master Choi's blessing, and I'm about to meet the man after all. I've broken free, I've transcended it all, and followed my conscience to get to Japan, and maybe I wouldn't have had the wherewithal to follow such a clear, heart-dictated path – and disregarding the risk! – had it not been for all that I'd endured at home.

Eight years! – of that woman telling me I should be ashamed, especially then, when I was following my conscience.

My love for family.

Squashed, and beaten down.

The risk!

After all.

The god of modern karate.

Could it be?

Will he send me away?

This in insanity!

"Nathan!" agreeing, my own voice in my head. "You *are* out of your mind!"

But good riddance! I laugh to myself, and laugh at the grief.

Out of my mind is a better place to be. "The one thing I can't overcome is the one thing that I must, in order to succeed." And what better way than leaving myself behind?

On Grandfather's peak.

That blood-curdling shriek in the night, that maelstrom of white blasting past, and cascading ice.

And suddenly then!

I'm back in the dojo, and it occurs to me.

After six whole years, and in a matter of moments, Mas Oyama will come down.

The god of modern karate.

I inhale and draw it in slow, I take in the universe, and then in a flash!

I transcend.

Nathan Ligo's out through the door. I'm standing there in fudo dachi, of course, but the intuitive, sensory ghost I've learned from Master Choi?

I've phase-shifted.

I've passed straight through the dojo wall and out into the

stairwell, my hearing and my eyes, and the vibrations through the floor, but far more than just that?

My newborn intuitive monster!

My very own psychic-psychotic back-scatter radar has reached out into the stairwell as trillions upon trillions of the subatomic particles of the air, the electromagnetic waves, the radio beams and the X-rays, my telepathic feelers in unison all bouncing and feeling in a million directions at once, and up the stairs, and around the bend at the speed of light, the forest green and the cracked linoleum of the stairs and the landing, those metal strips and those screw heads set, I reach out …

And I find.

The layout of the third floor of the building where Mas Oyama's offices are. Three dimensions I can see, in an electronic, glowing, cathode-ray-tube–incandescent green, the door to his apartment I've yet to see with my own eyes, but now that I know that it's there, that pane of glass that rattles in its frame, I can see it all in 3-D! I reach out and touch it and see.

Like as a sixth grader I once made it snow.

With a magical stone.

And now I know!

Mas Oyama is there! – the monster, the man, the god of modern karate, I can feel him before even I hear him step out into the stairwell. He's tucking in his shirt.

That's him! His slippers on the stairs!

Not the wise old Chinese philosopher, the Zen monk Takuan, or the kung-fu master on television.

It's an atom bomb!

An *explosion* of power and light, glowing out through the floor, the walls and the door, the stairwell!

An explosion, but silent like Grandfather's maelstrom of white, and contained in a ball the size of a bull, a supernova, a star, a black hole, Master Choi times a million! And now he's reached the third-floor landing, he's turning, his hand on the heavy oak rail. His feet shuffle, and halfway down, now, between the landing and the door.

My life passes before me!

Lorimar Street in Templeton, the log house, Cob Terrace and Ridgecrest. Cornelius, the Richies,' the Abbotts,' and the trailer by the lake. Templeton's dorm room, and Dillon's, and my basement apartment in Chapel Hill. The Main Street house kitchen and its purple paint stripper fumes. I'm nineteen, but six years of my life under Master Choi have been the most consistent, the longest run of them all. It's an eternity, and now here I am.

It's drawing to an end.

That chapter is closing and another one's creaking open like the door to the stairwell.

Mas Oyama's slippers, that tiny little clip, clip, clip on the stairs, like he's tip-toeing compared to his monster.

My ears this time, on fire!

A breath, and an exhale.

A sigh!

He's kicked off his slippers on the landing by the door, and he takes in and lets out that deep breath – I hear it! – and my back-scatter radar.

Suddenly there's something different altogether!

Those trillions upon trillions of particles, bouncing off and revealing the 3-D of the walls, the stairwell and the bull-sized man in the middle have suddenly been shaken up, twisted into a million-mile-per-hour maelstrom of white as the first breath of that beast, I hear it! – first enters the heartbeat of my new life.

Masutatsu Oyama.

The mountain.

The man.

The god of modern karate, and then suddenly I see him!

His gold-rimmed glasses. His cauliflower ear. His broad nose and broad shoulders, his forehead like a boulder. The ghost of Musashi's samurai sword at once in his grip turned outward, and its blade turned in against the flesh of his gut. Eyes like coal, and in a glance, he saw.

Me.

And all.

Everything!

The second floor dojo and every pair of eyes gathered there. A Hawaiian-print short-sleeved shirt, silk, a fresh coffee stain. Green trousers, and the threads at the button of his fly, stretching. The top centimeter of his zipper exposed.

Feet like bludgeons!

Trudging.

Lifeless lumps in through the door, everyone around me is already bowing it seems, and it dawns on me! These are feet rendered lifeless, bare flesh against a lifetime of ice and snow, and hundreds upon hundreds of miles pounded out on a lifetime of stone and the dojo floor!

A full half second late, the terrible, earth-shaking simultaneous echo of "Osu!", that of my roommates blasts its way in through the haze, and into my brain, and I realize I've forgotten to bow.

Me alone.

"Osu!" I take my turn a second late, and bend at the waist, my voice alone, my fists into stones out there in front of my hips like never before, and Mas Oyama!

Like a caricature!

I'm stunned.

He looks just like his picture!

He's real after all!

And he's a man after all!

My voice a beat late, he's taken his first stride towards his place at the front of the room, but his eyes swing then, they see all, but search and for an instant they find only me. The newcomer Nathan, the American, the unfamiliar voice in the room. My eyes are knocked out of focus, and my back-scatter radar array crumbles to the floor as those slate-gray piercing disks collide with the back of my skull.

He's turned away.

But it's enough.

I'm dumb, and struck staggered, and all but drooling stupidly for the next two days of my life.

My jet-lag haze, the exhaustion of finally finding Mas Oyama, and of finding him human.

One more time.

The second floor dojo, "Osu! Osu!" I shout, on Mocaram's heels, two days later and a different sort!

This time an actually *physical* maelstrom of white.

One hundred cheering karateka in white the day of the grading. A feeding frenzy, and two white belts, a full-contact fight exploding outwards from the middle of the room.

And Mas Oyama this time?

In a shirt and a tie, and sitting up there at a head table that wasn't there before, with his guests and two of my roommates squatting down at each end of his table, bodyguards there, it occurs to me, to prevent flying bodies from crashing into his table.

One of the fighters lands a good blow with a thump like a drum, and Mas Oyama straightens in his seat, nods in approval, and slaps the table with that same gnarled mass of flesh and bone that everyone knows the Japanese press deemed simply *God Hand* for his ability to smash stones. The same one that's sliced the horns off of raging bulls and bent quarters in half between that very thumb, and index and middle fingers of that hand. He's watching the fight in his shirt and his tie, those other distinguished gentlemen at the head table. There's a hundred in the room, karateka in white, and my "Osu! Osu!" near the top of my lungs, was, nevertheless, completely swallowed up.

And yet I have no doubt.

I've just stepped into a particle field, an array of master-fully arranged radar beams like I've never before seen, Master Choi's sensory powers on speed, peyote or LSD, and my feeble attempt beside it.

A joke!

Sosai didn't watch me come in, he didn't perk up his ears, he's watching the fight, he slapped the table, and yet he knows!

I've come in.

Not because of me, of course, but because he knows.

Everything!

He feels it! – his nephew Seong Soo's young student come all the way from America, that letter he's read that my mom wrote, expressing my parents' concern, his commitment, because he gave it, to take care of her son.

A punch to the jaw!

And that white belt stumbles back and his eyes roll back into his head. Mocaram has pulled me into a place by the door. Fudo dachi with one shoulder blade against a five-foot-tall mirror, five feet wide in a frame, and mounted to the wall, and my other against the dark, wood, wainscoting-like paneling of the wall.

And Mas Oyama's laughing, and slapping his knee!

And I consider Master Choi and the CMAC, my knees gone temporarily weak.

This full contact fight, I've never seen anything like it!

I've lost count, only one minute each, and this fight after fight, but they're so brutal! – they each seem to last an eternity. These are white belts, for God's sake, blow after blow, how many minutes have I been here already?

And still!

Every blow takes my breath away. I can feel them through the floor, the shock waves through the air, and my rib cage, because with every fight, I can see myself.

Out there.

On the floor.

100 pairs of eyes cheering, and shouting and encouraging me, and encouraging the guy that I'm fighting.

His mop of coarse, black Japanese hair.

His fists, slamming into me!

My own meager fighting experience flashed through my mind, once upon a time my brother and me.

My brother Aaron, so much bigger that me.

We're 13 and 14, and he's five inches taller and thirty pounds heaver, and his blocks are busting my shins, and he doesn't really have to focus like that, I tell him, and it hurts so much and I cry, and then Brian Moran. He's so much bigger than me, and kicks like Ninomiya on film, but he's patient and working with me, and Leticia Hawn, and I'm sparring equally *with the girl*, and then I'm 18. I'm sparring with everybody and no one can beat me. And Donald Whittier that time on the beach, and the jellyfish I picked up barehanded off the beach and tossed it away, and everyone was shocked. And then another time, at UNC, my head shaved, I'm so lean, and eating ginseng rice gruel, and failing out of school in that oversized dogi like a ghost, and Master Choi wants to bash me, I think, to teach me a lesson. And so it's Don, and we've got headgear on, and he comes at me with that Tae Kwon Do–like "Bahhh!" and he's flipping around through the air like a whirlwind, and whatever that was that he throws at me, it goes right past my skull, and I can't be sure.

If he missed me on purpose.

It would've taken my head off.

But fuck it, I'm so tired, and failing my classes! I can barely see from the Physics, the Japanese, and the Calculus, and as soon as his feet hit the ground, I kick him in the head so strong, with a solid, grounded Kyokushin-like kick to the skull, and only I can see it perhaps, because that headgear blocks everyone else's view of his eyes, but they fall out of focus, his pupils dilate, I've nearly knocked him out, and so for good measure.

I do it again!

He stumbles, and then Whack!

One more roundhouse kick to that same side of his head with a crack, I don't have anything against him, but fuck it, he threw that bullshit Tae Kwon Do "Bahh!" at me, I'm gonna kill him, I'm so tired! He's older than me and he doesn't go down, but I don't mind at all the tears in his eyes that no one else saw.

They encourage me.

Even though.

I see now.

None of that was anything at all next to what these white belts are doing!

I've never seen anything like it.

The bare-knuckled power is like nothing I've ever seen, they're trying their best to break each other's bones!

And then Mocaram.

He's bringing me back, he's hissing at me.

"Ligo!"

"They're calling you!"

"Go over there," he points at Mas Oyama's head table, "and stay low, and take Oshikiri's place, and stop any bodies from crashing into that table!"

"Me?"

"Osu!" I forgot.

I'm an uchi deshi, after all.

It's mine to work, for Mas Oyama, and Kyokushin.

But on only my third day?

I'm to protect Mas Oyama's table during the grading?

"Hurry up, Ligo!" Mocaram's voice.

"Osu!" I say, and kick my heels to the floor. A moment late, but I take off at a dash, and push off the wall. Oshikiri sees me coming, and rushes off into that maelstrom of white, to take care of whatever task it was he was sent off to do, and I'm ducking to pass in front of Mas Oyama's table and taking his place, squatting to stay low at the front corner of his table.

Dog of the dojo at Mas Oyama's feet, crouching there, and baring his teeth.

Mas Oyama's world headquarters dojo, and me.

A dog of Kyokushin.

xxxi.

Two fighters locked. Blow after blow, like cats! *Wild things* tearing limb out from limb. My head shaved, and there I am.

In the midst of it all.

Mas Oyama's uchi deshi, a defender of Kyokushin.

My teacher's uncle, the mountain, the man, the bare-handed bull killer. His presence radiating outwards towards me, and like a whirlwind!

A sigh of relief.

I settle into my spot, I realize I've faded in. I'm one in the spin, a cog, a piece at the top of this twelve-million-strong family that for six years has been calling to me.

"Family?" I laugh to myself.

What family?

My father's eyes glancing sideways just then. This endless line of full-contact blows have begun to blur into one.

All in one blink I see them, those eyes.

Mystified.

That pang in my gut.

Of not finding eyes that would have been proud to see where I am. A lifetime, instead, of all that's contained so tragically within.

The turning point.

My mind flashes by the scene of the crime, I'm thirteen. I'm in from Chapel Hill. The all-inconvenient Nathan Ligo tennis ball. It's summertime, and seventh grade at Phillips Junior

High, another year with my mom, and Bob, and the twins in Chapel Hill, has drawn to an end.

And here's Gatlin.

My brand-new stepmother Gracie across the table from me, our very first day of our very first week together in Templeton. That all-pivotal, paint-stripper summer at her duplex on Thompson Street, her brown Toyota Tercel, and a hard-core feminist attitude that's, well ... somehow sweet?

But I've just corrected her?

She's trying to show how well she can do parenting, and she's convened a meeting, first with my brother, and then with me, to ask us separately to outline what we might need money for that summer, and to establish the amount of our weekly allowance. But me, having listened outside secretly at the kitchen door as they met with my brother, I humor her for a minute, answer her questions, and then I pipe up in my best adult voice and say.

The obvious.

"But wait a minute, what are you trying to say? It sounds almost as if you're trying to make me participate in deciding an allowance amount that might be different from the one my brother got."

Taken aback, she holds her ground. Her knee jerk. She digs herself deeper into the ground, "But of course we are!" she says. "The amount of your allowance, independent of your brother's needs, is going to depend on the outcome of this discussion."

Oh, but my dad just then!

His sideways, concerned glance *speaks the world!*

His plan for our summer.

Three hours a day, we're going to work from 9 to 12 every day, scraping away layers of white paint from the windows and doors, their frames and their jambs, at the new red brick house across town, pulling up the staples and nails, the thousands upon thousands of them, when the urine-stained carpet comes up from the floor.

"Maybe it's better, Grace ..." he cuts in. I can see him discern, his mind sees the dark of that night not one year ago, when he and Martha sat us down by the wood stove in the log house, and he told us they were through, that what our mother had already told us was true, and that all of our parents were genuinely afraid of the damage their divorce might do to two elementary school boys, who'd been uprooted already so many times before, to lose yet another family home.

"Maybe it's better, Grace," his voice, his reasonable one, "that we *don't* try and introduce any shocking new routines right here at the start of this particular summer. Nathan and Aaron are only thirteen months apart. They've always gotten the same allowance before, they're too close in age. Nathan's right, we can't very well suggest that we'll give them some different amount."

Oh, but that look in her eyes then!

Talk about seeing somebody's stripes!

Shame and embarrassment that's so painful to see! This time it's me that's squirming in my seat, I've had two stepparents already but I've yet to see one with the capacity.

To feel so stung.

By the precocious counterpoint of a child.

Of course it's months if not years before I know it for sure, but this new one's gonna to try to assert herself like no other stepparent before.

And not only that?

From this day forward it's gonna be more about *her*.

Let alone what's right, or what's just, or what's "best for the kids." Interaction with this one's going to be about making her feel.

Big enough.

Secure in her skin.

One gigantic, full-contact punch.

My father's glance in a blink, here's two Kyokushin fighters in front of me. Nonstop punches and both of them beasts! A contest to see which one can hit the other more times, and which can hit harder, which one can break the ribs or rupture the spleen of the other one before …

Out of my skin!

I jump, as Hashimoto Sempai just then.

His drum!

A 110-mile-per-hour baseball pitch, and BOOM! one more time, it's so close to my ear it nearly knocks me off my feet, and I feel.

That gentle sway.

A summer breeze from a lifetime before. The drainpipe outside, Honbu's window beside me, my jet-lag haze, and my brother and me.

We're looking down through the branches of the big old magnolia tree, it's later that summer at the red brick house on Main Street. Its upper branches over the back porch which is not yet glassed in, and Gatlin's calling up to us, telling us to come down, explaining that we'd not be allowed any more.

To climb trees?

"Because it's too dangerous," she says.

And my dad, bless his heart!

He slips up.

His fatherly, his own confidant voice. It's a knee-jerk towards justice, so of course he pipes up, and he knows his sons' history so much better than she.

"Grace, it's okay," he says.

"It's normal for boys to climb trees. They've been scampering up and down trees since the day they were born."

And it's nothing for us?

But apparently.

Gatlin must be that sensitive, that look in her eye, she

thinks that we gloat ... We children who don't even know what that means?

And none of us would have wanted to be in my father's shoes that evening, apparently, because whatever happened between them, whatever discussion, that was the last time he *ever* contradicted her in our presence until the very last time when I was sixteen, and he slipped up again when I was learning to drive.

His knee jerk toward justice.

Stifled.

Our plight, I consider by fifteen, a father who's afraid from that very first summer to stand up to his wife, at least in regards to his sons. A stepmother that's going to endeavor to wear the pants at home, and insist. On pushing the envelope day after day, and challenging us. By venturing even to the verge of beyond-reason if necessary in all she asserts, in order to prove to herself that she's big enough, and to us that she's got total control, and that nobody can stand up to her, ever again, in her own family home.

And here, as a wedding present, my father gives her passive-aggressive himself and two jerked-around boys she can bully.

But she needs boys she can scar!

Ones who will never, so help her, ever once get the best of her.

I realize just then.

Japan.

Those two limping fighters are bowing to each other and shaking hands. "Osu!" they shout, and "Osu!" the next two are called up. I feel Mas Oyama's eyes burning in to me, I feel them like shame.

To be there in Japan, my teacher's uncle!

I stamp my foot internally and gnash my teeth – this dog of the dojo.

Heeling, at Mas Oyama's feet.

Hopefully no one can see! Maybe it was only a wince. I've blinked once. My eyes feel puffy. It's just been like twenty seconds since I've taken my place, but I've drifted in my past, and I see that worst side of everything that's become of me. The abuse, the condescending, the deceit, the lying, the insanity of always pretending for the sake of my dad. Purple paint stripper fumes, the burn of my flesh, my stomach lining, the loss of my dad ever once expressing pride in me, 'cause I can't close my eyes and let myself be.

Degraded, eternally, for the sake of his wife.

The rug pulled out from under me, an uchi deshi finally, and I wonder if I'll always be inferior?

To all the rest of them?

The next two are coming up and I wonder if I could take them in a fight. I wonder if I'll feel inferior to every peer that I have for the rest of my life, for the eight-year-steady erosion of what should have been that all-important support structure at home.

My brother and me.

I'm fifteen, and it's my brother's eyes this time, we're exchanging a look.

It's a little before twelve, and we're home for the night, just in to the Main Street house kitchen, its tunafish meat, and Gatlin's telling us we can't go out the next night, because "You're grounded!" she says, because we've been smoking cigarettes?

And Aaron and me exchanging that look.

It's not like we haven't before, but "What the fuck?"

We're wondering with grief and with horror in a look, "Weren't you with me all night?" We'd in fact not been smoking cigarettes that night, and we'd never experienced such an absurdity before, a creature who would draw an accusation out of thin air, and stick to it like she'd been out with us and we hadn't even been there?

And so.

Like so many other hundreds of times.

We're left there to pretend. To stand there and ultimately congratulate ourselves for being humble and polite, to bite our lips and pretend for the sake of our dad, since he looks so wounded whenever he realizes, and tries so hard to deny, how miserably she fails. For him we pretend, and fight tooth and nail to protect *him*, and show respect day after day for someone we don't. "Um, er, um, Gracie?" I say, the youngest of the two of us, "actually we weren't smoking cigarettes tonight. Why would you say that we were?"

And, even that!

Just like she planned it, she digs herself in, we've dared to stand up for ourselves! "Don't you lie to me!" her voice, her fists on her hips like Lynda Carter, and her boobs in our face. "Of course you were smoking! I can tell, I can smell it on your clothes!"

My brother and me in shock, and my father's hands over there, buried deep in his jeans. His head bowed slightly forward, and it's his turn to interject. He knows it because our father can see. His voice has been somewhat muted already, but his eyes are not yet gouged out. We were shaped in his mold and he taught us to see as clearly as he does in such situations. It's *his* sense of justice that flows through our veins, it's his turn to say.

"Excuse me, but Gracie?

"How can we possibly know if they were smoking tonight or not? We can't just call them out and blame them for something we don't really know. What'll they think of us if they weren't really smoking?

"Of course advising them on what's right, and what's safe for their bodies is another thing …"

But silence instead.

His hands in his jeans.

My brother and me, that instant, and 10,000 words in a glance.

Aside from knowing ourselves innocent, aside from knowing that thanks to our mother and father we tend to be more level-headed and into less trouble than most of our peers, aside from being injured and stunned that we were being punished for something we hadn't done, aside from the despair that we felt but couldn't yet put a finger on since *socially*, the Nathan and Aaron Ligo tennis balls that had never had a chance to fit in were finally at North Meck at last finding a home, and yet Gatlin!

Couldn't see.

Far enough past her own insecurity, to realize that every time she kept us in our rooms on a weekend night, or made us come home straight from school, or assigned us more punitive yard work to do, that she was standing in the way of two teens, and their last ever chance of finding a healthy level of teenage social self-esteem.

And aside from all that?

Contained in that glance.

There was also the grief of our father's silence to contend with.

His mute!

He knows better, that's why his hands are thus buried, deep down in his jeans and his forehead bent over. That's why he's standing by silent, and not saying anything at all.

He's over there looking for his balls!

Dad, can't you see?

By your silence, you're throwing *us* away, and year after year we're loving you, and respecting her *in act*, not because we do at all, but for you! – and waiting for you to get your feet under you again? Can't you see that your years-on-end tacit approval of your wife's degrading us is far more dangerous than any mere breakup of family?

"Shomen ni rei!"

The referee commands, that's "Bow to the front!" and this

latest set of fighters bows towards me and Mas Oyama's head table. "Osu!" they shout at the depth of their bow, their eyes out from under their brows, just one eyelash's height below where their gaze might be level with their teacher's, Mas Oyama.

A hundred karateka in white.

I scan the faces and wonder if anyone's noticing me, crouching here, the pale, the bald American, over here in his dog position. It's not been thirty seconds since I've taken my place, and I'm getting mad now my thoughts are of home.

And there's another one!

My brother Seth, I'm sixteen.

He's out of his high chair, he's three or four years old, and Cassie's the baby instead.

We're at the bar in the kitchen tonight, those brown ceramic tiles, and their tunafish meat. Seth's not behaving, but instead of scolding him, or shaking a finger, my stepmother Gracie's reached down and taken hold of an inch of his flesh. And she's twisting it, he's squealing in pain, she's got everyone's attention, and my dad's getting ready to burst.

His soda can.

And Seth crying out.

Boy child!

She's shown him who's boss, and I'm like, "No wonder my dad seems like he's about to explode whenever Seth misbehaves! I'd be like, 'Jesus Christ, this woman I'm powerless to stand up to is getting ready to reach out and pinch my son again, and making him cry!'"

Aaron's voice, one year older than me.

He's twenty now, and a Marine, and I'm at UNC.

"You have to remember that they're her kids," he explains, I think mostly to himself. "I think that probably they'll know well the same kind of psycho-manipulative treatment she's so comfortable using with us. But then for us it seems totally crazy and abusive, because she's not our mother, and we know better. We know that it's off. It the case of the kids, she's their mom. Presumably she won't be trying to get rid of *them*. If she resorts to it at all, they won't know any other way."

My pacifist dad.

The academic.

So afraid of failing in marriage again that he'd stand by and watch, for years on end, while his wife steamrolled over his teenaged sons and showed them the door time after time, and dared them to leave, since she'd preferred from the beginning to have them gone anyway.

It's clear that he loves them, but he's not gonna go there, it seems, at least not thus far, because to stand up for them is to suggest that he wouldn't do anything on Earth to stand up for her.

Even stand by silently and participate in the abuse of his sons.

Join her in her guilt trip and decide.

That the only way to address an ungrateful boy child is to show him who's boss, to break down his esteem by calling him names like "angry" and "maladjusted," and "you should be ashamed," to teach him that he'd rather see him heartbroken and gone than ever once have him stand up for himself?

My dad.

Who finally decides that he can't confront her, so he's gonna put himself aside? He's gonna use *her* words and *her* tone, and say what she says, and say it even louder than her. He's gonna dig in his heels, and look down from his pulpit and decree that he would have said the same things, no matter how hurtful they are.

He's gonna shut himself down and pretend not to see.

And hope beyond hope.

That my brother and me'd stop seeing too.

"You murdered your child," she says, I'm eighteen, but this time I've drawn her out, her stripes are totally inside-out, and who the fuck is she anyhow? My father's hands over there buried deep in his jeans, in the Main Street house kitchen again. Six years into our relationship already, but that woman!

To me and my life a total stranger. Still! Unwelcome in mine because she attacks and belittles, and constantly undermines any chance of my respecting her.

1990, and Mas Oyama's Japan.

My brother just into the Marine Corps and America on its way in to Iraq. Whatever happened, Dad, to "provide for and protect?"

Your sons are in harm's way, especially today, and you put them there.

Dad.

Only you have the power to shut it down. Only you have the power to silence that woman once and for all. Oh, let her talk, but tell your sons how that was a weak period of your life. Tell them how fucked up it all was that you couldn't stand up *for them*. Tell them that it was natural given the circumstances, that it wasn't selfish, or maladjusted, or immature, or injured, or weak, for your sons to object to being talked down to like that.

You have more sons than just me.

This full-contact slaughter in front of me?

The fists fall like bludgeons!

The abuse.

To the hollow drums and cracking ribs of our chests.

"What do you think, Nathan? Are you going to able to do that, too?

"This bare-knuckle full contact fight?"

This new pair of fighters are bowing to each other now, and shouting at the top of their lungs, and taking their stances and getting ready to fight. Mas Oyama's eyes burning into me, I turn to my left.

I thought so.

He's not even noticing me, his gold-rimmed glasses and his cauliflower ear.

That's Mas Oyama!

Damn right!

Twin white-belt fighters in front of me. Fuck 'em! I'll kill 'em all. Suddenly I see me that's out there getting ready to fight.

It can't be too much worse, I'm sure, than what I've been through before. It can't be much worse than the heartbreak of watching my dad.

Lost, and lose me.

No worse than being talked down to and degraded for the rest of my life.

But "Congratulations, Nathan, you're on your way!"

"Mas Oyama's Japan.

"The dog of the dojo, yes, but a chance for a future that's big enough.

"Big enough to make something important of all that you've lost."

LIGO DOJO OF BUDO KARATE
A 501.c.3 Public Charity Nonprofit

All proceeds from this and other Nathan Ligo titles support The Society for the Betterment of the Human Condition through the Training, Instruction, and Propagation of Budo Karate (d.b.a. Ligo Dojo of Budo Karate and Ligo Ink). Readers who want to know more, or wish to make a tax-deductible contribution, can find information online at:

www.ligodojo.com

Contributions go directly to make self-esteem- and discipline-instilling karate training available to young people who might not otherwise be able to participate.

About the Author

NATHAN LIGO (center) is a graduate of Davidson College in North Carolina, and the only American to hold a certificate from Mas Oyama's legendary Young Lions Dormitory in Japan (awarded, as Mas Oyama put it, "as a special case" after Nathan endured nearly 600 days in a program that when he started had never been completed by a non-Japanese). He is the founder of the 501(c)(3) nonprofit organization Ligo Dojo of Budo Karate in Chapel Hill, North Carolina, and a branch chief of Kyokushin-kan International Karate Organization under Kancho Hatsuo Royama in Japan. Nathan Ligo is pictured here with his teachers of the current era, Kancho Hatsuo Royama (right), Shihan Hiroto Okazaki (second from left), and Shihan Masahide Ishijima (left).

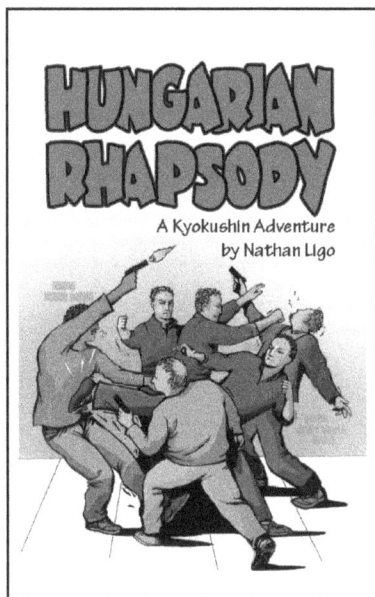

www.ingramcontent.com/pod-product-compliance
Lightning Source LLC
Chambersburg PA
CBHW030641150426

42811CB00076B/2007/J